Adjusting the contrast

MANCHESTER
1824

Manchester University Press

Adjusting the contrast

British television and constructs of race

Edited by Sarita Malik and Darrell M. Newton

Manchester University Press

Published by Manchester University Press
Altrincham Street, Manchester M1 7JA

www.manchesteruniversitypress.co.uk

British Library Cataloguing-in-Publication Data
A catalogue record for this book is available from the British Library

ISBN 978 1 5261 0098 6 hardback
ISBN 978 1 5261 4360 0 paperback

First published by Manchester University Press in hardback 2017
This edition published 2019

The publisher has no responsibility for the persistence or accuracy of URLs for any external or third-party internet websites referred to in this book, and does not guarantee that any content on such websites is, or will remain, accurate or appropriate.

Typeset by
Servis Filmsetting Ltd, Stockport, Cheshire

Contents

Figures

Notes on contributors

Kehinde Andrews is associate professor in sociology at Birmingham City University. His research specialism is race and racism and he is author of 'Resisting Racism: Race, Inequality, and the Black Supplementary School Movement' (Trentham Books, 2013) and co-editor of *Blackness in Britain* (Routledge, 2016). He is now director of the Centre for Critical Social Research, founder of the Organisation of Black Unity, and co-chair of the Black Studies Association.

James Burton is associate professor of communication at Salisbury University, Maryland. He holds a PhD from the University of Nottingham and is a contributing editor to *Literature/Film Quarterly*. His research focuses on representations of history in film and television.

Nicole M. Jackson is assistant professor of history at Bowling Green State University in Ohio. Her areas of expertise are African American history, African Diaspora History, post-Second World War and Black social movements. Her current book project considers Black British community activism as a challenge to understandings of a post-imperial Britain.

Susana Loza is associate professor of critical race, gender, and media studies at Hampshire College. Her recent publications include 'Playing Alien in Post-Racial Times', 'Vampires, Queers, and Other Monsters: Against the Homonormativity of *True Blood*', and 'Hashtag Feminism, #SolidarityIsForWhiteWomen, and the Other #FemFuture'. Her current project, *Speculative Imperialisms: Monstrosity and Masquerade in Post-Racial Times* (Lexington Books, forthcoming), explores the resurgence of ethnic simulation in science fiction, horror, and fantasy in a putatively post-racial and post-colonial era.

Sarita Malik is professor of media, culture and communications at Brunel University London. Her research explores questions of social change, inequality, communities and cultural representation. She has published widely on representations of Black and Asian communities on British television and also on diversity and broadcasting policy. She is currently leading a large international research project, funded by the UK government's Arts and Humanities Research Council, examining how disenfranchised communities use the arts, media and creativity to challenge marginalisation.

Darrell M. Newton currently serves as an associate dean at Salisbury University. He also teaches media and cultural studies, film, broadcast writing and international media as a full professor in the Communication Arts department. After extensive research on the British Broadcasting Corporation (BBC), Newton earned his Doctorate in Communication Arts in May 2002 with an emphasis in Media and Cultural Studies. Among other publications, he completed *Paving the Empire Road: BBC Television and Black Britons* (Manchester University Press, 2011) and essays for *Broadcasting in the UK and US in the 1950s; Historical Perspectives* (Cambridge Scholars, 2016), *Re-viewing Television History: Critical Issues in Television Historiography* (I. B. Tauris, 2007), *Ethnicity and Race in a Changing World* and the *Historical Journal of Film, Radio, and Television.*

Anamik Saha is a lecturer in the Department of Media and Communications, Goldsmiths, University of London. Prior to joining Goldsmiths he worked in the Institute of Communications Studies at the University of Leeds. Anamik's work can be found in journals including *Media, Culture and Society*, *Popular Music and Society*, *Ethnic and Racial Studies*, and *European Journal of Cultural Studies*. He co-edited a special issue of Popular *Communication* with Professor David Hesmondhalgh, on 'race' and ethnicity in cultural production. He is currently working on a book entitled *Race and the Cultural Industries*.

Gavin Schaffer is a professor of British history at Birmingham University. He is a specialist in race and immigration history and has a particular interest in racial science, race and the media and the history of racial violence. His present research also focuses on constructions of Jewish history and the treatment of minorities in Britain during the Second World War.

Acknowledgements

We originally conceived this book as an attempt to bring together in one collection a number of important discussions about how race is constructed and conceived on British television. A number of academics working in this field, including in the UK and USA, have shared their work and analyses here, in the form of this edited book. We must thank all of the authors who have worked with us on this project, and often against very tight deadlines. We would also like to thank Matthew Frost from Manchester University Press for his patience, support and guidance and for recognising the value in these kinds of reflections. Thank you also to Edinburgh University Press. We also greatly appreciate and clearly recognise the continuing struggle by media and cultural producers on both sides of the Atlantic, as they attempt to create more equitable opportunities for BAME people and more diverse representations of BAME communities. We thank them for their dedication, concern and resilience.

Introduction

Sarita Malik and Darrell M. Newton

National and cultural identity, ethnicity and difference have always been major themes within the national psyche, but have recently become even more prevalent in public discourse. Perhaps now, more than at any other time, how ideas of 'race' are constructed is at the centre of public debates, both in the UK and the USA. Cultural diversity is increasing alongside acute, ongoing, and often racialised, inequalities. In the midst of complex global flows and accompanying economic and social insecurity, we are witnessing the rise and visibility of far-right politics and counter-movements in the UK and USA. Simultaneously, there is an urgent need to defend the role of public service media, given its position in the multicultural public sphere.[1] This collection emerges at a time when these shifts and conjunctures that impact on and shape how 'race' and racial difference are perceived, are coinciding with rapidly changing media contexts and environments and the kinds of racial representations that are constructed within public service broadcasting (PSB).

Even in the midst of these contemporary political and cultural transformations, PSB remains an important part of everyday practice (public debate, private domestic rituals and market trends), of national order (how the national community is imagined, organised and addressed) and ultimately, of public interest. However, as delocalisation develops, the role of national broadcasting as a kind of 'social glue' that produces the ideological pursuits of national unity, and what Raymond Williams called 'common culture', has become increasingly problematic.[2] PSB's apparently unifying project based around a national public culture and identification is tasked with being entirely inclusive and 'representative' and grappling with the nuances of living with difference – cultural, racial or otherwise – in a multicultural, if not multiculturalist, society. At the heart of this ethical dilemma is the question of representation and the relationship between the nation's media and lived multiculture: how PSB adjusts and responds to the complexities and contrasts within the fabric of British society. At the same time, as Georgina Born reminds us, each element that goes into 'public' 'service' 'broadcasting', is being called into question;[3] as the very notion of 'public' has never been messier, the paternalistic idea of 'service' is being challenged in an apparently more 'citizen-led' media environment, and the end of the age of television itself is already being mourned. It is precisely in such uncertain and, in many ways, alarming times, that public service media needs to be defended, renewed and reflected upon. Michael Tracey suggests, in his scrutiny of the threats to public television, that the arguments about PSB matter because they are 'about the whole character of our lives, about principles and values and moral systems'.[4]

These important debates about the nature and role of PSB overlap with discussions around how one particular dimension of the 'public' is constructed – Black and Minority Ethnic (BAME) communities – and have not been a major focal point of critical studies in television. A broad focus on 'diversity' within scholarly, industry and public discussions often only obliquely references issues of race and representation. However, 'race' relates to important questions around the representative nature of PSB and the core question of media citizenship that also, of course, goes beyond a focus on BAME communities. This collection invites transnational interpretations of how Black people have been represented on British television. As has been previously pointed out, the early years of PSB in which it became a major aspect of UK cultural life developed at the same time as the mass immigration of people from the Commonwealth including the West Indies, India and Pakistan in the 1950s and 1960s.[5] This dual trajectory has produced a complex, dynamic relationship between Britain's post-imperial history and the institutional history of public service television. 'Black' communities come together in this discussion because of their shared post-colonial histories and the mass migration journeys that many embarked on after the Second World War. These communities have also remained at the forefront of debates about screen diversity, but have also traditionally been under-served as audiences and excluded as practitioners. The collection brings together a range of scholars who insist on foregrounding the role of public service television in a critical politics of racialised representations.

Contemporary critical concerns of race, representation and television

Recent studies point to the significance of these concerns and are reflected on here by the authors. Former studies that have addressed the matter of Black representation on British public service television include the work of Twitchin, Daniels and Gerson, Cottle, Malik, and Downing and Husband.[5] Issues of PSB policy have also been important for helping produce an understanding of the ways in which discursive frameworks and the public management of race and ethnicity are handled within the regulatory field.[7] Much of this work has also offered a wider European perspective.[8] Also noteworthy is the scholarly work examining other *loci* of cultural practices, beyond regulation, such as identity, production and consumption that foregrounds the connection between media, globalisation and cultural identities.[9] The role of diasporic media and cultural politics[10] and the transnational broadcasting marketplace as critical sites for the proliferation of difference[11] are especially useful in how we evaluate what is happening to nation-states and the idea of the national in relation to the media. Understanding processes of cultural production,[12] from a radical cultural industries perspective has also helped situate conditions of production within the dominant neo-liberal agenda that has been impacting public television since the 1990s. Saha's analysis, for example, suggests that ethnic minority producers are themselves implicated in industry shifts towards deregulation and the neo-liberal market models that we are experiencing.[13] All of these studies provide brilliant interventions into how we understand the politics of race and representation in the contemporary television space.

Significantly, the authors whose work is presented in *Adjusting the Contrast* are based in either the UK or the USA. This highlights the significance of British television for debates about cultural representation and also for non-UK scholars, but also provides a focus on the theme of comparison and translation that is apparent in this volume. On a basic level, the rationale for bringing together UK- and US-based scholars in one collection is because of shared research interests and a fascination with British television, both past and present. However, on a deeper level, and as the Black Lives Matter social media movement indicates, much is also shared and recognised in our different histories, politics and struggles. In 2016, Black Lives Matter activism – an articulation of anti-racist Black politics – seeped across from the USA to the UK. The politics of racisms, and indeed anti-racisms, that each country continues to be entwined in, along with the ways our respective media has the power to both reproduce and challenge such politics at this supposed post-racial time, is especially germane to what is actually a highly perceptible racialised contemporary climate.

But in any case, the UK has typically been at the forefront of public and scholarly debates around the politics of media representation and diversity in contemporary Europe. PSB was pioneered in the UK in the

1920s and has, since then, operated a particularly strong, civic-minded and globally recognised public service paradigm. By contrast, US broadcasting has been more overtly commercial in its frameworks and imperatives and, as Timothy Havens reminds us, increasingly seeks revenues abroad, including for the circulation of particular kinds of popular versions of African American 'blackness'. From its deep origins and first principles to its current reviews and repositioning, the public purposes that have underpinned UK PSB have been a major source of fascination beyond national boundaries. American scholars have, for example, long deconstructed and questioned the onus of public service undertaken by the BBC during its inauguration. Notable analyses of British television have been provided by Michele Hilmes, Darrell Newton, Christine Becker, and Jeffery S. Miller, among others.[14] Direct comparisons and contrasts have often been drawn within this work, of public service television origins and those of commercially driven networks in the USA – networks that began years before the advent of ITV in 1955. A principal concern within the literature has been the perceptions of American audiences who have long gleaned their ideas of British culture from a variety of radio broadcasts, and imported television programmes. These have included timeless favourites such as *The Prisoner* (Everyman/ITC, 1967–68), *The Avengers* (ITV/ABC, 1961–68) and the immensely popular *Doctor Who* (BBC, 1963–present).

As suggested by Michele Hilmes, national broadcasters such as America's A and E, ABC and CBS television networks have found it simpler to import popular foreign television shows at a relatively low cost, to place public funding into what she deems, 'original, nationally specific programs'.[15] It is also essential to note the co-production of many documentary and dramatic programmes, particularly in the 1970s, at first primarily for the public-service market. As independent broadcasting grew in the UK during the 1990s, Hilmes notes how digital platforms quickly created a 'new normal' of high-end co-productions. These have been particularly popular in the UK and the USA.[16] This continuing relationship between the UK and the USA highlights transnationalism, global audiences and cooperative productions, but also cultural engagement on an international scale; leading to the kind of further research this text seeks to initiate and subsequently interrogate.

There are, of course, wider domains around which contemporary debates about race and the media are taking place and which suggest that the focus of this collection is especially timely. We can loosely organise these into the following categories: the socio-cultural, the industrial and the regulatory, although we also understand these as interconnected terrains. The first falls to broader social, cultural and political developments that have called to question precisely what 'Britishness' is, and the media's role in framing such understandings. The most specific way in which this issue has not just surfaced, but shaken the UK to the core, is through the EU referendum that took place in June 2016. The result of that referendum demonstrated that nearly 52 per cent of the population wanted to leave the European Union (EU). While the hopes and motivations for such a desire to pull back from our European neighbours may have been diverse, and been driven by compelling, self-governing narratives around 'taking back control' – often fuelled by the more commercial aspects of the UK media, and most notably the UK tabloid press – what has materialised is a new mode of isolationism, a marked increase in hostility towards ethnic minorities and accompanying anti-immigration rhetoric, and a retreat towards a 'Little England' mentality.

The enactment of the EU 'in' or 'out' debates themselves and how these were mobilised and framed, also points to the significance and, indeed, power of the media in the processes whereby overlapping public identities are constructed and transformed; shaping public understandings of who we are and who we want to be as a nation. These seismic developments have coincided in the 2000s with a strong retreat from multiculturalism, a new discourse of global terrorism and terror/securitisation agenda, and a highly charged political climate wherever it touches on questions of racial and, increasingly, religious difference.[17] The ascent of Donald Trump to the US presidency in November 2016, just weeks after the 'Brexit' vote in June has highlighted new political commonalities hinged on new modes of nationalism and anti-immigration sentiment. Both of these events are of deep significance, described as a 'whitelash' energised by a move towards a politics of popular authoritarianism in which minority groups are increasingly being demonised. But there are also deep practical effects of these political developments. For example, on an operational level, the momentous implications of a 'Brexit' vote for UK PSB's relationship with European states outside a single market model are potentially huge and damaging.[18] In the USA, the role of the traditional news media has come under intense scrutiny and criticism, both by President Trump, but also be diverse publics who are pushing for more accountability and a questioning of the relationship between value, democracy and process.

Alongside these wider current political predicaments that suggest a move towards an exclusionary mode of politics, for the UK creative industries themselves, there is widespread agreement that not enough is being done to be sufficiently inclusive; specifically in terms of a crisis of diversity that is now apparent within the cultural industries. So the second domain pertains to industrial concerns that have been significant in the unveiling, and yet continued fact, of intense levels of inequality in the television sector. Another dimension that appears to be symptomatic of these deliberations about inequalities, shifting viewing habits among audiences and the cultures of production is what has been termed, 'Black flight' – where Black directorial and acting talent is actually moving to the USA for recognition and career progression, particularly to work in dramatic feature films, but also in prime-time drama series. Idris Elba and Naomie Harris (*Mandela*), Chiwetel Ejiofor and Steve McQueen (*12 Years a Slave*), Biyi Bandele (*Half of a Yellow Sun*), Amma Asante (*Belle*), Richard Ayoade (*The Double*), David Oyelowo (*Selma*), Archie Panjabi (*The Good Wife*, CBS) and Marianne Jean-Baptiste (*Without a Trace*, CBS) are all such examples. For Jean-Baptiste, Britain's first Black Oscar nominee for her performance in Mike Leigh's *Secrets & Lies* in 1996, the problem can be defined in one word: opportunity; a problem which also resonates for many of these Black and Asian actors who have moved between film and television roles within PSB and more commercial television projects. Jean-Baptiste says that,

> There needs to be more film directors of colour. They bandy about the word diversity a lot, but when I say of colour, I mean Asian, black, I mean people of *all* colour. We need to have those voices given the opportunity, not told that their films will not be distributed or will not sell well abroad. It's a very, very tricky subject, and it's one that I'm tired of.[19]

These predicaments about systemic inequalities and an opportunity gap in the UK general media sector are now very familiar. In 2013, the BBC's most senior Black executive, Pat Younge, echoed BBC Director General Tony Hall's concerns at an earlier select committee meeting: the BBC was not doing enough to provide programmes that Black audiences would find relevant.[20] At the time, Hall called for 'plans ... in how we reach those audiences'.[21] Younge highlighted the efforts put into employment and portrayal on screen in prime-time television leading to some real gains. However he also identified significant problems with both story lines that often do not resonate with Black audiences, and also with a white commissioning elite stronghold. He noted the lack of Black, powerful decision-makers in television, such as budget controllers, channel controllers and senior commissioners.

The Creative Skillset Employment Census (2012) indicated a significant drop in the proportion of BAME people working in the creative industries in the previous decade.[22] Between 2006 and 2012, Black, Asian and minority ethnic representation in the creative industries had declined by 30.9 per cent, to 5.4 per cent, the lowest figure since the body started taking the census. There has also been a decrease in BAME working specifically in TV. Figures fell from 9 per cent in 2009 to 7.5 per cent in 2012. At a diversity summit at the BAFTA headquarters in London in November 2013, Simon Albury, former Chief Executive of the Royal Television Society, said that diversity has become a game of 'pass the parcel'; it has no permanent leadership that is devoted to changing the industry. Since 2014, an important set of discussions about culture, value and inequality has partly been triggered by evidence of this still strong under-representation of BAME employees in the industry, raising questions about still unresolved inequalities within the structure of the creative industries at large, and about how best to tackle this.

As pointed out in the Warwick Commission on Cultural Value, 'representation of people with a disability, women and ethnic minorities in the cultural workforce has deteriorated over the last five years'.[23] Such depressing figures have triggered new campaigns to improve diversity within public service television – and in the light of the Creative Skillset findings, this has been targeted at tackling diversity in the workforce. In 2014, for example, the BBC introduced the Diversity Creative Talent Fund for projects to promote BAME employment and on-screen representation. On-screen targets have also been set up, including a 15 per cent target for on-screen BAME in 2017, the progress of which is measured by an on-screen diversity-monitoring tool (DIAMOND).[24]

One of the ways that these concerns have been carried forward relates to regulatory issues, which leads us to the third domain that we briefly consider here. The founding pillars of PSB – independence, universality, citizenship and quality[25] – are under intense scrutiny. Prior to its renewal in 2016, the actor and comedian Sir Lenny Henry, along with a large number of campaigners,[26] called for the BBC Royal Charter to better embed diversity into its remit. Henry's campaign called for a structural response to better represent communities, just as the BBC has responded to better representing nations and regions since it first identified a problem there in 2003. This would involve ring-fencing money specifically for BAME productions.[27] Henry, among others, noted how, in 2014, BSkyB pledged that by 2015, at least 20 per cent of writers and actors of UK-originated TV shows would come from a Black, Asian or other minority ethnic background. For many, this effort was considered more far-reaching than the BBC's plans to increase BAME on-screen representation to 15 per cent over a period of three years. Henry and others criticised the dismal percentage of Black and Asian people in the creative industries, and cast doubts over the BBC's plans ever coming to fruition without specified investment designated for ethnic minorities.[28]

The BBC Charter Review in 2016 stressed an improvement in audience appreciation and performance figures, and the organisation proudly reported that 'positive steps' in regards to diversity and representation had been taken in the form of proposals to enhance the World Service. However, the Review also noted that specific diversity obligations for the BBC and disparities in levels of service could be addressed through more representative employment, including BAME employment, and that departments must take an obligatory look at business and production units and their accurate reflection of the population demographics 'where they are based'.[29] As it turned out, the 2016 Charter Review more overtly entrenched diversity into its future strategy, placing diversity within the new Charter's purposes, and noting a 'new overall commitment to ensuring the BBC serves all audiences', and remaining a major advocate for representing diversity both on screen and behind the cameras. The problem remains, however, of how to make meaningful diversity interventions and encourage deeper, more critical ways of opening up debates around cultural representation, rather than 'quick-fix' solutions such as specialist diversity training or placing more BAME faces on, or indeed off, screen.

New claims and campaigns to improve diversity in these ways implicitly register the actual difficulties and contestations around how to produce real change within our public media. They also call into question the legitimacy and real impact of devising quantitative strategies to tackle deeper, structural inequalities, cultural bias and the kinds of cultural representations that end up being produced and, indeed, where they end up being placed in the schedules (see Saha's discussion in Chapter 2 of this volume). Nevertheless, it is also worth remembering that lobbying and debates about training and access for Britain's Black cultural workers helped to prepare the ground for the formation of Channel 4 which was heavily campaigned for by those who realised the importance of introducing a third space to the BBC and ITV duopoly. In 1982, the channel's commitment to 'say new things in new ways', its minority-based rationale formally inscribed in a Multicultural Programmes Department, along with its commitment to independent filmmaking, meant that it could offer a new form of cultural support to Black British film and programme-makers.[30]

Given the stealthy rise of commercial imperatives for 'serving audiences', reference should also be made here to the currently very fragile relationship between BAME audiences and PSB provision. A 2015 report by the UK media regulator, Ofcom, identified a marked concern among minority audiences about the ways in which they are represented on television, which suggests a deep sense of dissatisfaction and exclusion.[31] Further, when considering the rapid decline in television viewing by younger audiences in this new media world, it should be noted that many are choosing instead to watch on-demand services such as the BBC's iPlayer, Netflix and Amazon. Ofcom notes a 'widening gap' between younger and older viewers with a considerable reduction in television viewing, with the most significant drop being among the 16–24-year-old demographic.[32] This loss of traditional television viewership is just one of the many market challenges that PSB is currently implicated in. These socio-cultural, regulatory and market developments have raised new quandaries about the relationship among 'race', diversity and media culture. For all these current critiques of what it could be doing better and how, the status of public service television as a cultural form, 'public good' and democratic form of public service content provision is strongly defended by multiple publics, campaigners and, indeed, scholars.[33]

Focus of the collection

Through contextual and textual analyses, this collection explores a range of contexts and practices that address the ongoing phenomenon of 'race' and its specific relationship with public service television. Chapters address questions of textual representation and the ways in which meanings associated with cultural diversity are made on screen, such as that of the 'racial Other'. Further, authors address how television is implicated in such constructions. The analysis is broad-ranging and overlaps the concerns of media studies, sociology, cultural history, visual culture, film and television studies, cultural studies and race and ethnicity studies, reflecting television studies' 'disciplinary hybridity and continuing debate about how to conceptualise the object of study "television"'.[34] Contributions are diverse, ranging from the role of scheduling in 'race management' to how transnational relationships between the UK and USA are forged, and from key historical questions of representation to textual interpretations of race and 'blackness' in recent popular programming.

There is also a shared interest across the contributions in historiography, in reflecting on and bringing into view critical historical – albeit fairly recent – moments in what has been a fascinating and complex journey of cultural representation. This attempt to historicise some of the landmark moments in one collection represents an intervention on two fronts. First, there has, as John Corner notes, been a lack of 'historical scholarship on programme culture of British television' and this collection insists on catching moments and issues that reveal the complexities of the relationship among 'race', representation and

television.[35] And second, as already indicated, studies of Black representations on British television have themselves been further marginalised,
even within historical television studies, pointing to the existence of a
deep cultural amnesia in how the Black presence in Britain has itself
been historicised.[36]

Chapters deal primarily, although not exclusively, with the 1990s to
the early 2010s, a period that has seen significant shifts both in terms
of how PSB is framed and operates, but also in emergent discourses
around what it means to be 'Black and Minority Ethnic' in the UK today.
So while there is a strong impulse to 'look back' in what is presented
here, the chapters are produced within, and are informed by, what is
now a new age of television, replete with digital services, streaming and
on-demand downloads. For us, it is precisely the speed and capacity
of today's cultural turnover that intensifies the educational, social and
political value of looking back.

So the collection offers an opportunity to pause and reflect on some
of the landmark television moments in this intricate history. How
have minority ethnic communities been represented on public service
television, how do constructions of 'race', difference and multiculturalism shape our understandings of the nation and who we are? There is
a relaxed approach to terminology, particularly respectful to the often
divergent UK and US styles of presentation. In any case, categories and
terminology around 'race' are themselves socially constructed and can
further produce racial and cultural stereotyping.[37] Recognising these
confines, we use BAME, 'people of colour', 'visible minorities', Black,
Brown, Asian, but are always aware of the surrounding debates about
their relevance and value. When we use 'Black', it is used as a collective political working term to refer to those of African, Caribbean and
South Asian descent, although we accept its limitations several decades
on from the original anti-racist struggles in the 1970s and 1980s that
gave rise to this umbrella political term that was used within UK, and
indeed US anti-racist campaigns and strategies. We also use 'Asian' when
referring to those specifically from the Indian sub-continent. 'Race' does
not simply refer to what has traditionally been understood as compris-
ing the 'new communities', but is used as an analytical concept referring
to the social construction of ideas related to different ethnic and cultural groups and formations. As many of the chapters highlight, 'race'
intersects with a range of variables including class, religion, gender and
sexuality. We also recognise that a larger emphasis in this book is on
the specific representations that have materialised in relation to African
Caribbeans in the UK, although many of the issues of representation are
also pertinent to South Asian communities.

Together, the chapters help us to reflect on the framing of 'race' in wider contexts of production, but specifically in fictional genres, and most extensively in drama. As well as providing a potential space where 'racial typing' is challenged, drama has also provided a significant genre for debates around cultural representation. Examples would include multicultural content, integrated casting, narrative diversity and minority access. In 2016, much was made of the BBC drama, *Undercover*, because it featured two Black lead actors, Sophie Okonedo and Adrian Lester in a prime-time slot, and it was heavily promoted as a breakthrough. These kinds of historical television studies serve to remind us that there have been a few 'Black British television dramas' over the years, ranging from *Man from the Sun* (BBC, 1956) to *Luther* (BBC, 2010–) in which there have been Black leads, again pointing to the common gaps that tend to appear in media memories.

All the chapters present contemporary and up-to-date positions regarding conceptual debates, critical interventions and case studies. Bringing together a range of international scholars to explore questions of race and television is still, remarkably, virtually unknown. The significance is in presenting a diverse variety of perspectives and angles that together make a significant contribution to understanding how to research race critically and what the objects of analysis can be. All the contributors, even given the disciplines that they cross, also operate from a similar critical media and cultural studies perspective, and there is a unified endeavour to question assumptions and to provoke evaluation of the relationships we might have with different television programmes. The range of fictional examples and case studies presented here range from perhaps, more 'obvious' examples such as *Shoot the Messenger* and *Top Boy* to *Doctor Who* and *Call the Midwife*. Contributors, alongside textual analysis, also address issues of cultural production.

Chapter overview

The collection begins with Darrell Newton's chapter, which outlines how current studies of transnationalism highlight the importance of contemporary information societies, and the global consortiums of transnational corporations. Of particular interest to this research is BBC America; a channel launched in March 1998 via BBC Worldwide and its multi-million dollar partnership with Discovery Communications, launching several channels as global joint ventures. This chapter examines BBC America as a digital cable channel within the USA that offers a smattering of British comedies, sci-fi, reality programming and news for American audiences. The channel's advertising campaign identifies itself as 'eminently watchable programming' that 'pushes the boundaries to deliver high quality, highly addictive' programmes that are a 'little Brit different'. While the BBC seeks to increase revenues through its programme library, the offerings on BBC America feature shows that seemingly represent a Britain devoid of Black and Brown faces other than the occasional character actor or sidekick. Absent are controversial, yet thought-provoking BBC dramas such as *Holding On* (1997), *Babyfather* (2001) and *Shoot the Messenger* (2006), and other programmes featuring multiracial casting.

While the intention of BBC America may be to avoid heavier, thought-provoking dramas for lighter fare, the omission of these narratives seemingly contradicts efforts initiated by then Director General Greg Dyke to incorporate more diversity in programming and hiring practices (phenomena discussed in the chapter); a prime component of post-millennial cosmopolitanism. For Newton, this matter is particularly disconcerting when considering BBC's historic public service doctrine and its chosen responsibility of cultural education and integration. As BBC America interprets its notions of traditional programming for American tastes, its choices merely offer the occasional character of colour as an inoculation of the racial other, not as a naturalised part of British society. Within the collection, it is Newton's chapter that most directly addresses transnationalism and its associated politics and tensions.

The point in Newton's chapter about the cultural exclusions that perpetuate in these transnational politics –in spite of widespread expectations of PSB's status, as an instrument of cultural integration within PSB – is one that recurs in various ways within the book. While all the chapter address questions of production, representation and reception, using a range of approaches, Anamik Saha's focus on television scheduling provides a critical perspective because it reminds us how representation can be examined not just with regard to what is on screen, but also in how it gets there. Again, the point about what is – and what is not – included in prime-time public service television is significant. Saha explores, through a critical analysis of literature and new empirical research, how cultures of production steer the work of minority producers in ways that produce racialised tropes. He reminds us of the prevalence and persistence of traditional forms of television – and indeed traditional forms of viewing – in everyday practices in households in the UK. Saha talks about the marginalisation of representations of British South Asians, not just in terms of what is commissioned, but also in the hour in which certain programmes get scheduled. The focus is on the conditions of television production, produced through a dynamic among political economic structures, cultural policy, public service remits and wider discourses of multiculturalism and worker agency. It takes as a case study the scheduling of 'Asian' programming, including *Desi DNA* (BBC, 2003–), *Goodness Gracious Me* (BBC, 1998–2015), and *Indian Food Made Easy* (BBC, 2007–10), and focuses on the ways in which cultural producers feel their work is in the hands of schedulers, who effectively determine whether the programme in question will get attention or not. Based upon interviews with directors and producers, conducted by Saha, the chapter argues that schedulers – themselves working in increasingly commercialised and constraining cultures of production – have an indirect, though sometimes direct, effect on the type of narratives on race that enter the mainstream. The chapter usefully explores the politics of 'tick-boxing' especially in regard to public service remits. It therefore moves beyond the idea that we need more 'positive' representations of minorities on TV, in order to argue that bigger structural change is needed first if we are to achieve this.

Leading on from these two chapters, which provide a critical inter-rogation of some of the wider contexts of BAME representations, the collection assembles a range of discussions that focus on specific screen representations and position these in relation to wider social, cultural and political contexts. Dealing with especially timely themes around nostalgia, imagined communities and the nation, James Burton's chapter takes us back to reflect on how race is constructed on recent British television productions – including *The Bletchley Circle* (ITV, 2012–14), *Call the Midwife* (BBC, 2012–), *The Hour* (BBC, 2011–13) – that are set during the 1950s and purport to present a corrective to established notions of the nation at that time.

Contrary to the nostalgia that many Britons have for the post-Second World War era, Chris Waters has argued that attempts to secure the imagined community of nation amid a time of rapid change and uncer-tainty in 1950s Britain depended on reworking established tropes of little Englandism against the migrant other. Although ostensibly con-cerned with asserting gender politics, Burton argues that these series speak volumes about race and immigration both explicitly and implic-itly. Where discussions of 'heritage' programming often descend into reductive categorisation and knee-jerk mockery, this chapter critically interrogates the anti-nostalgic impulses of this programming, as well as the heroically rose-tinted version of the past that they often represent. The chapter further analyses the promotional discourses that surround, and subsequently shape, the reception of their narratives. Additionally, of central concern are the politics of representation and the dynamics of race that are present in, as well as absent from, these stories and how such dynamics speak to present-day racism, xenophobia and immigration debates.

Continuing the book's interest in issues of representation, Sarita Malik discusses the 2006 BBC drama *Shoot the Messenger*, based on the psychological journey of a Black school teacher, Joe Pascale, accused of assaulting a Black male pupil. The allegation triggers Joe's mental breakdown which is articulated, through Joe's first-person narration, as a vindictive loathing of Black people. In turn, a range of typical stereotypical characterisations and discourses based on a Black culture of hypocrisy, blame and entitlement are presented. Malik suggests that the text is therefore laid wide open to a critique of its neo-conservatism and hegemonic narratives of Black Britishness. However, she argues that the drama's representation of Black mental illness opens up the potential to interpret *Shoot the Messenger* as a critique of social inequality and the destabilising effects of living with *ethicised* social categories. The chapter considers audience reactions to the drama alongside the commissioning and production contexts. The aim of the analysis is to reclaim this controversial text as a radical drama and examine its implications for, and within, a critical cultural politics of 'race' and black representation.

Staying with British television's preoccupation with the Black/male/criminality nexus, Kehinde Andrews examines the Channel 4 'urban drama', *Top Boy* (Channel 4, 2011–13), Andrews draws on Elijah Anderson's work which explains that 'the ghetto is where "the Black people live", symbolising an impoverished, crime-prone, drug-infested, and violent area of the city.' Andrews suggests that, in the American context, such representations have become so pervasive that the ghetto has become an iconic feature of African American representation, whereby to be Black is synonymous in the popular imaginary with being 'ghetto'. For Andrews, Britain does not have as many reference points for Black culture on the small screen as the USA, but the iconic ghetto still features heavily in the representation of Black Britons. He comments that young Black men, in particular, are associated with crime and street violence in the British media. The chapter outlines how, while there are very few predominantly Black-cast television programmes on British television, those in recent years have all been concerned with stories from the 'iconic ghetto', for example, *Dubplate Drama* (Channel 4, 2005–7) and *Youngers* (E4, 2013–14). Channel 4's *Top Boy*, based on the story of a drug gang on an inner city estate in London, has been the most high profile. The chapter analyses and applies the key features of the iconic ghetto using *Top Boy* as an example of how these tropes appear on British television. Andrews concludes that the problem of representation is not just that there are so few spaces on British television, but also that the available space is also narrowly filtered through this representational lens of the iconic ghetto.

Just as Malik's chapter on *Shoot the Messenger* and Andrews's chapter on *Top Boy*, offer an in-depth analysis of particular texts, Susana Loza focuses on the case of the globally recognised BBC series, *Doctor Who* (BBC, 1963–). Loza suggest that the series has been fabricating and exporting British racial fears and fantasies across the globe since the 1960s. By utilising an interdisciplinary amalgam of critical ethnic studies, media studies, cultural studies and post-colonial theory, her chapter examines how the 2005 reboot of the classic series utilises deracialised and decontextualised slavery allegories to absolve white guilt over the transatlantic slave trade. Loza argues that the narrative reinforces xenophobic anxieties about post-colonial Britishness through the reinforcement of black racial stereotypes and by bolstering white privilege in demanding that viewers adopt the series' colour-blind liberal humanist standpoint. By carefully examining the imperial fictions and post-racial slavery parables of *Doctor Who*, she illuminates the programme's 'structural opacities', how its colour-blind universalism sustains and nourishes the boundaries of contemporary whiteness and colonial consciousness, and the full place of race in multicultural and ostensibly postcolonial Britain.

The myth of a multicultural England in BBC's *Luther* (BBC, 2010–15) is the focus of Nicole Jackson's chapter. In the run-up to BBC America's broadcast of the second season of Neil Cross's famed drama, the American press cast the titular character, John Luther, played by Idris Elba, within a long line of quirky, dark detectives who also seemed to be fading from US television screens. For Jackson, Luther's intuition was as spot-on as his personal life was a wreck. While a mild success in both countries when it debuted in 2010, the series became a cult classic, gaining a considerable following through word of mouth and social media. For all its commercial success, Jackson argues that one cannot view *Luther*, its characters or London as its backdrop, outside of history. Rather, she encourages a reading of John Luther's 'man-on-the-edge' within a historical development of London as a racially diverse city and the battles over the multiculturalism that this diversity precipitates. John Luther, she claims, stands in as the representative of a police force with a long history of antagonism with Black and Asian communities. London's modern-day reputation as a racially and ethnically diverse metropolis often obscures the racial antagonism within the city, much of which has centred on the police who often serve as gatekeepers of the nation. Luther's London is a place where race has ceased to matter; a tall tale with a long life. Thus, the absence of race in the show becomes curious in context.

Jackson reminds us that in the official reports on the 1981 Brixton disorders and Stephen Lawrence's 1999 murder, the authors posited that remaking the relationship between the police and Black and Asian communities was essential to improving race relations in the city. She outlines how the Metropolitan Police was encouraged to hire ethnic minority officers, but despite repeated recruitment schemes, officers of African and Asian descent have not flocked to the profession in droves and, in some quarters, beliefs that police are racist have not changed very much. Thus, besides the representation of a genius detective and man 'gazing into the abyss', Jackson's chapter urges an interrogation of how *Luther* signifies long-held myths about race, citizenship and nation in England. One of the myths about multiculturalism was that Black and Asian people could become part of the body politic by accentuating their Britishness and de-accentuating as many markers of 'foreign origin' as possible. Thus, John Luther is never a Black copper, in that blackness itself, with its ties to former colonies, has been inextricably linked to foreignness and the drama presents him as an example of the positive assimilative model. This chapter views Luther through the lens of multi-culturalism to mean assimilation, rather than a potentially transforma-tive radical process, where Luther's black body displaces historical and present-day complaints of institutional police racism, which makes race, as a lived reality, invisible; seemingly the ultimate goal of institutional multiculturalism.

Gavin Schaffer, while also considering fictional constructions, offers a close-up analysis of the comedy genre and formulations of race. His chapter examines the uses of race, immigration and multiculturalism as comic themes in British television sitcoms from the 1960s to the 1980s. Looking in depth at popular programmes such as *Till Death Us Do Part* (BBC, 1965–75), *Love Thy Neighbour* (Thames, 1972–76), *It Ain't Half Hot Mum* (BBC, 1976–81) and *Mind Your Language* (LWT, 1977–86), Schaffer argues that the genre of the racial sitcom privileged white constructions of racial difference and stifled the development of Black and Asian British comedy. Nonetheless, in the face of ambiva-lent attitudes and racism, Schaffer suggests that important comedy representations did begin to emerge in this period. This effort initially began through programmes such as *The Fosters* (LWT, 1976–77), which although it was not Black-British written, at least began to foreground black comedy talent such as Lenny Henry, Norman Beaton and Carmen Munroe. Building from these modest foundations, programmes such as *No Problem!* (LWT, 1983–85), *Desmond's* (Channel 4, 1989–94)

and *The Lenny Henry Show* (BBC, 1984–85, 1987–88) slowly began
to give voice to a wider experience of black and Asian British comedy.
Simultaneously, he argues, these narratives wrestled black and Asian
comedic constructions away from discourses of essential difference
and racial exoticism. By using these programmes as its core source, the
chapter considers the importance of humour and laughter as sites of
struggle in multicultural British society; reflecting on the meaning of
jokes and who tells them, and the thinking behind television comedies.
Finally, it evaluates the significance that has been, and might be, placed
on the laughter of television audiences.

As all of these chapters demonstrate, there is no simple progress model,
in terms of how televisual representations of 'Blackness' and lived multiculture develop. Recent developments in relation to, for example, the
renewed Royal Charter, suggest that there is still much to do in order to
build a more racially representative and inclusive public service media
culture and a large degree of contestation about how best to achieve
this. All of the chapters presented in this small collection encourage us to
read and re-read the important ways in which 'race', identity and difference are imagined and positioned in our national culture through public
service content. The potential value is in helping us to better understand
our historical and contemporary representations as well thinking ahead
about the future that we want for our public service television.

Notes

1 Malik, Sarita, '"Keeping It Real": The Politics of Channel 4's Multiculturalism,
   Mainstreaming and Mandates', *Screen*, 49:3 (2008), pp. 343–53.
2 Higgins, John (ed.), *The Raymond Williams Reader* (Hoboken, NJ: Wiley
   Blackwell, 2001), p. 17.
3 Born, Georgina, *Uncertain Vision: Birt, Dyke and the Reinvention of the BBC*
   (New York: Random House, 2005).
4 Tracey, Michael, *Decline and fall of Public Service Broadcasting* (Oxford:
   Clarendon Press, 1998), p. 33.
5 Daniels, Therese, and Gerson, Jane (eds), *The Colour Black* (London: BFI, 1989).
6 Twitchin, John (ed.), *The Black and White Media Show Book* (Stoke-on-Trent:
   Trentham, 1988); Daniels and Gerson, *The Colour Black*; Cottle, Simon (ed.),
   Ethnic Minorities and the Media: Changing Cultural Boundaries (Buckingham
   and Philadelphia: Open University Press, 2000); Malik, Sarita, *Representing
   Black Britain: Black and Asian Images on Television* (London: Sage, 2002);
   Downing, Neil and Husband, John, *Representing Race: Racisms, Ethnicity and
   the Media* (London: Sage 2005).
7 Malik, Sarita, '"Creative Diversity": UK Public Service Broadcasting After
   Multiculturalism', *Popular Communication*, 11:3 (2013), pp. 227–41.

8 Horsti, Karina, Hultén, Gunilla, and Titley, Gavan (eds), *National Conversations: Public Service Media and Cultural Diversity in Europe* (London: Intellect, 2014).

9 See Rigoni, I., and Saitta, E. (eds), *Mediating Cultural Diversity in a Globalised Public Space* (Basingstoke: Palgrave Macmillan, 2012); and Siapera, Eugenia, *Cultural Diversity and Global Media: The Mediation of Difference* (Hoboken, NJ: Wiley Blackwell, 2010).

10 Bailey, O., Georgiou, M., and Harindranath, R. (eds), *Transnational Lives and the Media: Re-Imagining Diasporas* (Basingstoke: Palgrave Macmillan, 2007).

11 Hilmes, Michele, 'Who We Are, Who We Are Not: Battle of the Global Paradigms', in Lisa Parks and Shanti Kumar (eds), *Planet TV: A Global Television Reader* (New York: New York University Press, 2003); Havens, Timothy, *Black Television Travels: African American Media around the Globe* (New York: New York University Press, 2013).

12 Cottle, *Ethnic Minorities and the Media*.

13 Saha, Anamik, 'Beards, Scarves, Halal Meat, Terrorists, Forced Marriage: Television Industries and the Production of "Race"', *Media Culture Society*, 34:4 (May 2012), pp. 424–38.

14 Hilmes, 'Who We Are, Who We Are Not'; Newton, Darrell, *Paving the Empire Road: BBC Television and Black Britons* (Manchester: Manchester University Press, 2011); Becker, Christine, 'From High Culture to Hip Culture: Transforming the BBC into BBC America', in Joel H. Wiener and Mark Hampton (eds), *Anglo-American Media Interactions, 1850–2000* (Basingstoke: Palgrave Macmillan, 2007); Miller, Jeffrey S., *Something Completely Different: British Television and American Culture* (Minneapolis: University of Minnesota Press, 2000).

15 Hilmes, Michele, 'Transnational TV: What Do We Mean by "Co-production" Anymore?' *Media Industries*, 1:2 (2014), p. 12.

16 *Ibid.*

17 See Bailey, Georgiou and Harindranath, *Transnational Lives and the Media*.

18 For a discussion of a post-Brexit television landscape, see Alison Harcourt, 'What a Brexit would mean for Europe's television channels', *The Conversation*, 3 June 2016, https://theconversation.com/what-a-brexit-would-mean-for-europes-television-channels-60388 (accessed 30 March 2017).

19 Jean-Baptiste discussed the ongoing lack of opportunity for Black British talent in, 'It's Not a Sob Story – I Could Have Stayed in the UK and Fought it out', *Guardian*, 15 June 2015.

20 Pat Younge, who served as the BBC's Chief Creative Officer until his resignation in 2013, was previously a series producer of current affairs programmes such as on Black Britain. He discussed these ongoing inequalities on 'The Media Show', BBC Radio 4, 23 October 2013.

21 Tony Hall speaking at the Select Committee, 22 October 2013.

22 See Creative Skillset. Employment Census of the Creative Media Industries, http://creativeskillset.org/assets/0000/5070/2012_Employment_Census_of_the_Creative_Media_Industries.pdf, 2012 (accessed 11 May 2016).

23 The Warwick Commission on the Future of Cultural Value. Enriching Britain: Culture, Creativity and Growth, www2.warwick.ac.uk/research/warwickcom mission/futureculture/ (accessed 20 November 2015).

24 BBC, *Equality Information Report 2016*, www.bbc.co.uk/diversity/strategy/eir-2016 (accessed 22 March 2017).

25 These were discussed at Georgina Born's paper, 'Rethinking the Principles of Public Service Media', delivered at the 'Future of Public Service Television Inquiry' seminar, Rethinking the Principles of Public Service Media', British Academy, 3 March 2016.

26 See the submissions on the issue of 'diversity' in the Future of TV inquiry, http:// futureoftv.org.uk/about/ and the *Future for Public Service Television: Content and Platforms in a Digital World* report, 2016.

27 http://stakeholders.ofcom.org.uk/binaries/consultations/psb-review-3/responses/ Campaign_for_Broadcasting_Equality_CIO.pdf.

28 Sweeney, Mark, 'BSkyB to Take 20% of Talent from Black, Asian or Other Minority Backgrounds', *Guardian*, 18 August 2004. https://www.theguardian. com/media/2014/aug/18/bskyb-20-percent-talent-black-asian-ethnic-minority (accessed 11 February 2016).

29 Anonymous, comp. BBC Charter Review Public Consultation: Summary of Responses. London: Crown Copyright, 2016.

30 Malik, 'Keeping it Real'.

31 See, 'PSB Diversity Research Summary', Ofcom, June 2015, pp. 7, 9, 15, 20, 34.

32 Plunkett, John, 'Third of TV Watching Among Younger Viewers Is via On-demand Services', *Guardian*, 11 July 2016. https://www.theguardian.com/media/2016/ jul/11/third-of-tv-watching-among-younger-viewers-done-on-demand-services (accessed 12 July 2016).

33 See *Future for Public Service Television: Content and Platforms in a Digital World* report, 2016.

34 Brunsdon, Charlotte, 'What is the 'Television' of Television Studies?' in Christine Geraghty and David Lusted (eds), *The Television Studies Book* (London: Arnold, 1998).

35 Corner, John, *Critical Ideas in Television Studies* (Oxford: Oxford University Press, 1999).

36 Malik, *Representing Black Britain*.

37 Parekh, Bhikhu C., *The Future of Multi-ethnic Britain: Report of the Commission on the Future of Multi-Ethnic Britain* (London: Profile, 2000).

1

A little Brit different? BBC America and transnational constructs of Britishness

Darrell M. Newton

I think it's very important for people to accept that Britain is a multicultural society. The sooner they realise that, the better. (South Asians from Glasgow interviewed by the Commission for Racial Equality, 2005)[1]

As noted by Barbara Selznick, the 1990s represented a decade in which the co-production of television programming for international audiences provided a catalyst toward a rapidly expanding global culture. In televising these projects, US cable television provided a smattering of programming essentially 'designed for international audiences'. These efforts created what she determined to be 'cultural constructs about the increasingly global world', and highlighted the 'means by which individuals could understand and navigate it'.[2] As BBC America (BBCA) began service in 1998, programmes were chosen that supposedly provided a smattering of popular British shows designed to appeal and inform American viewers. The channel advertised itself as offering 'eminently watchable programming' that 'pushes the boundaries to deliver high quality, highly addictive' shows that are a 'little Brit different' (figures 1.1 and 1.2) or 'completely British, completely different', as promotions for the channel boast.[3]

It was two years later that Director General Greg Dyke initiated directives for a new, more diverse BBC; one that is no longer 'hideously white' as he had famously – or infamously – stated during an interview.[4] These efforts included closer analyses of not only practices at BBC1 and BBC2 but BBC3, Digital Services and BBC Worldwide; the latter offering programmes for a variety of cable networks, including American providers A & E, and the Public Broadcasting Service (PBS). In 2002, when addressing the Commonwealth Broadcasting Association Conference in Manchester (CBA), Dyke again underscored the importance of ethnic diversity in programming and hiring, as 'one of the central defining characteristics of modern Britain – particularly among the young', a point echoed by BBCA's former CEO Bill Hilary. When considering globalisation, and television audiences free to access programming from a variety of nations, the issue of multiculturalism as 'simply a part of the furniture of their everyday lives', was noted by Dyke, as was the BBC's onus to 'actively reflect' this.[5] Realising the potential of the BBC to offer a programmes for a new, multi-ethnic Britain, Dyke imagined a BBC that could potentially expose audiences to what Barbra Selznick calls, 'television programmes that [shape] their understanding of how the world operates, how the world should operate, and what is possible'.[6] However, according to discussions with CEO Hilary, these directives did not include programming choices for BBCA, a commercially driven service based in New York City.

Since BBCA began at a time when the BBC and other British broadcasters began to further examine the need for cultural diversity, what effects did these notions have on BBCA's constructs of Britishness and race, if any? What market forces created a programming shift at BBCA from 'classic favourites' to more diverse representations of Britain during the mid-2000s, and then back again? How do these new efforts for increased representations of black and Asian faces affect BBCA's commercially driven programming choices for American viewers? How did Greg Dyke's notions of a 'hideously white' BBC affect the choices made by BBCA's management – if at all?

In this chapter, I examine how BBCA represents contemporary Britain in its programming choices since 1998 when it began service in the USA. With a healthy range of programming that featured black and Asian Britons from 2004 to 2011 no longer being offered by the channel, I argue that the diminished presence of these characters of colour directly affected cultural diversity on BBCA.[7] In turn, the changes in programming choices has constructed Britishness in a manner that reinforces a mostly white, nearly homogeneous nation-state; one that draws from an American fascination with 'Anglophenia'.[8] There has been limited research on the subject of BBCA specifically, but works by Christine Becker and Melinda Lewis provided insights on its efforts to represent Britain, and to capture a portion of the American television market. I also draw from an original interview with past CEO of BBCA Bill Hilary (2004–6) conducted in May 2016.

While BBCA currently offers little or no programming with Black or Brown characters in lead or prominent roles, the channel did offer programmes in which both groups were featured during the early to mid-2000s. However, this trend seemingly began to change after

2011, resulting in a failure to adequately represent the very diversity that was a principle concern for Dyke and UK broadcasters as Britain moved on into the new millennium. Further, as also addressed here, the programming choices made by BBCA since 2011 is a reflection of the rapidly diminishing roster of British programmes featuring people of colour; programmes available for acquisition from BBC Worldwide, Channel 4, BskyB, ITV or other production companies. These circumstances have drawn harsh criticisms from a number of Black British actors.

Also absent is a range of controversial yet thought-provoking BBC dramas that feature a multi-racial British cast, such as *Holding On* (1997), *Babyfather* (2001), *Shoot the Messenger* (2006), *Survivors* (BBC, 2008–10) and other similar shows with ensemble casts (figures 1.4–1.6). Though *Babyfather* and *Shoot the Messenger* were sharply criticised as full of racist stereotypes and shallow representations,[9] the programming at least provided opportunities for writers and directors of colour to construct a different view of contemporary Britain; one in which black and Asian Britons are commonplace. It remains true that many of these shows hail from previous seasons, yet fandom and the zeitgeist behind 'classic' or cult TV has reminded us of the power of audiences, their chosen reception and the pleasure gained from personal viewing habits.[10] This would include the viewing of perennial 'favourites' such as *Doctor Who* (BBC, 1963–), and *Absolutely Fabulous* (BBC, 1992–2012). I also briefly examine a history of BBCA and its dramatic programming choices; studies on British television's failures to provide images of a culturally diverse society; Dyke's diversity agenda and its possible effects on BBC's Worldwide and American services.

As suggested by Melinda Lewis's work on the channel, BBCA entertains audiences 'with the 'otherness' of British television', yet seemingly provides an 'educational tool to teach American audiences the ways of British', and despite depictions that are not 'wholly accurate, the expectation is that these programmes are representative of British culture'.[11] Christine Becker suggests that the service under past CEO Paul Lee endeavoured to become 'hipper' and more accessible to a younger demographic (figure 1.3). In her essay, she suggests that its identity was previously tied to BBC's older Reithian ideals of cultural refinement as BBCA's programming revelled in offering the low genres as has mainstream American television, but with 'greater cultural value'. Reality shows criticised for offering schlock and sensationalism were hyped by BBCA as 'vehicles for improvement and enrichment', presenting reality shows as what she called, 'an amiable elixir of civility, collective participation, and enrichment'.[12] However, considering the lack of cultural diversity, even in programming that is alleged to 'improve' a viewer's life, one must also consider the effect this absence of black and Asian faces has on American viewers, and their perceptions of modern-day Britain.

As BBCA interpreted what it considered popular British programming for American tastes, its earlier choices merely offer the occasional character of colour as an *inoculatory* presence,[13] thus avoiding criticisms that constructs of Britishness by the channel offers a reinforcement of whiteness as normative.[14] Various actors of colour, and Dyke himself, continue to criticise the BBC[15] for still failing to offer more opportunities to those of colour seeking to be represented on television.[16] At the time of writing, Black Briton and writer-producer-actor Sir Lenny Henry, who launched several initiatives to increase this participation in British television programming, continues to critique the industry for not adequately addressing similar issues that were current in the 1990s.[17] His initiatives have included a 'three-point plan' of how the British media could change to reflect diversity, as detailed later in this chapter.

BBC Worldwide added £123 million to the corporation's resources in 2004, a global commercial success that represents, as Sarikasis notes, a certain aspect of 'Britishness' designated as 'popular material', despite a public service mandate. While it is unclear why these two issues are implied as mutually exclusive, she also suggests that in the early 2000s the BBC faced 'threats' from a 'neo-liberal, market-driven ethos of British politics'. She criticises the restrictions that stunted the expansion of the BBC toward 'true public ownership', creating an inability to develop 'a greater degree of responsiveness to the needs of diverse audiences', and to treat them as 'citizens rather than customers or market niches'.[18]

The mid-2000s represented a possible departure from a televised Britishness immersed in whiteness as a normative social construct. However, BBCA's flirtations with younger, urban, upscale audience who wanted edgier television than that provided by US channels, as noted by Becker, are seemingly long gone. With the exception of *Skins* (2011), younger themed programmes offered only a smattering of BAME actors despite an acquisition of 49 per cent ownership by American Movie Classics Networks (AMC); home of a variety of programmes featuring diverse casts, such as the ever-popular *Walking Dead* franchises. Currently, AMC Networks consists of AMC, WE TV, Sundance and IFC networks. BBC Worldwide, the commercial arm of the BBC, will retain 50.1 per cent ownership.[19]

Though unrelated to Dyke's multicultural directives, Bill Hilary reportedly purchased several shows for broadcast throughout the mid-2000s that featured black and Asian Britons portraying varied roles, as opposed to the familiar Yardie crack-dealing criminal or maladjusted Asian torn between cultural mores.[20] More recently, however, offerings from BBCA have featured shows with predominately white casts, reinforcing a *Britishness* that is devoid of black and Asian faces, other than the occasional character actor or sidekick.[21] Fanfare from BBCA's website heralds the continued production of *Luther* with Idris Elba (BBC, 2010–), and the six-part series, *Undercover* (BBC, 2016) with Sophie Okonedo and Adrian Lester. Yet, these are recent additions featuring Black British leads, and only account for two programmes on the channel's new line-up. To understand the current direction of BBCA, I begin by briefly examining its origins.

The origins of BBCA

BBC America, or BBCA as it appears in American cable line-ups, was originally distributed through Discovery Networks, the parent company of the popular Discovery Channel. Discovery Communications and its operations in over 170 countries are considered rather robust, as evidenced by Discovery's profitability in its international operations.[22] The BBC planned to co-produce nearly 80 hours of programming with Discovery during the first year, and to increase output to 100 hours by year five.[23] BBCA was also launched on Dish Network in 1998, with a promise to offer 'the best of British television'. The channel was strategically placed on the package as part of its 'America's Top 100', at no additional cost. The agreement marked the first satellite carriage of the channel, which also represented a joint venture between Discovery Networks and the BBC, complete with dramas, comedies, documentaries and the highly respected BBC World News.[24] Discovery, which handled the affiliate and advertising sales through the New York office of BBCA, was advertising-supported, and like BBCA has edited programming segmented for commercial interruption.

When the service premiered, there were criticisms over the heavy repetition of its schedule which ran both night and day; creating 11 to 12 hours of content and advertisements. A typical episode of one drama had commercials at 10 past the hour, 20 past, 36, and 44 minutes past the hour, with the show ending at 51 minutes. Nine minutes of information about BBCA helped to fill the hours' worth of programming. Comedy shows (or 'Britcoms' as they were called by early promos for the channel) ran within two-hour slots, with one beginning at the top of the hour, and the second beginning 40 minutes in. The third programme began approximately 80 minutes after the first, with promos placed in between. Each show also had two or three breaks for advertisements.

The first season included the long-running hospital drama *Casualty* (BBC, 1986–), *The Inspector Alleyn Mysteries* (BBC, 1990–94), and the police drama *Hamish Macbeth* (BBC, 1995–97) with Robert Carlyle as the counter-cultural Scottish sleuth. However, of great popularity with audiences was *EastEnders* (BBC, 1985–), which ran daily only weeks after their screening on British television; a programme that clearly offered a different view of British life as it featured middle- to lower-income characters with daily problems and issues that many average viewers could relate to. Half of a 'classic' episode was also telecast to fill out an hour slot and to potentially draw in American audiences unfamiliar with the long-running tale. However, the soap was removed from the schedule in 2003, leading to angry letters and calls from American viewers who came to enjoy the programme.[25]

Doctor Who also 'premiered' on BBCA and advertisements for the show touted it as being shown 'only on BBC America' after the programme had run for sixteen years on public television stations around the country. These same stations and the Arts and Entertainment Network (A&E) offered *Jeeves and Wooster* (Granada, 1990–93), *The Two Ronnies* (BBC, 1971–87), *Are You Being Served?* (BBC, 1972–85), *Touching Evil* (Anglia, 1997–99), and *Inspector Morse* (Carlton, 1987–2000). Early comedic offerings included older repeats of favourites from the 1980s, including *Blackadder* (BBC, 1982–83), *Yes, Minister* (BBC, 1980–84), and *French and Saunders* (BBC, 1987–2005). Reality based home improvement shows popular with British audiences were also early staples, including repeats of *Changing Rooms* (BBC, 1997–2004) and *Ground Force* (BBC, 1998–2002). BBCA also offered *Antiques Roadshow* (BBC, 1979–), occasional documentaries, and made for TV films.

As American appetites for British programming grew, Paul Lee, the first general manager and chief operating officer of BBCA, felt compelled to offer programming that drew from hit programmes in the UK. These included the original version of *The Office* (BBC, 2001–3) *The Graham Norton Show* (BBC, 2007–), TLC programmes *Trading Spaces* (TLC, 2000–11) based on *Changing Rooms*; *What Not to Wear* (TLC, 2003–) and others.[26] However, under the leadership of Bill Hilary, BBCA was restructured and received a larger programming budget. Kathryn Mitchell was appointed to oversee marketing and programming as General Manager after serving at Comedy Central where she also oversaw scheduling and acquisitions until 2004.[27] Hilary believed that the BBC needed to narrowcast more niche programming that non-UK viewer found appealing. Calls for diversity on British television, and Dyke's directives, are necessary to examine as we consider BBCA's past programming choices, and its current failures.

Findings, and a continuing need for cultural diversity

As indicated earlier in this study, there remains a need to address diverse
images on British television, and subsequently on BBCA. In 1989 the BBC
launched the 'Step Forward' programme, designed to allow more Black
comedy-writers to gain positions in television. The idea was a combined
effort between BBC Controller Jonathan Powell and Henry who considered this problem after 'turning up for the first script readings' of a
comedy pilot, and finding that out of '90 writers in the room, not one of
them was black or Asian. There were only a couple of women there, too,
come to think about it.'[28] The comic's film production company, Crucial
Films, and BBC Television sponsored a two-day comedy workshop
aimed at writers 'who will reflect Britain's multicultural society, noting
that 'Black people are often misrepresented on television and that's
because there are very few black writers.'[29] Despite some improvements
at the start of the 2000s, an ongoing struggle continues, as evidenced by
more recent concerns over casting and opportunities, as detailed later in
this study.

In 1991 Channel 4, in conjunction with the Centre for Mass
Communication Research at the University of Leicester held a conference, 'Ethnic Minorities and Television: A Study of Use, Reactions, and
Preferences – A Report for Channel 4', resulting in a report written by
Professor James Halloran and others. The document included a rather
negative evaluation of programming on Channel 4 and BBC2 as it
related to ethnic minorities.[30] Professor Karen Ross considered most
British programmes to be prejudiced towards ethnic minorities, in that
they were usually portrayed as criminals or drug abusers.[31] She was also
highly critical of the negative stereotyping present on *EastEnders* and on
the hard-hitting crime drama *The Paradise Club* (BBC, 1989–90).[32] Ross
cites an example of an Asian family who ran a successful grocery shop in
East London, but left after a scandal. Also discussed was a Turkish character who lost all his money gambling and a Black West Indian character
dealing in stolen property.[33]

In February 1996, another report called *Ethnic Minorities on Television*
was authored by Guy Cumberbatch and Samantha Woods of the
Communications Research Group at Aston University in Birmingham.
The report surveyed spending habits, advertisements, and ethnic audiences for BBC1, BBC2, ITV and Channel 4.[34] The highly influential
Commission for Racial Equality (CRE) in conjunction the Independent
Television Commission (ITC), and BBC also released a seminar report
called *Race and Television in Britain: Channels of Diversity*. This report,
based on a 1996 seminar, examined implications drawn from previous

research into representations of ethnic minorities on British television. This included the findings of a qualitative survey of ethnic minority opinions regarding television output. Common outcomes included that: (1) ethnic minorities desperately need more diverse representations on British television; (2) Black British audiences, much like Black American audiences, were now realising that there were alternatives to the disappointing programmes being offered on regular or terrestrial channels; and (3) if white production and programming staff cannot rise to the challenge of diversity in programming and opportunities, then ethnic minorities should be given autonomy through funding.[35]

In an effort to provide more programming that reflected the growing cultural diversity of the UK, a new cable and satellite TV channel was granted a licence from the ITC to specifically target the UK African-Caribbean community in the same year BBCA began. The African Broadcasting Corporation, or ABC TV, would be a channel dedicated to African-Caribbean culture and the contributions made by this community to Britain. Director of the channel, M. Soyode, said ABC TV hoped to provide a platform for British African-Caribbean programme-makers, and its offerings would show the 'more positive side of African people, and so break down the barriers which are created by the negative side currently show on TV'.[36] The new channel had predicted that 90 per cent of viewers would be of African-Caribbean descent, with the other 10 per cent representing those with an interest in Africa. These efforts clearly indicated the importance of these audiences, and their ultimate desire to find more balanced representations on UK television. As the new millennium approached, it became important to examine the direction the BBC would take under its new Director General, Greg Dyke, particularly given Dyke's explicit criticism of the lack of cultural diversity within the organisation.

The BBC, BBCA and Dyke's directives

In April 1999, Dyke accepted the position as the new Director General of the BBC, eventually replacing Sir John Birt. His primary tasks would include 'the challenges of maintaining the BBC's prominence in the face of a massive expansion of digital channels and international competition'.[37] Upon his appointment, he unveiled the BBC's new management structure announcing that the organisation would be spending at least £100 million more on BBC programming and services in the coming year.[38] As Dyke made the transition, more criticism was being levelled against the television industry, which was accused of 'lagging behind society and failing to reflect the multicultural nature of the country'. As a partial response during the Race in Media Awards ceremony in April 2000, Dyke served as keynote speaker, and Sir Trevor McDonald, ITV's Black anchor for their nightly news, hosted.[39] The new Director General told attendees that he planned to head up 'a BBC where diversity is seen as an asset not an issue or a problem; a BBC which is open to talent from all communities and all cultures; a BBC which reflects the world in which we live today not the world of yesterday'. He had also expressed concern that 'young people' were ahead of the organisation in terms of recognising change. He reminded the audience that 'in London and Birmingham ... within less than 15 years, African-Caribbean and Asian people will make up at least 40 per cent of the youth population' and that '[they] the media don't understand the implications of that'.[40]

Within months, British channels began to launch new initiatives designed to increase the number of ethnic minority faces on screen, and behind the camera. The project would be called the 'Cultural Diversity Network' or CDN, and named as its first chairman, Carlton TV's chief executive Clive Jones. The CDN (now called Cultural DN) became a joint initiative involving the BBC, ITV, Carlton Television, Granada Media, Good Morning Television (GMTV), Independent Television News (ITN), Channel 4, Channel 5 and Rupert Murdoch's British Sky Broadcasting (BskyB). Via a mandate, each company produced an action plan, with employment targets and commitments to increase the number of Black and Asian screen actors and broadcasters. ITV said it would begin directing programme makers to consider how they portrayed issues of cultural diversity in their shows. The 'TV chiefs' as they were called, were 'concerned that black and Asian viewers are deserting them quicker than others', and 'admitted that not enough has been done to reflect the changing culture of Britain'.[41]

As examples of their efforts, the highly popular soap *Crossroads* (ITV, 1964–88; 2001–3) would now have a much stronger multicultural theme. Channel 4's plan was to increase its ethnic minority staff from 9 per cent of its payroll to 11 per cent by 2003, and Channel 5 said it aimed to reach 13 per cent. BskyB pledged to introduce a 'mentoring system'.[42] Echoing Dyke's concerns, Jones reminded broadcasters that they would 'lose even more viewers if change is not made now'. Britain was rapidly facing a change in demographics described as a 'revolution', which clearly signalled a need for rapid change. However, despite these efforts figures had worsened as Channel 4's employment of ethnic minorities fell during a period of economic downturn, from 13.5 per cent in 2000 to 6.6 per cent in 2001. By 2002 seven of the ITV franchises had no ethnic minorities in management at all, leading the broadcasting union BECTU (Broadcasting, Entertainment, Cinematograph and

Theatre Union) to call British television 'institutionally racist'. Within a year, Dyke accepted the chairmanship of the CDN, and by 2004 the BBC had met Dyke's higher targets, allowing him to raise them higher, but with ultimate redundancy in the coming years.[43]

Programming initiatives sought to normalise ethnic diversity as a part of British life on television screens, drawing black and Asian actors into mainstream dramas such as *Holby City* (BBC, 1999–), *EastEnders* (BBC, 1985–) *Merseybeat* (BBC, 2001–4), and as leads in shows like *Babyfather* (BBC2, 2001–2). While the Asian-themed *Kumars at No 42* (BBC2, 2001–4) was considered to be insightful (yet not appropriate for BBCA, as suggested by CEO Hilary later in this chapter), the black family sitcom *The Crouches* (BBC, 2003–5) was slammed by many in Briton's black community as shallow and bizarre. Critics included past BBC diversity manager Cyril Husbands, and other members of BBC Black Forum.[44] Also, in regard to increased representations of black and Asian faces on British television (the source for BBCA programming), a revitalisation and reinvention of classic genres may have incorporated more minority representations, yet these were still considered 'token characters'. Those programmes touted as signalling some degree of progress and change (i.e., *Hope and Glory* from BBC1 and the mini-series *Babyfather* from BBC2) did not last more than two seasons. Also, these programmes by no means 'represent a wholesale revolution in British televisions drama'.[45] Varied representations of these characters, and images of a multicultural Britain addressed by BBCA's Bill Hilary, are covered in the following section, as are discussions of American audiences, and their reception of this particular version of the UK.

Bill Hilary and BBCA

Six years after the start of BBCA under then CEO Paul Lee, Bill Hilary was hired away from Comedy Central to replace the incumbent. His immediate agenda, beside increased profitability, was to reach out to young, American audiences (as was Lee's), but with an eye toward multiculturalism. As an 'independently held commercial company', Hilary noted that BBCA's 'goal is to make money [for BBC Worldwide] and to support the production, marketing and programming efforts of the BBC'. In an interview that took place in May, 2016, Hilary stated that during his years as CEO, PBS and the Sci-Fi Channel, that first featured *Doctor Who* on American television, 'had more content than anyone', calling BBCA 'a British channel that attempted to represent Britain with a BBC title'. Hilary noted that BBCA 'in those days did not create their own programming, and instead purchased programming from the BBC,

Channel 4 or ITV, freeing the company to acquire programming from a variety of sources'. He noted that *Footballers' Wives* (ITV, 2002–6) was one of the most successful programmes offered, which featured a diverse cast, noting that BBCA was not designed merely to be a showcase for BBC content.

Expressing empathy for the racialised other 'as an Irishman', Hilary noted that before moving to America seventeen years earlier, he thought of life in London '30 years ago, [when he] was protected under the race discrimination act, as an [Irish] ethnic minority'. Then, when moving to New York, he found himself in the majority as 'white and Irish'. [When considering representations of race] Hilary notes again that his staff 'didn't set the agenda. [They] merely followed the British agenda, and what we thought would work in America.' He also noted that it was hard to find a drama series with a Brown or Black lead in 2004, and he called this absence, 'a kind of culture shock', to see how British programming 'really was in terms of diversity', and 'probably behind the times when compared to America. When I think of what was available to buy, I would have wanted much more diverse programming.' Demographic analysis was vital for ad sales in a commercially driven channel, and ethnic demographics were considered. However, he noted that Brown and Black viewers were not considered 'with any level of importance due to the limited exposure of BBCA to American homes'. At that time, he noted that 57 million homes were watching the channel, and 'seeing to a much younger audience, was essential'. Hilary noted that the effort to provide programming that reflected modern multicultural England 'was like a two-edged sword. [It] was very political organization'. He noted Director General Dyke's 'strong support' for his efforts in America, but with some concerns over how Americans view global programming, citing a lack of cultural competence.

As for Dyke's specific directives for cultural diversity, he explained that BBCA 'didn't control representations of Britishness to American audiences', forcing the channel to 'buy into whatever [constructs] the British considered racial equality – as it related to ethnic minorities – that existed. You bought into whatever the BBC, Channel 4 or ITV had already decided, because you simply bought what was already available.' He explained how the programme, *The Kumars at Number 42* (BBC, 2001–6), was a possibility for purchase and broadcast on BBCA, but he did not acquire it, for what he called 'ethnic reasons', because the programme wouldn't 'work here', due to certain cultural differences inherent to British life. He also noted that comedian and director Caroline Aherne's popular sitcom, *The Royle Family* (Granada, 1998–2008, and later ITV) was 'very, very British', and 'wouldn't be clearly appreciated', in the USA. Reminding himself that he was seeking to acquire programming that would relate to the 'widest possible audience', he did acquire 'lots of drama series. My decisions were not based upon what I could develop, but what I could buy.' BBCA tended 'not to do period pieces', at the time, 'because that was kind of PBS's brand'.

After being asked if he recalled programming that may have been available like *Babyfather*, *Shoot the Messenger* or *Holding On*, he wasn't aware of these titles, and felt some programming was 'before [his] time'. He again noted that perhaps these shows weren't picked up because they were so quintessentially British. However, after an explanation of the premise of *Babyfather* and the principal characters, he felt the programme could still work presently on BBCA, provided it wasn't too 'colloquialised or localised' to work for American audiences, including Blacks. Dyke's concerns about the lack of cultural diversity at the BBC had no bearing on Hilary's efforts at BBCA. The only correlation mentioned was that recent programming was failing to reflect the very modern-day Briton that Dyke acknowledged. He also suggested that certain programming he considered during his time at BBCA was too difficult for American audiences to comprehend.

When noting the spate of programmes during the early to mid-2000s that featured characters of colour, Hilary notes, 'that was me', as the person responsible for the acquisition of these shows. Though some weren't telecast under after he left, they were mostly purchased on his watch. He noted the success of *Luther* (BBC 2010–) as an example of successful programming that spanned the ocean, yet featured a Black lead. The offering of the show was thought by Hilary at first to be 'brilliant, but not really brilliant – just keeping up with the times'. It should be noted that seventeen Black Britons appeared in BBCA programming between 2002 and 2016, including lead dramatic roles. Many of these programmes were acquired by Hilary during his tenure at the channel as CEO. When asked if he could imagine a day in which BBCA featured more programmes with Black and Asian actors in lead, such as *Best Boy* and others (or perhaps even secondary roles), Hilary noted that BBCA has entered into the production of some programming, but still relies on British imports primarily. Licence agreements with BBC, Channel 4 and ITV still exist, and shape the choices made by BBCA, and now AMC. He notes that if he was still at BBCA:

> I would absolutely develop more programming featuring Brown and Black British characters, because that's the way America is changing. America is kind of in a weird position. Having just run millennial and multicultural channels for two years (Fuse) with a very large, like 45 percent African American, 20 percent Hispanic, and 30 percent white audiences,

[I see] the truth about American millennials. I don't know about the UK since I've been away so long, [but younger American audiences] don't see [race] the way an older generation did. They are part of a multicultural society, and I almost feel that what's happening is a reaction against that by an older generation. [For example], the rise of Donald Trump, and the rise of what is really right wing fascist elements is a reaction against a new generation – a generation that is digitally aware, but not aware of race the way an older generation was. There is a movement – a young movement happening which is very exciting. I think that that BBCA needs to keep up with these younger, multi-ethnic audiences, if they want to stay young in America.[46]

Addressing public service, and BBCA as a bastard child of the public service agenda and America commercial interest, Hilary noted that BBCA was a truly *commercial* venture, often placing it 'at odds' with certain BBC directives. He also noted that a commercial agenda does not necessarily mean 'anti-ethnic minorities', something he realised from years in advertising:

[Advertisers] want young, multicultural millennials. That is the 'hotbox' at the minute. If you can't provide that, you're seen as old fashioned. When I was there, as well, it was very important in America to represent all of America, not just a small part. With 270 million people in America, it's a much larger cross section and you do need to represent as much as you can, every part of that society.

Hilary noted that the present management of BBCA might find it difficult to find 'younger shows in the UK that would appeal here. If you look at the British imports that work, its things like *American Idol, Dancing with the Stars* – those big, glossy entertainment shows. Further, shows like *Downton Abbey* are popular due to its quintessential Britishness.' As an example, he noted that in its early years, during the 1980s, BBCA ran *EastEnders* which, despite shallow and staid representations, included a range of black and Asian characters that had previously rarely been seen on British television.[47] Despite criticisms of how *EastEnders'* multi-ethnic community is displaced within the narrative by white *EastEnders'* characters, the series also moved beyond Blackness as representative of social problems, and instead created dramatic roles that were significant to the plot. While the programme has traditionally revolved around these citizens, as Daniels and Gerson suggest, this narrative seemingly displaced those characters as an actual part of the community.[48] However, the programme, one of the early offerings by BBCA, at least featured people of colour as being very much a part of contemporary Britain.

Hilary noted that the BBC prides itself on not being commercial, yet it often features people of colour in roles that are 'worthy' of respect or honorary Britishness. However, he noted that 'much greater goals' could account for managerial decisions that reflect a fear of diversification of programme offerings – which is 'strange because America is definitely changing'. He noted how proud he was to have worked in an industry that reflected a very young, vibrant generation that is 'different than anything that has gone before'. He warned that, 'this is the future', and if BBCA and the nation doesn't 'head in that direction', including programming and representations, 'we're in trouble'. I noted that the programming he had commissioned was far more diverse; leading him to remind me that it was 'likely a reflection of what was going on in the UK at that time'. He also expressed frustration at the BBC not reflecting the changing Britain as more multicultural. It is possible, he feels, to 'reflect both kinds of England to audiences there and in America. It's not an either, or.'[49] Ideally, these images of black and Asian Britons as a normal part of contemporary life in the UK, should remind viewers of how culturally diverse the UK is. Further, the deconstruction of notions of Britishness, particularly on the part of black and Asian/Indian American viewers is fundamental to this study of BBCA and US audiences. Through a re-examination of globalisation, transnationalism encourages efforts toward the deconstruction of nationalism, and subsequent naming of citizenry.

Transnationalism, British programming and BBCA

Within this section, I examine how – despite a waning amount of black and brown faces on BBCA – transnationalism has a huge economic and intercultural effect on global audiences; touted as an ideological site for ethnic groups to negotiate power and agency. Similar notions apply to the potential agency for black and Asian Britons to shape the future of British television programming, and by proxy, shape American ideas of Britishness. This effort lends itself to what Shih and Lionnet call minor globalisations when discussing the work of Jenny Sharpe on rural Jamaica.[50] The authors discuss how Jamaican radio, unlike cyberspace, becomes a site for the negotiation of black female subjectivity and agency. I would argue that similar circumstances takes place for those international audiences of Blacks and Asians who choose to use 'global forms of transnationalism' that correspond to a virtual network of urban spaces, conglomerates and multinational media companies. Similar kinds of 'minor' globalisations allow for a detailed examination of BBCA and its choices of international television programming;

programming watched by black and Asian/Indian Americans seeking
to build communities; even if imagined, as suggested by the work of
Benedict Anderson.[51]

As an example, radio programmes created by West Indian producers
during the 1940s and 1950s, were broadcast by the BBC from production centres based in London; targeting indigenous West Indian audiences in Jamaica, Barbados and other islands. Each programme's live
broadcast constructed individual notions of ethnicity and empire whilst
highlighting discourses of transnationalism and citizenry. Ultimately, the
London-based show *Calling the West Indies* shifted focus and began to
offer an intrinsic view of the West Indian experience in the UK during
the segments *We See Britain* (1949) and *West Indian Diary* (1949).
Authors, servicemen, teachers and others who visited or lived in England
discussed their personal experiences and views on Britishness for the
benefit of those considering immigration. These narratives provided rare
opportunities for West Indians to discuss their personal perspectives on
life among white Britons and subsequent social issues. The BBC situated these segments within programmes they ultimately controlled; yet
producers and talent used these sites as locations for messages packed
with intrinsic value for hopeful citizens; citizens who developed strong
transnational ties to both countries.[52]

It is this moving of boundaries, and movement between social spaces,
that have ultimately allowed global audiences to glean what they choose
from global media industries and from growing, or ebbing trends in
media representations, and identities. Studies in media consumption
among diasporic communities highlight the immense possibilities for
those Americans viewing BBCA for not only cultural cues of familiar
Britishness, but for comparative contexts of race and imagery.[53] Paul
Lee's determination to highlight how BBCA 'blazed a trail for American
networks to follow', only tends to show that the channel did not accom-
plish its goals, and instead began to offer similar, safely homogenised
constructs of a white Britain so near and dear to many older Americans.
While the BBC may have tried to 'prove on American soil that it could
do what the American networks do, only better' current management
ultimately retreated to period pieces, endless marathons of *Star Trek: the
Next Generation* and James Bond films; *Top Gear*, and recent science
fiction narratives that revolve around sultry, white heroines such as
Orphan Black (BBC, 2013–), and *Thirteen* (BBC, 2016). As a welcome
departure from this formula, a growth in multicultural programming
seemingly occurred on Hilary's watch; increasing the number of black
and Asian Britons in various non-comedic roles that did not highlight
their 'otherness' but instead merely positioned them as Britons of colour.

Lee considered the knowledge of the BBC by Americans to be 'confined mainly to older, more highly educated urban-based viewers who watch *PBS' Masterpiece Theatre* (PBS, 1971–) or *Mystery* (PBS, 1980–), and little has changed.'

The cultural predilections held by American audiences have been historically shaped by mediated representations that range from the *Masterpiece Theatre* and its rebroadcasts of *Sense and Sensibility*, *Brideshead Revisited* and other costume dramas that, as Cooke reminds us, proved to be a financial boon to the BBC and its 'heritage exports', selling to 45 countries (including the USA) and reaching over 165 million viewers.[54] It is these very allusions to British upper class and privilege as normative values that make the counter-cultural forays and unruly behaviour of Pasty and Eddy in *Absolutely Fabulous* and the fumbling efforts of Hyacinth Bucket in *Keeping up Appearances* (BBC, 1990–95) so humorous to American viewers. As mentioned, programmes building on heritage (i.e. *Pride and Prejudice*, BBC, 2005), attracted what Selznick considered 'older, more traditional female audiences', whereas programmes like Granada's *Cracker* (A&E, 1993–96) were more appealing to younger, male audiences. Both were framed as 'high quality' programming, allowing for the targeting of vast audiences through 'branding', and by casting its 'cultural net' as widely as possible.[55] Further, as class and race often form a social nexus or outside constitutive that link those of colour with the problematic circumstances of poverty, crime and mindless violence, these allusions to higher-classed Britishness form an inclusion that typically does not incorporate black faces.

The public sphere that is *supposedly* national media, as suggested by Morley, 'is central in the mediation of the nation-state to the public, and that which is excluded from those media are excluded from the symbolic culture of the nation'.[56] If this culture is racialised by one largely undeclared principle form of ethnicity (which Catherine Hall argues Englishness truly is)[57] then only citizens who identify with this construct truly find this nation 'home'. As Dyer reminds us in his essays on privilege, this universalised whiteness becomes invisible; yet it is 'everything and nothing – a source of representational power'.[58] Particularly problematic is the linking of Britishness with a higher-class status as advertisement after advertisement in the USA attempts to market specific commodities and products with voiceovers that ooze resplendent British accents as a badge of better, more aristocratic endeavours. This is the case with advertisements for programmes on BBCA as well. Journalist Suzanne Moore's critiques of Anthony Smith's inability to accept the sociability of 'ordinary persons' appearing on American daytime talk programming provides an inverse example of the representations of Britishness American audiences are often shown.[59]

Beyond the need to hire and promote people of colour within the private club of British television, the degree of diversity in editorial and production processes clearly influence content, but also promote a skewed representation of Britishness yet again, for American audiences, in the case of this study, via the BBC. Surely A&E, PBS and Sci-Fi channel programming choices are also severely affected by these limitations. However, the casting of Britons of colour who are not framed as ghettoised criminals/victims/community leaders or hypersexualised denizens of the night, remain rare due in large part to what Born argues is an inability to gain participation in the production process. Whether the kind of 'home grown' production processes, such as the BBC's *Open Door* series (BBC2, 1973–75),[60] which allowed access to cameras and lighting to self-produce programming of an alternate variety, 'the camera and editing decisions' need to be placed 'directly in the hands of under-represented groups'. She noted that the issue becomes how 'adequately are Britain's publics' represented as 'producers and participants'. However, she also notes how diversity in relation to public service broadcasting offers a 'provision of a diverse range of genres on mass channels', drawing from the notion of 'broadcasting as culture', particularly when being shown to a global audience.

> [Whether] in the vicarious explorations of other lives offered by observational documentary, or in the daring subversions of common sense given by parodic comedy, or in the resonant imagery and imagined worlds generated by innovative drama, good television condenses a variety of expressive commentaries that extend the way we understand the human condition.[61]

As the BBC was driven by Greg Dyke to become more multicultural in its programming and hiring practices, BBCA began under Paul Lee with less diverse, older, more familiar favourites. By 2004 and Hilary's tenure, BBCA changed to showing multiracial programmes popular with UK audiences. As noted within this study, recent BBC programmes are far less diverse, once again. Programming for BBCA has also reflected this, and has fallen back upon representations of classic Britishness (i.e. a barrage of Bond films), American favourites (previously top grossing movies), and nature programmes from the Discovery Channel. Efforts to present a multi-ethnic Britain are not currently reflected in these programmes offered by the BBC leaving newer programmes featuring Black leads (*Undercover*, *Luther*) of value, but not reflective of either country's true diversity, or of those younger audiences suggested by Hilary. Further, considering the origins of BBC public service directives, the commercialised versions of British programming on BBCA, particularly those not segmented for advertisements as shows from Channel 4 and ITV are, can be awkwardly interrupted by commercials, rupturing the televisual flow of narrative storytelling.[62]

The future, *TV to go*, and the shifting paradigms

The younger, multicultural audiences that Hilary longed for during his tenure at BBCA, and that Dyke praised as essential to the future of the BBC, are slowly abandoning not only network television, but cable as well; choosing instead to stream, watch on line, and to 'TiVo', skipping ads along the way. As suggested by Levine and Newman's discussions of television's future and portability 'away from home' as a concept dating back to the 1960s with the advent and marketing of portable television sets.[63] Yet, the future of viewing in the convergence era allows for on-line purchases through streaming, and downloading; 'accessing files rather than of audiences for televised flow, and storing and accessing this content on a laptop or iPod', thereby 'keeping television shows in your purse or pocket'. It is channels like BBCA that stand to lose the very young, hip viewers they seek to attract.

A shifting, nearly indeterminable schedule of programming, inundated with nature shows, an aging roster of American films considered favourites, and a barrage of Bond films won't assure the continuance of the channel, particularly as even more technologies pull viewers away from traditional viewings habits. At the time of writing, a start-up company is working with Hollywood studios to initiate the 'Screening Room', where for a flat fee, new releases will be available in the home on the same day they are released in movie hit theatres, complete with a secure, anti-piracy technology. If audiences still choose to watch ad-driven shows on BBCA, they had better see more images like themselves; multicultural, multiracial and with fresh, innovative stories.

As Hilmes mentions when considering the 'battle of the paradigms' between 'the privately owned, competitive commercial system of the United States', and the 'state-charted public service monopoly of Great Britain' that was the BBC, the choice of non-commercial public service systems modelled after the BBC were considered 'the only defence against not only direct American influence', and 'the uncontrolled outbreak of popular culture', along with 'oppositional national ideologies and identities', that commercial systems might incite.[64] When considering the mere history of television in both nations, it seems almost unfathomable for these two models of broadcasting – as divergent as they are – to merge efforts under the umbrella of BBCA. The channel seems to have abandoned public service efforts, at least under the rubric of Dyke's diversity agenda, and instead chooses to operate as commercial channels do; with respect to advertisers and their concerns.

BBCA's interpretation and interpellation of American audiences' tastes for this cultural fabric reinforces a nearly homogenous culture – one that is friendly and foreign, yet familiar. When constructing a Britain that is devoid of ethnic diversity and multiracialism, ideological constructions rely upon whiteness as a normative construct, and seemingly assume that American viewers expect to see *this* kind of Britain. In doing so, a disservice is done through a kind of de facto racism; one that reinforces constructs of post-millennial Britain as nearly devoid of issues and narratives that incorporate those of colour. Furthermore, an assumption is seemingly made that white or majority American audiences don't have a desire or curiosity to examine these *Other* lives. As these audiences draw upon transnational images of race, gender and class from other nations, representations of whiteness and nationality are surely challenged (or at least disrupted) as brown faces and eyes gaze back into the camera's lens.

Lee suggests that BBCA 'was not beholden to the same standards and formulas as network television, striving to be much more innovative'. However, it seems very difficult to accept when considering Bill Hilary's insistence that BBCA is also 'incapable of taking risks' because they too are reliant upon advertising as a means to 'make money', and serve the needs of both BBC Worldwide and AMC. Clearly, advertising is a rather important part of BBCA's programming schema, and, as a result, the channel is beholden to the influence that advertisers wield, and that Reith hated so deeply.

The notion that American audiences responded to British programming according to their own cultural values and accents, creates a stronger argument for the power of reception, not those cultural producers who seek to shape Britishness in a manner less disconcerting to those American viewers steeped in ideas of what Britishness should, or used to be. Miller suggests that in the programme *The Avengers* (ABC Weekend Television, 1961–69), its Mrs Peel (played by Diana Rigg) 'was a character speaking to the changing roles for women in American society [reaching] an audience unconcerned with the deliberately placed British elements of the show'.[65] In this same manner, the desire of younger audiences (as suggested by Hilary), to potentially view Britishness in any manner they choose often includes a more multicultural manner. This agency allows for a reaffirmation of how viewers may *choose* to be hailed seeking BBCA's programmes, particularly through the mid-2000s. While images of blacks in America and Britain are continually linked with crime, or the presence of social problems, there is always an element of ambiguity in the representation of race, as suggested by Barker. Positive representations of black people are linked to sports, music (especially rap) creating a possible 'celebration and acceptance of black success', this process is also rife with the ghettoisation of black and Asian characters or icons.[66] BBCA's choice of programming during the 2000s seemingly offers the best possible disruption of this tiresome trend. As suggested, British television producers and the industry continue to be criticised by Henry, David Harewood and many others for not continuing to offer more opportunities for people of colour;[67] leading the BBC to again offer targeting for inclusion, along with BskyB.[68]

Henry noted a need to, first, create financing through 'ring-fenced money' earmarked for black and minority-ethnic programmes and productions. This would hopefully include placing 'a set number of hours and money aside to make these programmes', yet recognise their importance 'to the wellbeing of the UK'; noting that they must be protected from commercial pressures. He argued that the BBC has again failed to represent a multicultural Britain, by not dedicating funds to 'fulfil this part of the charter', thus devaluing 'the importance of diverse programmes and the role they play in creating a better and more cohesive society'. Second, he called for a 'centre of excellence' for diversity productions that would cross a broad range of genres; thereby allowing dramas, comedies, daytime programming, news and more to be considered a 'diverse production', if created by that unit. Finally, Henry noted the importance of accurate quantitative measurements of the amount of ethnic minorities working in the industry; an amount he argues is 'far lower than the broadcasters' estimates'. Citing a study in the *Guardian*, he noted that calculations from the BBC were 'greatly inflated by people who work in finance and in programmes for foreign audiences outside the UK, including the World Service, BBC Persia' and others. Once these departments are excluded, he argued that ethnic minorities working on BBC programmes fell to 'just 9.2 per cent'.

Henry also noted the immense support for these efforts by listing over fifty names of British industry figures, including Idris Elba, Emma Thompson, Marianne Jean-Baptiste, Charlie Hanson, Lynda La Plante and many others, who signed an open letter asking broadcasters to devote monies toward these and related efforts, including an increase in 'Black, Asian and minority ethnic (BAME) people', both on British television screens and behind cameras.[69] These issues and other were addressed by Culture Secretary John Whittingdale when unveiling a White Paper on the future of the BBC. He noted that the organisation would be required to focus on serving BAME viewers, making the BBC the 'leading broadcaster in addressing diversity issues', and ensuring that diversity would become a definitive part of the new charter.[70] Again, this effort does not include BBCA.

While the original intent of BBCA may be to avoid heavier, thought-provoking dramas for lighter fare, the omission of these narratives seemingly contradicts the essence of cultural diversity in programming; a prime competent of post-millennial and Dyke-influenced cosmopolitanism. As Malik and Corner have both suggested, Black characters within multiculturalist narratives, are often framed as 'part of the fabric of everyday institutional British life in integrated workspaces', including hospitals, the fire brigade, schools, and so on. Long-running mainstream dramas have been situated within these diegetic spaces, helping to normalise their presence in British daily life. However, Malik also notes that the differences underscored by race, both within the narrative, and the sheer imagery of Black and/or Brown performers creates an additional responsibility to these televisual authors to carefully and skilfully balance difference. When considering the soap opera, Corner notes how notions of routine lives and ordinariness help to craft these stories in a manner that draws from the parasocial, drawing pleasure from social realism. Each of the soaps studied have come to be understood within discourses of a 'particular, national version of "community"', grounded within 'cultural meanings surrounding locality, social class, wealth, and family'.

The balancing of race becomes far more complex, particularly as British television offers its spin on the constructs of race, and Blackness for the benefit of American audiences. Malik notes how Black soap opera characters, likely seen on BBCA's early broadcasts of *EastEnders*, the intertextuality inherent within the marketing of such shows via fanzines, talk programing, and news magazines help to bolster an interest in these programmes. More important is the ability of these texts to normalise the presence of these citizens. However, their ratings appeal is limited not only through a diminished presence, but a marked absence in popular programming; the mostly Black exclusion she notes occurred in the UK and USA until the premillennial years.

A saving grace may have been the workplace drama in which issues of race and socio-economic status were a given; a part of the overall narrative and premise of the programme. Malik and Corner note shows such as *Casualty* (BBC, 1986) and *London's Burning* (ITV, 2002) combining 'documentary strengths' with the daily 'routines of work within the rhythms of living, central to the British television experience'. Cable television and its many digital offerings expand this platform of reasoning and hopeful enlightenment through narrowcasting; which, though specialised in its content, offers alternatives to the staid, shallow diet of syndicated sitcoms, Movies of the Week, and vertically controlled films on HBO, Cinemax and Showtime. Offerings from the Independent Film Channel (IFC), Logo, Sundance and other cable channels seeking to provide voices to struggling film makers and alternative voices are easily sampled from one's family room or bedroom.

It should also be clearly noted that efforts by the BBC or by Henry to increase diversity have little to do with the choices currently being made by BBCA when programming for American audiences, especially since the channel currently draws programmes from a variety of sources, including BBC Worldwide, Channel 4, ITV and BskyB. According to Bill Hilary, the organisation was not bound by directives that speak to needs for cultural diversity. As mentioned during a personal interview, the channel was solely in the business of 'making money' for their commercial advertisers – a very different mandate from that of the BBC.[71] As Hilary noted, BBCA can only obtain what the BBC allows. However, at the time of writing, BBCA hardly offers any new, multicultural entertainment. It must also be noted that after agreeing to an interview to discuss current trends at BBCA and AMC, management cancelled the appointment after reviewing my questions, in advance.[72]

None of these perspectives suggest that BBCA deliberately avoids programming that features black and Asian Britons. However, these digital channels must learn to feature a multiplicity of voices and persona, or they will fail; particularly when considering the vast number of cable channels no longer holding audiences because of increased competition from Amazon, Netflix and a host of new 'a-la-carte' services forthcoming.[73] This is particularly disconcerting when considering BBC's historic public service doctrine, and recent efforts toward an increase in cultural education incorporating racial issues. This is a responsibility BBCA has surely not adopted; and as their line-up of new shows being ordered indicates, nor have their commercial sponsors.[74]

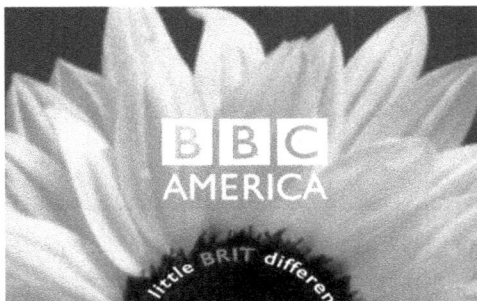

Figure 1.1 The BBC America flower logo (promotional image)

Figure 1.2 The BBC America jacket with RAF influenced logo (promotional image)

Figure 1.3 The Union Jack tongue and 'hipper' logo (promotional image)

Figure 1.4 Phillip Rhys and Chahak Patel as *Survivors* (BBC, tx. 23/11/08)

Figure 1.5 Julie Graham and Paterson Joseph as *Survivors* (BBC, tx. 9/12/08)

Figure 1.6 (Left to right) Paterson Joseph, Max Beesley, Zoë Tapper, Julie Graham, Phillip Rhys make up most of the multi-ethnic ensemble cast of *Survivors* (BBC, tx. 23/11/08)

Notes

1 Commission for Racial Equality, 'Citizenship and Belonging: What Is Britishness?' 2005: 22–39 (www.ethnos.co.uk/pdfs/9_what_is_britishness_CRE.pdf).

2 Selznick, Barbara J., *Global Television: Co-Producing Culture* (Philadelphia: Temple University Press, 2008), p. 177.

3 As indicated by a series of promotions messages about BBCA to US audiences. Other promos include mention of 'BBC America's superlative, sensational programming' (2011); the 'Britannica Man for BBC America' (2005); 'BBC

America: Television From the Other Side' (2011); and the oddly worded, 'We Speak English – and the World is better for This' (2013).

4 'Dyke: BBC is "Hideously White"', BBC News, 6 January 2001. http://news.bbc. co.uk/1/hi/scotland/1104305.stm (accessed 29 March 2017).

5 Dyke, Greg, 'Diversity in Broadcasting: A Public Service Perspective'. BBC Press Office. N.p., 3 May 2002, www.bbc.co.uk/pressoffice/speeches/stories/dyke_cba. shtml (accessed 30 March 2017).

6 Selznick, *Global Television*, p. 178.

7 Without including chat shows, the following Black actors (for the benefit of this study) played secondary roles, or leads in the following programmes during these seasons: Adetomiwa Edun – *The Hour* (BBC, 2011–12); Adrian Lester – *Undercover* (BBC, 2016); Ariyon Bakare – *Jonathan Strange & Mr Norrell* (BBCA, 2015); Ashley Walters – *Outcasts* (BBCA, 2010); Ato Essandoh – *Copper* (BBCA, 2012–13); Ben Bailey Smith (aka Doc Brown) – *Law and Order* (ITV, 2014); Britne Oldford – *Skins* (Channel 4, 2007), Colin Salmon – *Hex* (BskyB, 2004–5), David Harewood – *Robin Hood* (BBC, 2009); David Oyelowo – *Spooks/MI-5* (BBC, 2002–4); Idris Elba – *Luther* (BBC, 2010–15); Kevin Hanchard – *Orphan Black* (BBCA, 2013–16); Michael Obiora – *Hotel Babylon* (BBC, 2008–9); Nikki Amuka-Bird – *Luther* (BBC, 2011–13), *Survivors* (BBC, 2008–10); Nonso Anozie – *Occupation* (BBC, 2009); Paterson Joseph – *Law and Order UK* (ITV, 2013–14), *Survivors* (BBC, 2008–10), *Peep Show* (Channel 4, 2003–15); Sophie Okonedo – *Undercover* (BBC, 2016). A partial list of non-black minorities include Natalie Mendoza (*Hotel Babylon*), Yuki Kushida (*Little Britain*), Shelley Conn and Laila Rouass (*Mistresses*), Alexander Siddig (*Primeval*), Naoko Mori (*Absolutely Fabulous, Torchwood*) and African American Mekhi Phifer (*Torchwood*).

8 Anglophenia is a website, considered the 'Official tumblr for BBC America's Anglophenia: British culture with an American accent'.

9 Ahmed, Kamal, 'Black Writer Raps BBC over Race Bias', *Guardian*, 27 October 2002, www.theguardian.com/media/2002/oct/27/bbc.broadcasting (accessed 10 August 2015).

10 Jenkins, Henry, *Textual Poachers: Television Fans & Participatory Culture: Studies in culture and communication* (New York: Routledge, 1992); Gray, Jonathan, Cornel Sandvoss and C. Lee Harrington (eds), *Fandom: Identities and Communities in a Mediated World* (London, Routledge: 2007); Lotz, Amanda D., *The Television Will Be Revolutionized* (New York: New York University Press, 2007); Jancovich, Mark and Lyons, James (eds), *Quality Popular Television: Cult TV, the Industry and Fans* (London: BFI, 2008); Thompson, Ethan, and Mittell, Jason, *How to Watch Television* (New York: New York University Press, 2013).

11 Lewis, Melinda, 'Renegotiating British Identity through Comedy Television', thesis (Bowling Green State University, 2009), n.p.: n.p., n.d. Print, 19.

12 Becker, Christine, 'From High Culture to Hip Culture: Transforming the BBC into BBC America', *Anglo-American Media Interactions, 1850–2000* (Basingstoke: Palgrave Macmillan, 2007), p. 282.

13 As suggested by Roland Barthes, the notion of inoculation allows for a small quantity of outside influence into an institution to ward off cognisance of its essential shortcomings, or flaws. Bathes, Roland, *Mythologies* (Paris: Editions du Seuil, 1957), p. 136.

14 Gabriel, Deborah, 'Challenging the Whiteness of Britishness: Co-creating British Social History in the Blogosphere', Academia.edu., 2 May 2016; Clarke, Simon and Garner, Steven, *White Identities: A Critical Sociological Approach* (New York: Pluto Press, 2009); Roediger, David, *Towards the Abolition of Whiteness: Essays on Race, Politics, and Working Class History* (New York: Verso, 1994); Gilroy, Paul, *The Black Atlantic: Modernity and Double-Consciousness* (Cambridge. MA: Harvard University Press, 1993); Hall, Catherine, *White Male and Middle Class* (Polity Press, 1992).

15 'Time for Action', C21 Media, 30 September 2015 (published in *Features*), 'After decades of words but not much action, it seems the UK television industry is finally tackling ... take action.' The BBC director general at the time, Greg Dyke, said the BBC 'was still ... in 2009'. The situation is equally unsettling for the disabled, says Creative Skillset TV.

16 'BBC More "Hideously White" than Ever as Number of Black Executives Drops to All Time Low', *Evening Standard*, 11 January 2008, www.standard.co.uk/news/bbc-more-hideously-white-than-ever-as-number-of-black-executives-drops-to-all-time-low-7279102.html (accessed 17 November 2009).

17 Clarke, Steve, 'Lenny looks for Wicked New Talent', *Guardian*, 29 August 1990, p. 31.

18 Sarikakis, Katherine, *British Media in a Global Era* (Arnold, 2004), p. 113.

19 Villarreal, Yvonne, 'AMC Networks Pays $200 Million in Deal to Operate BBC America', *Los Angeles Times*, 23 October 2014, www.latimes.com/entertainment/envelope/cotown/la-et-ct-amc-networks-pays-200-million-in-deal-to-operate-bbc-america-20141023-story.html (acessed 12 January 2015).

20 Malik, Sarita, *Representing Black Britain: Black and Asian Images on Television* (London: Sage, 2002); Bourne, Stephen, *Black in the British Frame: Black people in British Film and Television 1896–1996* (London: Cassell, 1998); Gillespie, Marie, *Television, Ethnicity and Cultural Change* (London: Routledge, 1995); Pines, Jim (ed.), *Black and White in Colour: Black People in British Television since 1936* (London: BFI, 1992); Hall, Stuart, 'The Whites of their Eyes: Racist Ideologies and the Media', in Hugh Mackay (ed.), *The Media Reader* (London: BFI, 1990).

21 The schedule for Tuesday 17 May to Monday 23 May 2016 features a host of repeated programmes from past years, including: *Star Trek: The Next Generation* (Paramount, 1987–94) shown 35 times; *Planet Earth* (BBC/Discovery Channel, 2006–) shown 11 times; *Top Gear* (BBC/BBCA, 2002–) shown 12 times; *Orphan Black* (BBCA, 2013–) shown twice; *After the Black* (BBCA, 2015–), *Orphan Black*'s answer to *Talking Dead*, which routinely follows the popular *The Walking Dead* (AMC, 2010–); *The Graham Norton Show* (BBC, 2007–) aired once during the week, with *Man vs. Wild* (Channel 4/Discovery, 2006–) airing twice. *Weird Wonders* (BBC, 2014) aired once. American films

shown included *Apocalypto* (2006); *Aliens* (1986); *Terminator 3: Rise of the Machines* (2003); *Black Hawk Down* (2001); *The Monuments Men* (2014) and *Mad Max* (1979).

22 Selznick, *Global Television*, p. 168.

23 Katz, Michael, 'The British are Coming'. *Broadcasting and Cable*, 21 April 1997, p. 41.

24 Anonymous, 'BBC America Launches on DISH', *Broadcasting and Cable*, 2 November 1998, p. 41.

25 Bill Hilary in a personal interview suggested that BBCA underestimated the appreciation Americans would feel for 'Cockney East Enders', noting the show's large, 'cult' following – evidence of the often eclectic viewing habits of Americans. Lynn Smith, 'Missing "EastEnders"', *Los Angeles Times*, 4 October 2003. http://articles.latimes.com/2003/oct/04/entertainment/et-smith4 (accessed 5 October 2015).

26 Shows included *Doctor Who* (BBC), *The Graham Norton Show* (Channel 4), *Kitchen Nightmares* (US; Channel 4), *Man vs. Wild* (Channel 4), *Planet Earth* (BBC), *Ramsay's Kitchen Nightmares* (UK; Channel 4), *Star Trek: The Next Generation* (Paramount) and *Top Gear* (BBC).

27 'Bill Hilary Returns to BBC to Become New Head of BBC America', BBC Press Office, 4 October 2004, www.bbc.co.uk/pressoffice/pressreleases/stories/2004/10_october/04/hilary.shtml(accessed 22 September 2015).

28 Stoddart, Patrick, 'A Crucial Step for Black Comedy', *Sunday Times*, 28 October 1989, p. 15.

29 Clarke, 'Lenny looks for Wicked New Talent', p. 31.

30 Halloran, James, Bhatt, Arvind Bhatt, and Peggy Gray, 'Ethnic Minorities and Television: A Study of Use, Reactions and Preferences – A Report for Channel Four', Centre for Mass Communication Research, University of Leicester, April 1991.

31 Ross, Karen, 'In Whose Image? TV Criticism and Black Minority Viewers', in Simon Cottle (ed.), *Ethnic Minorities and the Media: Changing Cultural Boundaries* (Buckingham and Philadelphia: Open University Press, 2000), pp. 133–48.

32 Anonymous. 'EastEnders Accused of Racism', *Daily Mail*, 20 June 1992, p. 3.

33 Newton, Darrell, *Paving the Empire Road: BBC Television and Black Britons* (Manchester: Manchester University Press, 2011), p. 394.

34 Ouseley, Herman (ed.), 'Race and Television in Britain: Channels of Diversity-Seminar Report', Commission for Racial Equality, March 1996.

35 Cumberbatch, Guy, and Samantha Woods *et al.*, 'Ethnic Minorities on Television: A Report for the ITC', The Communications Research Group, Aston University, Birmingham, England, February 1996.

36 Dams, Tim, 'ABC to target Afro-Caribbeans', *Broadcast*, 7 March 1998, p. 8.

37 Anonymous, 'Greg Dyke is new BBC Boss'. BBC News, 24 June 1999. BBC Online Network, 17 August 2001, http://news.bbc.co.uk/hi/english/uk/newsid_377000/377424.stm.

38 Anonymous, 'Dyke Unveils Moves to Build "One BBC"', BBC News Release, 26 June 1999. BBC Online Network, 17 August 2001, www.bbc.co.uk/info/news/news231.htm.

39 Anonymous, 'New BBC Addresses Race in Media Awards', *Guardian*, 17 November 1999, www.theguardian.com/uk/1999/nov/17/race.world2 (accessed 30 March 2017).

40 Dyke, Greg, 'The BBC: Leading Cultural Change for a Rich and Diverse UK', Race in Media Awards 2000, 7 April 2000. Commission for Racial Equality, 17 August 2001, www.cre.gov.uk/media/nr_arch/gregdyke.html.

41 Wells, Matt, 'TV Chiefs Promise Broader Cultural Picture', *Guardian*, 13 October 2000, www.theguardian.com/media/2000/oct/13/raceintheuk (accessed 20 August 2001).

42 *Ibid.*

43 Born, Georgina, *Uncertain Vision: Birt, Dyke and the Reinvention of the BBC* (New York: Random House, 2005), pp. 470–1.

44 Husbands and others railed against the programme in personal interviews for Newton, *Paving the Empire Road.*

45 Cooke, Lez, *British Television Drama: A History* (London: BFI, 2003), p. 84.

46 Hilary, Bill. Personal Interview, 3 May, 2016.

47 As suggested by a variety of researchers, including Malik, Sarita, *Representing Black Britain: Black and Asian Images on Television* (London: Sage, 2002); Newton, *Paving the Empire Road*; Bignell, Jonathan, *An Introduction to Television Studies* (London: Routledge, 2012); and Schaffer, Gavin, *The Vision of a Nation: Making Multiculturalism on British Television 1960–80* (New York: Palgrave Macmillan, 2014).

48 Daniels, Therese and Jane Gerson (eds), *The Colour Black* (London: BFI, 1989).

49 Hilary, Bill, personal interview, 3 May 2016.

50 Lionett, Francoise and Shih, Shu-mei, *Minor Transnationalism* (Durham: Duke University Press, 2005), p. 19.

51 Anderson, Benedict, *Imagined Communities: Reflections on the Origin and Spread of Nationalism* (London: Verso, 1991).

52 Newton, Darrell, 'Calling the West Indies: The BBC World Service and Caribbean Voices'. *The Historical Journal of Film, Radio, and Television*, 28:4 (2010), p. 495.

53 Selznick, *Global Television*, p. 114.

54 Cooke, *British Television Drama*, p. 98.

55 Selznick, *Global Television*, pp. 71–3.

56 Morley, David, *Home Territories: Media, Mobility and Identity* (London: Routledge, 2000), p. 118.

57 See Hall, Catherine, *White Male and Middle Class* (Polity Press, 1992).

58 Dyer, Richard, 'Is the Camera Racist?' *Guardian*, 18 July 1997: sec. 2, 13.

59 Moore, Suzanne, 'Barking up the Family Tree', *Guardian*, 9 March 1995.

60 The BBC approved, as an experiment, 13 weekly programmes, broadcast as the community series, *Open Door*. The programme ran at a non-peak hour on BBC2, Mondays at 11.30 p.m. beginning 2 April, lasting for forty minutes.

Specific shows related to groups of colour and immigrants included the Black Teachers' Group, who expressed concerns about the English education system as it affected black children (16 April 1973). Other programmes included a show on Immigrant Workers' Rights (25 March 1974) featuring criticisms from Indian immigrants on the lack of support shown by the trade unions for 'coloured workers', mainly in Nottingham. *Black Feet in the Snow* (8 April 1974) was a musical drama made by the West Indian Radical Alliance of Poets and Players (RAPP). *The Nite Blues Steel Band* (29 September 1974) told the history of the West Indies through steel band music played regularly in Essex. The Standing Conference of Asian Communities in the UK were given two successive weeks (28 April–5 May 1975) in which they discussed solutions to difficulties faced by Asian communities in Britain. Newton, *Paving the Empire Road*, p. 286.

61 Born, Georgina, *Uncertain Vision: Birt, Dyke and the Reinvention of the BBC* (London: Random House, 2005), pp. 380–1.

62 See Butler, Jeremy, *Television: Critical Methods and Applications* (New York: Routledge, 2001).

63 See Spigel, Lynn, *Welcome to the Dreamhouse: Popular Media and Postwar Suburbs* (Durham, NC: Duke University Press, 2001).

64 Hilmes, Michele, 'Who we are, Who we are Not: Battle of the Global Paradigms', in Lisa Parks and Shanti Kumar (eds), *Planet TV* (New York: New York University Press, 2003), p. 54.

65 Miller, Jeffrey S., *Something Completely Different: British Television and American Culture* (University of Minnesota Press, 2000), p. 45.

66 Barker, Chris, *Television, Globalization, and Cultural Identities* (Maidenhead, Open University Press, 2005), p. 81.

67 Godwin, Richard, 'David Harewood Nearly Quit Acting before Homeland', *Radio Times*, 1 March 2016, www.radiotimes.com/news/2016-03-01/david-harewood-nearly-quit-acting-before-homeland (accessed 10 April 2016).

68 Conlan, Tara, 'Lenny Henry Calls for Law to Boost Low Numbers of Black People in TV Industry', *Guardian*, 17 March 2014, www.theguardian.com/media/2014/mar/18/lenny-henry-black-asian-television (accessed 23 April 2016).

69 Henry, Lenny, 'My Three-point Plan for BBC Reform', *Guardian*, 12 May 2016. www.theguardian.com/commentisfree/2016/may/12/three-point-plan-bbc-reform-lenny-henry (accessed 23 May 2016).

70 Plunkett, John, 'BBC White Paper: Key Points at a Glance', *Guardian*, 12 May 2016. www.theguardian.com/media/2016/may/12/bbc-white-paper-key-points-john-whittingdale (accessed 23 May 2016).

71 Hilary, Bill, personal interview, 3 May 2016.

72 In an attempt to discuss this essay with current BBCA management, I wrote on 30 November 2015 to request an interview. After a series of emails, a date was set. At the request of the organization, I forwarded these questions in advance: 1) When considering the myriads of programmes available through the BBC, ITV and Channel 4, what kinds of considerations are made when it comes to the ultimate choices for BBC America? What kinds of demographic analyses has

BBCA undertaken that justifies its programming choices? How do audience reactions to popular programming in the UK translate into what American viewers may enjoy? 2) Past Director General Greg Dyke once called the BBC 'hideously white', and also noted that the organisation had a role in reflecting a '21st century Britain', as 'multi-channel, and multi-cultural'. In what manner does BBCA attempt to reflect the modern day, multi-ethnic Britain? 3) BBCA programming has primarily featured shows with predominately or all-white casts; reinforcing a Britain devoid of black and brown faces other than the occasional character actor or sidekick. Whilst *Luther* with Idris Elba has done well, absent are the controversial yet thought provoking BBC dramas *Babyfather* (2001), *Shoot the Messenger* (2006), *Holding On* (1997) or other shows that feature a multiracial or black British cast. What are your thoughts about these omissions, and the future of BBCA's choices?

Several days later, the interview was cancelled by a corporate VP with partner network, AMC Networks, indicating, 'Thanks for being in touch but we are going to pass on this.' No actual reason was given.

73 LaFayette, John, 'Turner CEO Says U.S. Has Too Many Networks', *Broadcasting and Cable*, 4 May 2016, www.broadcastingcable.com/blog/currency/turner-ceo-says-us-has-too-many-networks/156186 (accessed 11 May 2016).

74 Stanhope, Kate, 'BBC America Orders Dramas from "Murderball," "Hitchhiker's Guide" Creators', *The Hollywood Reporter*, 31 July 2015, www.hollywoodreporter.com/live-feed/bbc-america-orders-dramas-murderball-812407 (accessed 11 May 2016).

2

Scheduling race

Anamik Saha

Writing in the mid-1980s, Nicholas Garnham describes broadcasting as the 'heartland of contemporary cultural practice'. While television in terms of its production and – especially – consumption has been radically transformed by the impact of new digital technologies, Garnham's point about the centrality of television to a nation's cultural life still remains. This is not least 'because of the high proportion of consumers' time and money devoted to it and because, as a result of that concentration of attention, it is itself both directly and indirectly the major cultural patron'.[1] In terms of this book's interests, British public service broadcasting in this role as 'cultural patron' has a particularly critical role to play in determining the extent to which racialised minorities are recognised, represented and catered for within the national imaginary. This chapter's concern is the extent to which public service broadcasters – specifically the BBC and Channel 4 – achieve this and contribute to the formation of what might be described as a progressive 'multicultural public sphere'.[2]

This is a matter of regulation in the UK since public service broadcasters, whether publicly or commercially funded, have a remit to represent 'its nations, regions and communities' – in the case of the BBC – and appeal 'to the tastes and interests of a culturally diverse society', in the case of Channel 4 (Communications Act, 2003). Yet it is widely understood – by academics and industry itself – that television has a problem with race. This can be measured in terms of the declining numbers of minorities working in the industry, or in analysing the quality of the nature of representations of minorities, where racial and ethnic groups, when not rendered invisible, tend to be framed within racialised tropes and historical constructions of Otherness. In paralleling the industry's recognition of its own failings with regard to the experience of minorities on and off screen, scholars are increasingly examining cultural production itself for clues as to why representations take the shape that they do.[3]

Yet this remains a frustratingly marginal area of research that needs further development. When the focus is not solely on issues of representation, which is the dominant mode in studies of race and the media, the tendency in studies of diversity and the media is to place the cultural producer or symbol creator at the centre of the analysis. Yet artistic/cultural practice is just one part of the production process. For Garnham, the 'cultural process is as much, if not more, about creating audiences or publics as it is about producing cultural artefacts or performances'.[4] In the context of broadcasting Garnham's comment switches the spotlight onto scheduling – and the search of audiences – as the key site where 'cultural plurality' is achieved or not achieved. Yet in television studies and broader studies of production, scheduling and cultural distribution in general is a neglected area of research. In the still growing field of race and production studies, the discussion on scheduling is almost non-existent, except for one telling contribution by critical media scholar Tim Havens. This is a significant omission. In this chapter I argue, following Garnham's lead, that the scheduling of – for want of a better term – 'minority programming', and the commitment to finding, or rather, creating audiences for this type of programming is a much more crucial moment in the cultural process than receiving the commission to make the programme in the first place. In the relatively small amount of research literature on scheduling the process is stressed as an 'art form' or, as Jonathan Ellis puts it, the last creative act. But I want to go further and emphasise the ideological role of scheduling – specifically in relation to the representation of racialised minorities. Using a case study of British South Asian[5] television workers reflecting on their experience of scheduling, I demonstrate how this neglected and particularly opaque stage of production has a determining effect on the recognition and representation of minorities on television.

From the art of scheduling to the politics of scheduling

It feels anachronistic to talk about scheduling in a time of DVRs, online streaming and 'catch-up TV', where 'television viewers become schedulers themselves'.[6] Yet, as is often the case in evangelical pronouncements about the revolutionary impact of new digital media, the death of traditional forms of television viewing has been greatly exaggerated. According to Ofcom's 2015 Communications Market Report, those belonging to the 16–34 age group still watch two-thirds of television live and not time shifted – and 77 per cent of the whole population does the same. So while there is undoubtedly a significant increase in the volume of time-shifted viewing, it is also fair to say that schedulers and scheduling still shape television consumption in the majority of households. As Bignell says, 'for the moment it seems likely that viewers will still want to see the free programmes which are available simply by switching on the television when the daily routines of life in British households allow them the opportunity to do so. Scheduling remains a crucial activity in shaping audiences.'[7] Indeed, while the research for this chapter was conducted in the mid-2000s – at a time where time-shifted television was in its relative infancy – the narratives collected on scheduling still resonate in contemporary times. Broadcasters, of course, increasingly factor in the issue of time-shifting television when commissioning programmes. But the scheduling of live television remains a crucial part of broadcasting.

For those researching and writing about scheduling it is de rigueur to begin by stressing how little has been written about the subject. Nonetheless, literature on scheduling, despite its limited size, can be split into two fields of research. First, there is the field of television studies, which has made an important contribution in drawing attention to scheduling as a significant force in how we view and experience television. The field in turn can be characterised by two approaches. The first explores television programming in terms of how it shapes and fits within the rhythms of modern life.[8] The second focuses on the process of scheduling itself, and the scheduler's task in finding audiences for programmes, whether in terms of maximising ratings and advertising revenue, or fulfilling public service remits. This literature draws attention to the historical shift that has occurred in scheduling practices, from a process of trial and error, based on perceptions of what audiences wanted, or needed, to watch and when 'without much thought to the fact that they might want different kinds of programmes to those on offer',[9] to a more rationalised process where the grid pattern of 30-minute slots became commonplace.[10]

In this second period, different types of programmes, or rather, genres of programmes would be slotted within the grid according to common-sense ideas about everyday life and indeed, gendered understandings of the heteronormative family.[11] Other factors that determined which programmes are scheduled, and when, include national holidays/traditions (e.g. Christmas), live events (e.g. the Olympic Games), policy (e.g. when the news or children television should be broadcast) and increasingly, competition with other channels. The particular focus of researchers in television studies is the role of data in shaping television schedules, not only television ratings and audience breakdowns provided by the

Broadcasters' Audience Research Bureau (BARB), but also the increasing use of focus groups, and the way that the process of scheduling is then rationalised and narrated by television executives using somewhat peculiar industry jargon such as: 'echoes' and 'pre-echoes', 'junction points', 'tent-pole programmes', 'peeling away audiences' or 'hammocking'.[12]

Studies of scheduling tend to follow in the 'production of culture' tradition and, as a consequence, are descriptive and neutral in tone rather than critical. Yet we can identify two important arguments in this literature. The first important finding by television studies scholars is that despite the dominance of data in determining scheduling decisions, the process 'is still riddled with uncertainty'[13] where the role of schedulers and executives in interpreting data and then rationalising the process in which programmes are scheduled is still central. It is in this sense that scheduling is often referred to as an 'art' in this literature, not in terms of 'placing individual programmes into the itinerary, but in creating a seamless televisual flow that secures channel loyalty'.[14] Ellis describes scheduling as both a 'black art' in its lack of transparency and the 'last creative act', which he compares to editing a film, as the 'principles involved are broadly similar to those of narrative construction'.[15] The second important contribution of this research is on the impact of competition and how this increasingly determines scheduling. The emphasis again here is on uncertainty and how 'television schedulers are wary of taking risks by making decisions that run counter to their expectations about time slots and the positions of programmes within television seasons'.[16] There is an even more bold suggestion that schedulers have the most influence in television production. As Bignell and Orlebar state: 'The power to commission new programmes is in the hands of broadcasting executives, but schedulers have an important role to play in identifying programmes that are likely to gain audiences, based on information schedulers have about what audiences have watched in the past. So schedulers provide recommendations of commissioning executives and thus influence which programmes are made.'[17]

This produces conservatism leading to oversupply of certain types and formats of programmes. For Calvert et al., 'Predictability is important, as one of the core aims of scheduling is to assist broadcasters in capturing the biggest audience possible, the maximising advertising revenues.'[18] In light of this, Ellis defines scheduling as 'the locus of power in television, the mechanism whereby demographic speculations are turned into a viewing experience. And it is more than that as well, for any schedule contains the distillation of the past history of a channel, of national broadcasting as a whole, and of the particular habits of national life.'[19] He goes on to say, 'the facts that make every nation's television specific ... are produced and reproduced within the dynamic process of scheduling'.[20]

Thus the important contribution of television studies is in shedding light on the opaque nature of scheduling – a process that is crucial to the habits of national life, as Ellis puts it, though he is unwilling to go as far as saying national identity itself. Indeed, this particular approach is descriptive rather than critical. This makes it no less valuable, and the reason for covering this literature in relative depth is because it provides the context for the empirical material to follow in the next section. Yet the television studies research of the type that I cite is more interested in describing the practices of scheduling, rather than thinking through this process in relation to questions of power. In light of this chapter's concern with the ideological function of scheduling in relation to the programmes made by racialised minorities, I want to draw from the second field of research that tackles scheduling, which comes from a critical cultural studies perspective. I am specifically referring to the work of critical media industries scholar, Tim Havens.

Drawing from Raymond Williams's influential work on television, and programming as experienced as a 'flow' rather than the individual consumption of discrete units, Tim Havens in *Black Television Travels* applies a 'critical analysis of program schedules', not unlike Williams's own study, to see how 'they privilege particular discourses and position viewers'. [21] Of particular pertinence for this chapter is Havens's interest in representations of race, and specifically, the journey of African American television in the context of international syndication. His concern is with what he describes as 'industry lore' – a distinct form of power/knowledge – that informs what gets bought and sold in domestic and international markets. Havens argues that 'African American television', despite sometimes huge domestic success, has struggled to be syndicated in international markets because it is considered too culturally specific. Yet, Havens finds various exceptions to this overall trend, including the case of South African television during apartheid in the 1980s – and, in particular, the scheduling strategies of 'renegade' black South African broadcasters Bophuthatswana Broadcasting Corporation (Bop-TV) who went against the grain and bought several African American television shows during the 1980s.

To reiterate, Havens is not just interested in the shows that were syndicated, but in how they were placed in the television schedule. Echoing Williams's work, Havens states that 'while an analysis of a single program or genre tells us only how that program or genre imagines society, a reading of program schedules tells us how entire changes or entire national broadcasting systems imagine viewers' identities, sympathies, and relationships'.[22] Havens focuses on Bop-TV's counter-programming techniques through 'vertical' strategies and the creation of its brand by creating a mix of local productions and integrated African American television. The effort sought to bring together English speakers and black viewers; exploiting lingering tensions between white English speakers and Afrikaners. 'Horizontal' strategies were also a consideration, where Bop-TV 'Counter programmed' American imports and other programmes against white TV1, black TV2 and TV3 as part of a 'concerted effort to imagine and assemble an integrated viewing audience, while maintaining its primary identity as a black channel'. Therefore Bop-TV succeeded in using imported US series, scheduling them in a strategic way that helped 'bring together certain segments of the black and white viewing public, and to project an integrated, cosmopolitan channel identity', which, as Havens describes, some commentators argue contributed to the fall of apartheid nearly a decade later.[23]

For Havens 'scheduling, then, serves as a primary site where institutionalised perceptions of viewers' tastes, affiliations, and identities become available for analysis'.[24] This is particularly pertinent for my own study into the programming of British Asian television and what it might say about the experience of living with difference in the UK. My approach is different, though, in two ways. First, rather than taking television schedules as objects to examine critically, as Havens and Williams do, my interest is in Asian filmmakers, producers and executives. I consider how they reflect on scheduling practices in relation to their own experience; what this reveals about the challenges facing people of colour working in television and how the scheduling process itself is racialised. As a result, my approach differs methodologically from Havens. Whereas Havens's study is historical, reliant on archives, and in particular, trade magazines for the insights of television executives into scheduling strategies, mine is based on qualitative interviews with over twenty predominantly Asian television workers to see how they describe, reflect on and narrate their experience of scheduling and schedulers.

I also work with a different theoretical model from Havens, adopting the 'cultural industries' tradition of the political economy of culture. Such an approach emphasises the particularities of cultural industries – as distinct from other industries – framed within a broader of discussion of the relations between capitalism and culture, according to a 'properly sophisticated reading of Marx',[25] which recognises the ambivalence of markets. The cultural industries approach is grounded in social theory, and empirical in nature. In terms of this chapter there are three particularly pertinent characteristics of industrial cultural production that the cultural industries approach draws attention to. First it emphasises the inherent riskiness of cultural production, since the use value of cultural goods is based on their difference and novelty.[26] When production costs are so high this generally means that media owners tend to be conservative and risk-adverse – this is particularly true of television schedulers – but there is always the potential for unexpected successes that go against the grain, either in terms of content or form. This is the ambivalence of cultural production.

Second, the cultural industries approach characterises industrial cultural production as employing a form of 'loose/tight control'. This refers to how, in the main, symbol creators are given a lot of autonomy – or are loosely controlled in contrast to other workers in other industries – in order to produce products that are original and novel. But it is when the product is handed over that media owners and executive enforce strict control over the marketing/publicity/distribution process, employing techniques of rationalisation such as data and 'formatting' techniques (e.g. the use of the star system or genre conventions) that determine how the product is received in the marketplace, or indeed where it is placed in a television schedule.

This leads on to the third important insight that the cultural industries approach brings: it is, as Garnham puts it, 'cultural distribution, not cultural production, that is the key locus of power and profit. It is access to distribution which is the key to cultural plurality'. Garnham describes this as the 'editorial' stage of production. Based on this comment, this chapter seeks to demonstrate how scheduling, as a form of cultural distribution, ultimately determines the ability for minorities such as British Asians to produce narratives that can contribute to cultural plurality, and a progressive/radical multicultural politics.[27] I show that the forms of rationalisation employed by schedulers and executive producers contain within them racialising dynamics. Specifically, I am thinking of the way British Asian texts are dispersed, where they literally come to be placed at the centre of discourse, or on the periphery, depending on their narrative. This chapter aims to bring into sharp focus the decisive nature of distribution for British Asian cultural production. As I have already stated, scheduling has an ideological function that is missed in the television studies literature outlined above.

Scheduling British Asian television

When it comes to the scheduling of what I broadly label British Asian television programmes – that is, programmes about a facet of British Asian experience – we find that such programmes rarely featuring in prime time, and are frequently marginalised to the 'efnik graveyard' slots.[28] This view is based on an industry perception of British Asian television as niche, with little mainstream appeal. In this section I highlight how, in order to appear on prime time, an Asian programme needs to exhibit crossover potential, usually by producing a particular representation of Asian identity and culture that executives imagine will be something that the 'white mainstream' audience can understand and relate to. I demonstrate that this has physical effects, where those pro-grammes that provide particular Indophilic (as discussed by Prashad) representation of Asianness are more likely to be allocated prime-time viewing over more complex representations, which are side-lined to non-mainstream timeslots.[29]

The fundamental aim of television scheduling is to boost ratings and prevent a viewer from switching over to the competition. Scheduling is therefore a structured task with its own position, constituted by a range of considerations and constraints. As Fanthome states, 'Schedulers must be able to analyse audience data, find the right time slots for programmes and programmes for the right slots, locate "new" audiences, and ensure that the viewers are able to navigate the schedule with relative ease.' Since the proliferation of satellite, digital and cable channels, audience groups have become more fragmented and the 'art of scheduling' has become an even more inexact science.[30] Hence, schedulers are assuming an increasingly influential role in the commissioning process. Whereas in the past scheduling was offer-led, and schedulers would construct a schedule out of the programmes handed to them, in more recent times, this has shifted to demand-led scheduling, where the audience needs are anticipated, and the timeslots filled appropriately. As one interviewee from the BBC said to me, the scheduler has become the 'controller's right-hand man' (sic). The role of the scheduler is to outline the kinds of programmes that are needed to fill specific slots, based on various sources of statistical infor-mation, such as historical and up-to-the-minute ratings data, audience demographics and so on. Thus schedulers represent the growing quanti-fication and rationalisation of editorial decisions – an attempt to bridle the unpredictability of the market.

The intensely competitive marketplace that characterises the contem-porary television industry means that executives – even those working in public service broadcasting (PSB) – are pressured to produce 'main-stream' output, or, inversely, ensure that niche stories can cross over to the biggest potential audience. This is the particular way Aaqil Ahmed, former head of religion at Channel 4 (figure 2.3), makes sense of his work in relation to scheduling. Speaking in front of the BBC Charter Review Select Committee on the subject of religious programming,

Ahmed described how the Channel 4 religion unit had commissioned '50 hours of programming of which only 4.4 hours are not broadcast at 7, 8 or 9 p.m. during the week or on a Saturday' (UK Parliament, 2005). In light of this, I wanted to see in my interview with Ahmed how he explained his success in gaining coveted prime-time slots. This produced the following account:

> Well, the honest truth is you have to deliver. ... If you go to your bosses and say we've got Inside the Mind of a Suicide-Bomber, Children of Abraham, Karbala, Priest Idol, God is Black with Robert [Beckford] – these are the first five things we commissioned. If you go to them with that then they are going to turn around to you and say, alright, we'll have all of those in primetime! They're not going to want put those on the periphery of the schedule because they are just too bloody good. So all you've got to do is convince them that these things are bloody good [...] look at the cookery show [*Indian Food Made Easy*] – the cookery show is on primetime. All the factors that make that work are: it's mainstream enough for a wide-enough audience and its subject matter that everyone is going to be interested in. And I think they have got an interesting presenter and it just feels right, so go for it. Sanjeev Bhaskar wants to do something on India, put it on primetime because he's Sanjeev. It's all about what you are selling.[31]

The initial part of this narrative is based on a normative sense of quality; Ahmed matter-of-factly attributes his success in acquiring prime-time positions to simply making programmes that are 'bloody good'. Yet towards the end of this account, the respondent provides more detail about what he believes are the factors that ensure prime-time programming: content that is 'mainstream enough for a wide-enough audience', preferably fronted by a celebrity such as Sanjeev Bhaskar. It is interesting that Ahmed uses BBC cookery show *Indian Food Made Easy* – produced by the now defunct Asian Programming Unit (APU) – as an example of 'mainstream' Asian programming, especially since he is critical of the BBC's 'flagship' Asian programming *Desi DNA* (BBC Asian, 2003–) (also produced by the APU) for not having the same cross-over appeal (figure 2.1). Indeed, a Pact[32] report on 'minority ethnic-led' independent television companies noted how the industry was 'moving towards mainstreaming cultural diversity',[33] following a rationale 'that mainstream and minority tastes are no longer divided'.[34]

This is a trend delineated by Sarita Malik who highlights a shift in public service broadcasting in its remit to cater for minorities, from a policy of multiculturalism, where programming is designed to cater for specific minority groups, to a policy of cultural diversity, where 'minority programming' is brought into the centre, with racial/ethnic diversity as just one of many diversities incorporated into mainstream programming. Malik in fact argues that we have entered a further stage defined by 'creative diversity' policy, whereby diversity is yet again reconceptualised, this time as a quality that can produce innovation, originality and excellence in output. For Malik this is a deeply ideological shift where policy that was originally designed to address the experiences of racial and ethnic minorities has been gradually diluted so that it no longer attends to issues of marginalisation and racism.[35] Moreover, in my view, the shift towards the mainstreaming of British Asian programming acts as a form of racialised governance, where cultural practices are shaped in a way that transforms the potential radical hybridity of British Asian cultural expression into predictable, reified, absolute difference. This is enacted through a normative commercial rationale that follows a neo-liberal trend in the cultural industries which states that free market and free trade are the most efficient means of producing and distributing cultural works. The focus here, then, is on how the politics of British Asian cultural production are affected by the supposed convergence of mainstream and niche; or rather the subsumption of the latter by the former, as it manifests in the process of scheduling.

'Mainstream' vs. 'niche'

Implicit in Aaqil Ahmed's recipe for securing prime-time slots is an assumption about what is perceived to be 'mainstream' and 'niche': as he states, prime time is ensured by producing content that is 'mainstream enough for a wide-enough audience and [has] subject matter that everyone is going to be interested in'. Further implied is that 'mainstream' is equated to the white majority, with 'niche' associated with ethnically defined communities; according to Channel 4 Commissioning Editor Nasfim Haque's definition, '[niche] is anything that is of a different culture'. Thus, a recurring theme in the research presented here is how British Asian cultural works are by default regarded as niche or, put another way, how its success is measured by its ability to cross over into the white, mainstream market. When put in these terms, the ideological dimension to the 'mainstream' and 'niche' binary becomes evident. Several respondents cited two BBC programmes that were broadcast at the time of this research – *Indian Food Made Easy* (BBC Asian, 2007–) and *Lost World of the Raj* (BBC1, 2007) – as examples of how Asian programming can obtain prime-time scheduling. Yet these programmes seem to present a more recognisable – or indeed Indophilic – representation of Asianness deemed suitable for mainstream, white tastes. Vijay Prashad in his historical overview of Indophilia, refers to the West's long-held fascination with the 'ghastly and beautiful mystery' of the Indian sub-continent.[36] This would suggest that it is only those versions of Asianness judged 'beautiful' (e.g. Indian cuisine or ancient history) or 'ghastly' (e.g. honour killings, religious fundamentalism) that are able to secure mainstream, prime-time coverage. It is the normative terms in which this is rationalised during the scheduling process – via notions of 'mainstream' and 'niche' – that dictate how the counternarratives of difference are governed, foregrounding the more complicit narratives, and side-lining the potentially challenging disruptive ones.

Thus, scheduling is a critical area for British Asian programming, providing an example of how commercial logic governs the narratives of difference within racialised hierarchies of inclusion. One critical industry development that has affected the narratives of British Asian symbol creators is how channels are placing less priority on one-off films/documentaries. Since the 1980s television schedules have been organised according to a grid split into 30-minute/one-hour slots. This in effect shapes the structure of television programmes that have to fit into these slots. Arguably, this implicitly serves to close down the space for more experimental, risky programmes; which include minority/niche-interest programming. But the point I want to raise here is how this development has contributed to a shift towards serialisation that has had a negative impact on minority programming. An increasingly competitive environment means that broadcasters are looking for format-based series, which have proved a lucrative market since they cost less to make, and can be sold abroad. Since British Asians wanting to explore British Asian issues are unlikely to receive a commission for a whole series, with a few notable exceptions, producers and directors are confined to making one-off films. In terms of scheduling, such films very rarely get prime-time slots, despite receiving relatively large budgets. This issue unravels in an exchange with British Asian producer/director Minoo Bhatia (figure 2.6) who reflected on her award-winning BBC2 documentary *Who Do you Think You're Talking To?*[37] in which call-centre workers in Bangalore and Norwich swapped jobs:

AS: Were you happy with the way your films went out?
MB: No. I feel with the call centre film it went out on a really late slot. 11:20pm. Which is a real shame because it was a really well resourced film – it's not as if it was on a tiny budget – I do feel the BBC should have put on that film earlier …
AS: Do they tell you in advance when they plan on showing the film?
MB: Sometimes.
AS: What did they tell you with this one?

MB: <pause> It was all scheduled to do with the end of the financial year …
    it's so complex how they make scheduling decisions. So one single film is
    not a big priority for them. They are going to be worrying about schedul-
    ing big series and stuff. Yeah, I was disappointed.[38]

The reference to how the decision to schedule the film at that particular time was informed by the 'end of the financial year' – whether or not
this was the real reason for the late time slot – pulls into sharp focus
the complex, rationalised processes that underpin the scheduling stage
of production. Moreover, Minoo's comment stresses how under such a
rationale, single films – particularly ones on cross-cultural entanglements
– are not a 'big priority' for the major channels. Editor and filmmaker
Nasfim Haque describes a similar experience with her film *Don't Panic,
I'm Islamic!* – part of a new director's strand on BBC3 – which was a
humorous and irreverent look at representations of Islam in the UK,
through the premise of setting up a fake Muslim PR company called
Jihad Media.[39] Despite being well received by the senior executives the
film was nonetheless scheduled for 12:30 a.m.:

The whole strand was going on late [at night] because it was difficult to
bring in audiences for single films – which I agree with: it is difficult to
bring in audiences for single films if they're not advertised. But I think
it could have gone on at 11 o'clock and if you can watch the first few
minutes just out of curiosity, I'm pretty certain the audience would have
stuck with it. Actually it got the biggest audience out of all the films [in
the strand]. I had some really nice feedback from the commissioners and
the controllers. They all said the film was well produced and very well
made but the subject matter was so difficult … I think that if I made a
programme about fat people having sex they probably would have put it
on earlier![40]

What is striking about these stories is how, despite being 'well
resourced', as Minoo states, the BBC still scheduled the films for late
at night. Such a narrative is intended to imply that the commissioning
of these films appears tokenistic; the BBC's public service remit says
it needs to commission programmes that appeal to all the communities of Britain, but there is no regulation over what time they should
be shown.[41] Nasfim told me later that her film also received a decent
budget. What is made apparent is a sense that executives are unwilling to take a risk on subject matter they find 'difficult'. Commercial
pressures mean that audiences need to be maximised, and even in the
case of public service broadcaster, the BBC, scheduling has become
demand-led rather than offer-led. The commercial circumstances of
such scheduling decisions is stated in quite unequivocal terms in the

following comment from a commissioning editor, speaking in the context of Channel 4:

> If you say, alright, instead of *Jamie's Kitchen* we will put out *Narinder's Kitchen* and it only gets watched by one million then, why are you going to do that if you are a commercial broadcaster? No, you put *Narinder's Kitchen* out at a time when it hasn't got to bring in as many viewers because Channel 4 is a commercial broadcaster. It has to survive on advertising; there is no handout, no licence fee. If you want to see it survive on advertising and you don't think that they are going to make all their money from populist programmes then we will be making programmes for a quarter of the budget because that is what the market will pay.[42]

Such an account perhaps explains why Nasfim believes broadcasters would rather schedule a programme about 'fat people having sex' at 9 p.m. rather than an original, funny and provocative look at representations of Islam in modern-day Britain. In the rationalised schema of television production, the former is, somewhat perversely, deemed more mainstream and 'commercial' than the latter.

Desi DNA and the racialisation of niche

Again, the experiences of Minoo and Nasfim relate to a normative institutional understanding of what is 'mainstream' and what is 'niche'. Despite appearing as common-sense knowledge, such a discourse is not so clear cut, exemplified by the debate over the scheduling of *Desi DNA*. *Desi DNA* was a BBC2 series produced by the APU that ran between 2003 and 2008, covering British Asian art, culture and entertainment. Wanting to break away from the old Network East strand that catered for an Asian audience, which he found staid and boring, commissioning editor Tommy Nagra created *Desi DNA* 'as something with a really strong British Asian identity, that was confident and brash … comfortable in its own skin'.[43] Waheed Khan, one of the original directors on *Desi DNA*, stressed how the show's aesthetic was purposefully designed to obliterate prevailing images of Asian youth as 'uncool' and conformist, making it appear 'slick', 'pushing the limit and putting the money on screen, and having great talent and good stories and good journalism and making it better then, or as good as MTV'. [44]

However, five series later, despite critical acclaim[45] for its fresh and vibrant representation of British Asian youth cultures, the programme was still shown late at night, at 11:20 p.m. The most cited reason given by my respondents was because it has been unable to break away from the perception that it is only of interest to Asians. As Aaqil Ahmed said, 'the mere fact that it goes out at 11:20 p.m. to me would suggest that everybody who has watched that at the BBC thinks this is a show just for Asians. That's why we can't put it out at 8 o'clock because it's just not wide enough.'

However, this perception was also challenged by many of my respondents. Waheed stated unequivocally that *Desi DNA* would have been a success if it had been shown earlier, but it was hampered not only by the late timeslot but the lack of publicity the BBC afforded it; as he said, 'You can make the best thing in the world, but if people don't know about it they're not going to watch it. So you're kind of dead in the water'.

Echoing the issue of tokenism discussed earlier, one freelancer I interviewed makes a similar point regarding the lack of faith executives and schedulers have in the show, to the extent that it is commissioned just so the BBC can tick a box: 'Do they think they are not going to get the audiences, so "let's stick it on a late schedule, because let's be seen to be doing our bit"? So they'll put it on and, "Oh well the viewing figures are shit, we've done our best"?' Yet *Desi DNA*'s creator, Tommy Nagra is forced to agree with Ahmed and concedes that '*Desi DNA* is seen as a specialist kind of programme which probably doesn't have mainstream appeal.' He also stresses that this is not a problem for all APU productions, since the BBC had broadcast *Indian Food Made Easy*, and a series of films relating to the sixty-year anniversary of the partition of India, at prime time. But even though he believes that *Desi DNA* 'could work at 7:30 p.m., or 10 p.m.', Tommy makes a revealing point when he gives one last reason for why it might not get scheduled earlier: 'maybe it's the title?'

The idea that the appearance of the word 'Desi'[46] inadvertently compounds the programme's perceived difference and Otherness – and therefore its status as 'niche' – which is why executives were unwilling to take a risk on scheduling it at prime time is certainly compelling. The recurring theme from respondents' narratives is that schedulers are generally conservative, and do not trust Asian programmes – or rather certain kinds of Asian programmes – to attract big ratings. Screenwriter and director Neil Biswas, experienced this first hand, when his two-part Channel 4 drama, *Second Generation* – one of the first British television dramas to centre solely on British Asian characters – got bumped from its scheduled 9 p.m. broadcast, to 10 p.m. This was even though the film – and its original 9 p.m. timeslot – had already been publicised in a significant marketing push, including newspaper adverts, television trailers and a billboard campaign. The reason for this switch, according to Neil, was because Channel 4 ultimately decided that *Second Generation* would fail in the ratings battle against its competitors for the 9 p.m. slot: 'they lost their bottle right at the end and put it out at 10 which I think screwed with the people who watched it. I was always heavily critical of that. Because they spent all this money but then decided to put it out at 10.' Despite the publicity and excellent reviews, the drama managed to generate a relatively disappointing one million viewers for the first episode, which dropped to 900,000 for the final episode. The last-minute rescheduling of *Second Generation* represents the literal repositioning of the narrative from the centre, out to the periphery; the temporal governance of difference in real-time.

The innate cautiousness of television scheduling is suggested in another story from Haque, who described how she wrote an email to the scheduler behind the broadcast of her film *Don't Panic, I'm Islamic!* during the 'graveyard slot' – 12:30 a.m.:

> NASFIM HAQUE: He emailed me back, really sweet actually, saying, really liked your film, it very well made and very funny, but it's very difficult to bring an audience for this kind of film. [But] I think it's really difficult to bring an audience in if it's half past midnight!
> AS: What did he mean by 'difficult to bring in an audience'?
> NH: I think in terms of subject area. And I met him subsequently at a commissioning meeting and I introduced myself and he put two and two together and realised who I was. And he said, I bet you're pissed off with me because I scheduled your programme on late. And I said I bloody well am! But he was very sweet. Again he said […] the subject is very difficult. Even though I used humour … there's Bernard Manning and Max Clifford in it! I don't know how niche it is! Again, the wider picture is, I do feel as though, it's always kind of, managers, commissioners, execs, anything that is of a different culture is niche. The word 'niche' comes up. And unless you wrap it up in middle-class Marks & Spencer's, like [presenter of *Indian Food Made Easy*] Anjum Anand, you're not really going to get it out on air. I love Anjum Anand, but who eats chicken paneer wraps or whatever it is? Nobody eats that! But it has to be wrapped in that façade.[47]

This comment is a further illustration of how certain kinds of Asianness are perceived to have mainstream appeal. Those narratives that appeal to a certain class sensibility; the tastes of whom are symbolised by middle-class shopping institution Marks & Spencer with regard to the consumption of South Asian cultures. Unless it's 'wrapped in a façade' that appeals to bourgeois tastes, it is regarded as 'niche' and 'difficult to bring in an audience'. There is a clear racial dimension to this; returning to Nasfim's definition, what is considered as 'niche' is simply 'anything that is of a different culture'.

What I find particularly striking about Nasfim's quote, however, and why I choose it to conclude this chapter, is how it stresses the human dimension to scheduling decisions, through the character of the scheduler, who was empathic and in fact, 'really sweet actually', and who guessed correctly that Nasfim would be 'pissed off' over his decision to schedule her film at 12:30 a.m. However, while the quote alludes to individual agency and self-reflexivity, it is set against the hierarchy of production and the networks of 'managers, commissioners, execs' who in turn are identified as having tastes that belong to a particular social class (i.e., 'middle-class Marks & Spencers'). In this way, niche is identified as anything different from their own culture, and is scheduled as such – on the margins of terrestrial broadcasting, and public discourse. It follows that 'difficult' films about cultural entanglements, such as Minoo Bhatia's award winning *Who Do you Think You're Talking To?* and Nasfim Haque's *Don't Panic, I'm Islamic!* (figure 2.2) get pushed out to the 'graveyard efnik slots', whereas more palatable and recognisable – and indeed, Orientalist – forms of difference such as *Indian Food Made Easy* (figure 2.4) and *Lost Days of the Raj* (figure 2.5) are scheduled for prime time.

To return to the point raised at the beginning of this chapter, even in this new age of television viewership where time-shifted viewing increasingly characterises our television consumption, scheduling nonetheless remains a crucial part of broadcasting. Indeed, in an increasingly commercialised environment, scheduling practices take on a greater significance, as it is one of the key ways through which channels compete with each other. Scheduling is arguably less a discussion about the cultural diet of the nation and more about the battle for lucrative audiences.

It is surprising how little attention is paid to scheduling in research into race and television, since it is a more decisive factor for producers from minority backgrounds than receiving a commission or a decent budget for their production. Scheduling effectively decides where the programmes of black and Asian filmmakers feature in the national conversation, which in turn, depends on the particular representation of race/multiculturalism/nationalism that they offer. Those programmes that produce a narrative that is complicit with a particular bourgeois Eurocentric worldview tend to receive favourable treatment, and will be given a premium position in discourse. Those programmes that produce an oppositional narrative that potentially disrupts the nation's sense of itself will be marginalised to the periphery and broadcast in the graveyard slot. Moreover, black and Asian filmmakers suffer from the emphasis on formats and serials rather than one-off or more experimental productions, where the perceived inherent riskiness of programmes dealing with issues of racial and ethnic identity – let alone racism – are immediately deemed' 'niche'.

That is not to say that these productions have no impact in these periphery positions, but their capacity for producing an alternative representation of Asianness/blackness or more progressive form of multiculture is nevertheless governed by the 'art' of scheduling. Moreover, it is precisely the normative and common-sense terms in which decisions over scheduling are rationalised that hide its ideological function and ensure the further reproduction of the dominant culture. In other words, the rationalised processes behind scheduling contain racialising dynamics. The negative scheduling of television programmes that attempt an alternative representation of black and Asian life and experience is literally the means through which the counter-narratives of difference are physically governed within the conditions of capitalistic cultural production. If, following Ellis, scheduling reflects 'the particular habits of national life', then the placement of programmes depicting black and Asian experience well away from prime-time slots exposes scheduling as a technology of racialised governmentalities. Reiterating the argument of Nicholas Garnham, the neglected 'editorial' function of cultural production is the key to cultural plurality, but in the experience of black Asian cultural producers, it is more likely to be the space where the cultural political possibilities of their work are limited and constrained.

Figure 2.1 Anita Rani, *Desi DNA* and British Asian culture (BBC2, tx. 13/2/08)

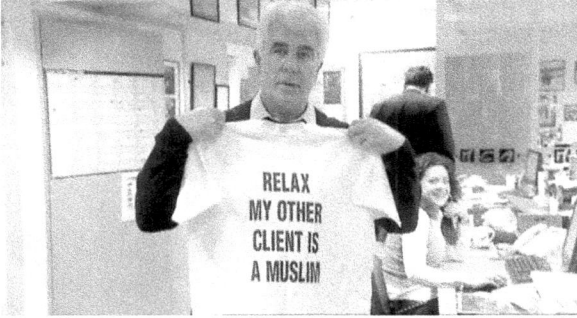

Figure 2.2 *Don't Panic I'm Islamic* and Max Clifford (BBC, tx. 7/7/05)

Figure 2.3 Aaqil Ahmed, past BBC Commissioning Editor, Religion and Head of Religion and Ethics (promotional image)

Figure 2.4 *Indian Food Made Easy* and Anjum Anand as the 'Asian Nigella' (BBC Asian, 2007–)

Figure 2.5 *The Lost World of the Raj* series marked the 60th anniversary of the partition of India, featuring activist Pratima Vedi (right) (BBC2, tx. 3/7/07)

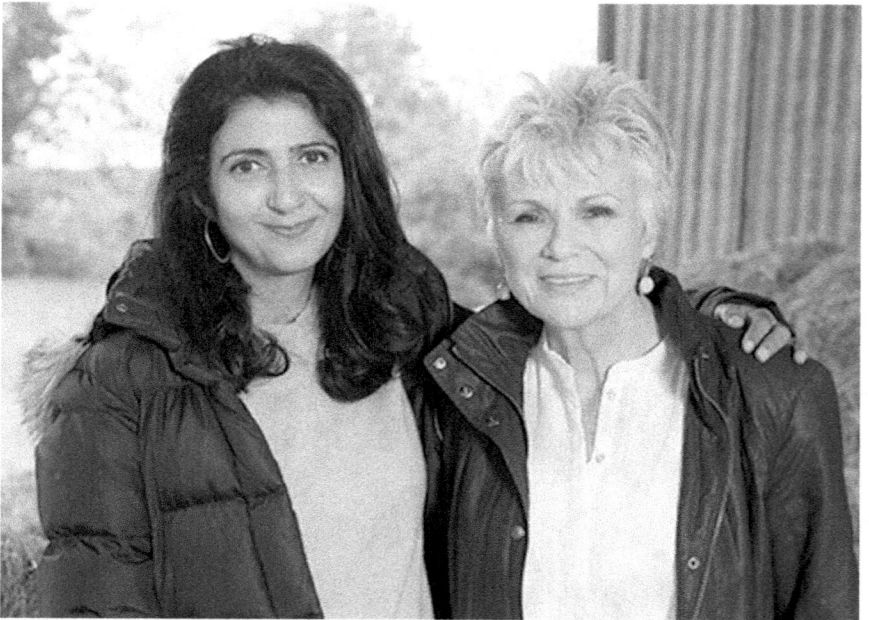

Figure 2.6 Minoo Bhatia and the award winning film, *Who Do you Think You're Talking To?* (BBC2, tx. 30/3/05)

Notes

1 Garnham, Nicholas, 'Concepts of Culture: Public Policy and the Cultural Industries', *Cultural Studies*, 1:1 (1987), p. 36.
2 Malik, Sarita, 'Keeping It Real: The Politics of Channel 4's Multiculturalism, Mainstreaming and Mandates', *Screen*, 49 (2008), p. 344.
3 See Hesmondhalgh, David, and Saha, Anamik, 'Race, Ethnicity, and Cultural Production', *Popular Communication*, 11:3 (2013), pp. 179–95.
4 Garnham, 'Concepts of Culture', pp. 31–2.
5 In this chapter all references to Asian or British Asian refer specifically to South Asian cultures (i.e. as originating from the Indian sub-continent), as is the case in the UK.
6 Bignell, Jonathan, and Orlebar, Jeremy, *The Television Handbook* (Philadelphia: Taylor & Francis, 2005), p. 76.
7 Bignell, Jonathan, *An Introduction to Television Studies* (London: Routledge, 2012), p. 289.
8 See Scannell, Paddy, 'Radio, Television, and Modern Life: A Phenomenological Approach', *Google Scholar*, 1996.
9 Ellis, John, 'Scheduling: The Last Creative Act in Television?' *Media, Culture & Society*. 22:1 (2000), p. 25.
10 See Bignell and Orlebar, *The Television Handbook*; and Ellis, 'Scheduling', pp. 25–38.
11 See Calvert, Ben, Casey, Neil, Casey, Bernadette, French, Liam, and Lewis, Justin, *Television Studies: The Key Concepts* (New York: Routledge, 2007).
12 See Ellis, 'Scheduling', p. 26; and Bignell and Orlebar, *The Television Handbook*.
13 Bignell and Orlebar, *The Television Handbook*, p. 34.
14 Calvert *et al.*, *Television Studies*, p. 241.
15 Ellis, 'Scheduling: The Last Creative Act in Television', p. 25.
16 Bignell and Orlebar, *The Television Handbook*, p. 75.
17 *Ibid.*, p. 82.
18 Calvert *et al.*, *Television Studies*, p. 241.
19 Ellis, 'Scheduling: The Last Creative Act in Television', p. 26.
20 *Ibid.*, p. 36.
21 Havens, Timothy, *Black Television Travels: African American Media around the Globe* (New York University Press, 2013), p. 62.
22 *Ibid.*
23 *Ibid.*, p. 74.
24 *Ibid.*, p. 75.
25 Hesmondhalgh, David, 'Cultural and Creative Industries' in Tony Bennett and J. Frow (eds), *The SAGE Handbook of Cultural Analysis* (Los Angeles: Sage, 2008), p. 556.
26 Garnham, 'Concepts of Culture', p. 31.
27 *Ibid.*
28 Campion, M. J., *Look Who's Talking: Cultural Diversity, Public Service Broadcasting and the National Conversation* (Nuffield College, 2005), p. 51.

29 See Prashad, Vijay, *The Karma of Brown Folk* (Minneapolis: University of Minnesota Press, 2000).

30 Fanthome, Christine, 'Commissioning Television Programmes', in Douglas Gomery and Luke Hockley (eds), *Television Industries* (London: BFI, 2006), p. 86.

31 Aaqil Ahmed, personal interview.

32 A UK trade association that represents and promotes the commercial interests of independent feature film, television, children's and animation media companies.

33 Pollard, E., Barkworth. R., Sheppard, E., and Tamkin, P., 'Researching the Independent Production Sector: A Focus on Minority Ethnic Led Companies', Report Produced for Pact and the UK Film Council (London: Institute for Employment Studies, 2004), p. 18.

34 *Ibid.*, p. 30.

35 Malik, Sarita, '"Creative Diversity": UK Public Service Broadcasting After Multiculturalism', *Popular Communication*, 11:3 (2013), pp. 227–41.

36 Prashad, *The Karma of Brown Folk*, p. 32.

37 The film won best documentary at the CRE's Race in Media Awards.

38 Minoo Bhatia, personal interview.

39 The film has many notable moments, including interviews with Bernard Manning and Max Clifford, and an opening spoof of the Bjork track 'It's All So Quiet'.

40 Nasfim Haque, personal interview.

41 Ofcom are responsible for schedules but these are in terms of enforcing standards of impartiality, and the avoidance of offence and harm (and the 'watershed'). Additionally, they make sure that certain quotas are met, regarding the number of hours of certain genres are too be shown. However, since the 2003 Communication Act, channels have taken responsibility over their own schedules and assess their own performances in relation to Ofcom guidelines. See Fanthome, 'Commissioning Television Programmes'.

42 Quoted in Campion, *Look Who's Talking*, p. 53.

43 Tommy Nagra, personal interview, 5 September 2007.

44 Waheed Khan, personal interview, 14 April 2007.

45 The series won 'Best Lifestyle Programme' at the 2004 Royal Television Society Awards.

46 'Desi' is originally a Sanskrit word but is nowadays used colloquially referring to anyone belonging to the South Asian diaspora.

47 Nasfim Haque, personal interview.

3

Reframing the 1950s: race and representation in recent British television

James Burton

Television broadcasting in Britain has traditionally been the 'primary site where the nation is imagined and imagines itself'.[1] Central to such constructions of national identity are the collective media memories presented and represented in fictional historical programming. In this chapter I interrogate a small, but interesting, group of programmes broadcast since 2011 that engage with the domestic realities of London in the 1950s and present a corrective to established notions of the nation at that time. My particular purpose is to critically examine the representation of race and immigration in these narratives that are ostensibly about gender politics. Since heritage programming has traditionally 'excluded a significant Black narrative presence', even when its aims have been progressive, it is important to map the ways in which these programmes represent race and, as Sarita Malik notes, construct the immigrant 'Other'.[2]

All three programmes – *The Hour* (2011–12), *The Bletchley Circle* (2012–14), and the phenomenally popular *Call the Midwife* (2012–) – are primarily created by women, written by women, feature women in most of the lead roles, and forcefully reassert the place of women in British history. I see them operating in a similar way to *Mad Men* (2007–15), in that they take as their setting an era that prompts nostalgic responses and proceeds to pull back the comforting veneer to reveal uncomfortable truths about the place and treatment of women in society at that time. Although each show conjures a longing for the era that they represent, I see their function as something beyond the notion of nostalgia, as being 'essentially inauthentic, ahistorical, sentimentalizing, regressive and exploitative', characterising much of the acritical debate around heritage screen fictions.[3] Moreover, they encourage audiences to engage cognitively and critically as well as emotionally. *The Bletchley Circle*, for example, emphasises that the women who worked breaking Nazi codes at Bletchley Park during the Second World War were expected to return to domestic roles once the war ended. At the same time, the programme's protagonists work together in secret to solve crimes against women. Audiences are invited to enjoy the clothes, the simpler times, and other period trappings, but cannot ignore the critical consideration of the era's sexual politics and 'a woman's place'. Essentially, with regards to gender politics, each of these three programmes presents a paradox of histori- cal revisionism in a progressive sense, alongside a heroically rose-tinted version of 1950s Britain that is predominantly white.

This is not in itself surprising. Like the nostalgia that many feel for the Eisenhower 1950s in the USA, the sense of community and national spirit that inspired and followed victory in the Second World War is fondly recalled in Britain, especially in London. However, much like the politicised nostalgia for the American 1950s that Daniel Marcus recounts, such a perspective requires a certain 'whitewashing' of the past, and a representational absence of colour in programmes that revisit the past serves to re-emphasise the dominant cultural ideals of that era.[4] Indeed, Chris Waters has argued that attempts to secure the imagined community of nation, amidst a time of rapid change and uncertainty in 1950s Britain, depended on the reworking of established tropes of little-Englandism against the migrant 'Other' as the Black population of Britain rose from an estimated 74,500 in 1951 to 336,000 by the end of 1959.[5] The idea of 'ordinary people, defined by their modesty, kind- ness to others, loyalty, truthfulness, straightforwardness, and simplicity' was a creation of the BBC and wartime propaganda that gendered the nation as more feminine than in the past (and susceptible, therefore, to Black male sexuality).[6] At the same time, Waters argues, images of the stalwart and stoic working class, previously considered a race apart, and became central to national identity.

My consequent objective in this chapter is not to downplay the impor- tant gender work that these programmes carry out. As Julia Hallam has observed, it has taken a long time for female writers and producers to break out of the soap-ghetto. The role of women in producing these improvements is enthusiastically applauded, and the gendered revision- ist histories presented within these programmes are highly significant.[7] Rather, I am more concerned with the complex and somewhat contra- dictory ways in which they deal, or fail to deal, with race, especially as they are set within a decade so formative in shaping British identity and in which that identity was shaped against the racialised 'Other'. At stake are the ways in which these programmes engage with the histori- cal reality of 1950s, in the dialogue with the constructions of national identity created in that decade, and how they speak to present-day racism, xenophobia and immigration debates.

I begin with an examination of *Call the Midwife* and how its strategies of representation evolve from the omission of racial difference to consider particular episodes that examine the experiences of recent immigrants. I then move on to discuss the place of racial politics in the grander narrative concerns of *The Hour*. Since it includes no representation of Commonwealth immigrants, I only return to *The Bletchley Circle* briefly at the end of the chapter.

Call the Midwife

Sunday-night television in Britain is almost a genre of its own, as journalist Julia Raeside observes. 'The British love to huddle', she suggests, 'in a collective onesie and warm themselves in front of the TV equivalent of a big log fire' with programming that takes their mind off going back to work the next day.[8] It is the traditional timeslot for period drama. Since the broadcast of its second episode in January 2012, *Call the Midwife* has been the nation's top-rated show, regularly garnering an astonishing 30 per cent share of the total viewing audience. It is based on the memoirs of Jennifer Worth (née Jennifer Lee), memoirs that subsequently became bestsellers about a newly qualified midwife who goes to work in the East End of London in 1957.[9] Jenny Lee moves into Nonnatus House, a nursing convent that is home to a small order of nuns and a few other young midwives. *Call the Midwife is* an incredibly cosy, occasionally saccharine show set in a comforting, simpler time, thus incorporating hallmarks of the genre. However, its presentation of a world of poverty, filth and unmedicated women straining to give birth, mean that there is just enough grit to balance out the sugar, especially as the programme smuggles in some fairly radical commentary about the importance of the National Health Service at a time when its future is being threatened today.

Each episode of *Call the Midwife* begins and ends with a montage of scenes of everyday life – streets, docks, markets – accompanied by a voiceover that comments on the particular mood of the time and sets the stage for the thematic content of the episode. These introductions appear designed to comfortably ease the audience into the nation's communal past, with the soothing, familiar voice of Vanessa Redgrave as the older Jenny. They also reflect the programme's claims to historical authenticity, both in terms of time and place, as well as the true origins of the storylines in the memoirs of Jennifer Worth that were focal points of the promotional relay.[10] A parallel can be drawn here with the way in which the openings of historical documentaries combine 'distant materiality and forms of subjectivity at once both alien and familiar' to historically orient viewers and provide them with historical knowledge.[11] Given that these bookends – the episodes end with similarly poetic summaries – are essential to establishing the verisimilitude of the programme, and its particular history, it is problematic that they rarely include non-white faces. In fact, aside from the three plotlines that I discuss here (only one of which features a Black protagonist), the world of the *Call the Midwife*'s East End contains only four fleeting glimpses of racial difference across the show's first three series, totalling twenty-two episodes and two Christmas specials (figures 3.1–3.4). These hints indicate the invisible nature as the extras are looking away from the camera or moving so quickly through the frame. Collectively they have less screen time than Sr Monica Joan's gollywog in the second episode of the first series. These examples underline what Malik notes as the exclusionary tendencies of heritage programing that often omit race altogether.[12]

What makes the lack of racial difference particularly noteworthy, in addition to aforementioned immigration into the country and construction of the parallel ethnocentric imagined community, is that *Call the Midwife* goes to great lengths to address and represent diverse groups and topics that are often absent from historical drama. In addition to its re-emphasising of women's stories, it has been lauded for its depiction of the elderly, poverty, mental health issues, both postpartum and otherwise, cystic fibrosis, spina bifida, female prisoners, and the discarded disabled. Furthermore, two of the three plots that explicitly address racial issues involve a married white woman who turns out to be pregnant by a Black man, not her husband, following isolated incidents of infidelity. Ignoring the fact that each of these babies can be read as punishment for crossing racial lines and exemplifying the fear of black male potency, neither plot investigates the reasons for these infidelities or presents these men on screen. The first of these plots occurs in the show's third episode. Winnie marries Ted to be a father for her children after her first husband is killed in the war. This is to be Ted's first 'proper child' but the midwives discover that Winnie has been tempted by 'a navvie with a nice smile'. All ends happily as Ted takes on the role of the holy fool, accepting the baby as his own to the bewilderment of the midwives. The second plot from the third series does not end quite so happily as dock foreman Cyril demands that his wife Doris get rid of the baby. The audience witness the pain of Doris's giving the baby up for adoption and the distress of her other children as she lies to them that the baby has died.

When the second of these episodes aired, Alyssa Rosenberg questioned the show's wisdom in returning to this storyline in the *Washington Post*'s

TV blog. She noted the rigour with which the show explains how policy and social conditions play out in the domestic lives of its many characters and asked that it apply the same rigour and empathy in the stories that it tells about race. Commenters immediately responded that she was missing the point of the episode. Among these claims was that it was not a show about race but about pregnancy and the midwives' lives, that she should not look to create controversy around such a brave show, and how typical it is of a woman to give these cheating women a pass and change the conversation to something totally different. Of course, one should not rely on comment threads for rationality, but these responses to Rosenberg's criticism do underline the ambiguity with which these plots are presented and the absence of a clear editorial statement. An explanation for *Call the Midwife* returning to the idea of miscegenation can be found in Worth's memoir. The first volume features three chapters that recount births 'of mixed descent', the two incorporated into the series and a third in which the expectant mother fears 'the baby's goin' to be black. [My husband]'ll kill me', only for her baby to be born white and the midwife sworn to secrecy.[13] Immigration is rarely broached in Worth's memoirs and it is only when the programme deviates from her memoir that stories of immigrants are told, especially in series four once Jenny has left Poplar.

A clearer statement is provided in the seventh episode of the second series, albeit in the six shortish scenes that make up the episode's B-story. *Call the Midwife* typically features two stories or 'births of the week', alongside the serialised arcs of the midwives and nuns, which in this episode include: the procurement of a new moped and training for the midwives; the deterioration of Sister Monica-Joan's faculties; Sister Bernadette's fight against tuberculosis and her desire for Dr Turner; and the return of Nurse Chummy from her missionary work in Sierra Leone. The A-story, which covers domestic abuse and a returning son who has 'married up', is discussed by the sisters and midwives outside of the work, thereby enabling editorial comment, whereas Monique Hyde's story is witnessed by Jenny alone so the programme's statement on the subject is limited to their encounters.

We first meet Monique Hyde sitting apart, isolated from the other mothers in the clinic waiting area. Monique observes another mother, Rita Bailey, hit her daughter and smiles sympathetically at the child who silently mouths 'hello' back. Rita sees this silent interaction and asks, 'That coloured woman bothering you again, Sylvie?' Immediately, Monique is thus presented as isolated from the other mothers on clearly vocalised racial grounds. We subsequently learn that Monique and Rita are neighbours in a particularly grim basement slum. Jenny's

conversation with Monique during her examination covers many familiar experiences of new immigrants during the 1950s: Monique is not
greeted at Dover by Dame Vera Lynn; her husband has served in the
RAF during the Second World War and could not wait to get back to the
'Mother Country' despite being refused by the air force after the war;
and working-class Londoners were not who she expected to encounter.
In fact, the conversations between Monique and Jenny in the episode so
closely echo the oral testimonies of immigrants during the 1950s that
it appears that they have been written using a checklist of the experiences of the Windrush generation that the writers wanted viewers to be
reminded about. The exchanges between Monique and Jenny also serve
to emphasise the vast difference between a utopian ideal of England and
the realities of 1950s London.

The polemic nature of these opening exchanges is clear and rare in
heritage programming. Their second conversation occurs when Jenny
visits Monique to ensure that the dwelling is suitable for a home birth.
Before she enters, Jenny is informed by Rita that, 'every time a boat
comes in, there's another one. Six coloureds in there now.' Monique
reluctantly admits that there are six living in the room, but that they are
prevented from taking rooms of their own by the 'colour bar'. Rather
than disprove Rita's assertion as more unfounded prejudice, the programme uses this as an opportunity to engage, albeit fleetingly, with the
broader social practice of discrimination. Jenny and Monique bond over
the similar china that their mothers had, and Monique laments that she
misses home, and that her mother had led her to 'believe that everyone
in England drank tea and grew flowers in their gardens'. When Jenny
visits again briefly she brings Monique a bunch of flowers cut from the
garden of Nonnatus House and is greeted as the 'English lady my mother
told me about', again emphasising the elusiveness of a utopian England.
Monique has reluctantly called complaining of pains that turn out to be
Braxton Hicks contractions, a reluctance that she explains is due to her
'neighbours think she gets too much for nothing'. As Jenny leaves, she
is intercepted by Rita who requests, on behalf of the other expectant
mothers, that Jenny visit them first so that they do not catch anything
from 'the coloured girl'. Jenny, who has clearly formed a bond with
Monique, responds that 'I'll come to you first Mrs Bailey ... because
then at the end of my round, I'll be able to sit with Mrs Hyde and have a
conversation with an intelligent, well-mannered woman. A proper conversation, one that isn't full of narrow-minded judgement. It'll help me
get through my other visits.'

There is clear engagement with prejudice here, although it is drawn
along class lines rather than in institutional terms – upper-middle-class

Jenny is able to see beyond colour and is the 'best of England', whereas the working-class women are ignorant. This narrative choice reinforces the long-held myth of racism as a working-class disease from which the enlightened middle classes are immune. Louise Fitzgerald has observed that this problematises the claims of those who read *Call the Midwife* as a feminist text because 'laying of the blame and shame squarely on the shoulders of the working-class women' is indicative of white middle-class privilege.[14] Events later turn around, however, once Monique catches the pregnant Rita as she falls backwards down the stone steps that lead from their dwellings to the street; and they both bond over the council's failure to clean the steps as promised and their mutual preference for Clark Gable. The relationship between the two is cemented when Monique's waters break and she is unable to call the midwife because the forgetful sister Monica Joan answers the phone. Rita helps Monique to Nonnatus House, ignoring the other working-class women's warnings, and chastises the midwives upon arrival: 'Where the hell were you lot leaving a decent woman in this state?' The innocent victimised and the ignorant victimiser are united in the challenge of birth and we see them celebrating together, along with our first glimpse of the baby's father, in the episode's closing montage (figure 3.5).

As Jenny Lee leaves Poplar at the end of *Call the Midwife*'s third series, so the screenwriters leave the memoirs behind, although the programme does maintain the authorial voiceover of the aforementioned bookends. Set in 1960, the fourth series is more inclusive in terms of the diversity of its extras and presents two stories of non-white mothers. The second of these presents the experiences of *Call the Midwife*'s first South Asian woman, albeit as the B-story to a baby with brittle bones born to a Christian Scientist couple in the fifth episode. Ameera Khatun is a Sylheti woman who has come to London with her husband, against the norm which often saw women delay their travel until the husband was established. Ameera is geographically disconnected from her support network and her inability to speak English means that she relies on her son, Faruk, for communication. This narrative strategy significantly slows down the pace of the episode and provides the viewer with space to contemplate the everyday reality of non-English speaking immigrants, both in terms of their inability to communicate easily and in terms of the visual representation of Ameera's home.

Ameera's inability to speak for herself (or denial of a voice) is compounded as we learn of her situation through the new midwife, Nurse Barbara Gilbert. Barbara first speaks to the headmistress of Faruk's school who informs her that Ameera is fairly isolated because her husband works long hours. 'I can't imagine what it must be like',

Barbara tells the headmistress (and, by extension, the audience), 'to leave everything behind, to come to a country where you can't understand anyone.' This exchange prepares us to witness the frustrations of Ameera and Barbara's need to communicate through Faruk, especially when it comes to discussing the need for an internal examination and when Ameera contracts diphtheria. However, the delayed nature of a translated conversation which reduces the amount of plot that can be covered also gives the audience time to appreciate the complexity of Ameera's experience and Barbara's attempts to overcome the language/cultural barrier. As Barbara is thanked for her efforts with a bowl of samosas, the audience is rewarded with opportunities for empathy.

If the Monique Hyde story is read as a cataloguing of the experiences of the Windrush generation for contemporary audiences, the story of Abigail and Terence Bissette in episode two of the third series can be seen as an attempt to counter the myth that immigration had 'jeopardized what little stability had hitherto existed within West Indian family life', and the perception of irresponsible West Indian men in general.[15] In an interview with *Enstars*, Cherrelle Skeete, the actress who plays Abigail Bissette, suggested that her story would centre 'around the racism she experienced, but how she handles it with dignity'. In an early scene at an expectant mothers' group, Abigail tells the other mothers that she has spent her maternity grant on a washing machine, to which another mother snidely remarks that she 'got a new council flat too'. Abigail's happiness about her impending arrival appears to prevent her from noticing their judgement. This is the only instance of prejudice in the episode, which suggests that it may have been reworked to remove overt racism. Regardless, Skeete is correct in her expectation that the episode 'portrays those first Windrush settlers in such a positive light … as hard working people who were pursuing their own British version of the American dream'.

The Bissettes' story begins with Abigail chasing after a bus to give her husband Terence, the driver, his lunch. Terence is grateful, but advises Abigail to go home and rest. The baby is clearly more important than his sandwiches. The couple share a tender scene when Terence returns home that evening. In a slightly exaggerated Caribbean accent, Terence tells her that she is a magnificent woman, suggests that they dance, and that their 'calypso baby' already knows where she comes from. Abigail insists that 'this baby is going to be a Londoner', as they dance awkwardly yet lovingly. These scenes take place within the first ten minutes of the episode and firmly establish the Bissettes as a loving and committed couple, living in a clean flat, and keen to assimilate to their adopted country.

Their story is also at the centre of the episode and our emotional investment is with them as Abigail's pregnancy becomes difficult (as the pregnancies in the programme often do). Abigail's 'dancing baby' has calmed its movements and although the foetal heartbeat is detected, her high blood pressure leads to her being admitted to hospital for bed rest. Further underlining his commitment to Abigail, Terence is immediately there by her side, trying to lighten her mood with jokes and advising her to 'keep smiling girl, it's good for the baby' as he is forced to leave when visiting hours are over. Abigail endures a difficult experience overnight in the hospital – she is treated as a prisoner by an authoritarian nurse and then she witnesses the horrific consequences of a self-inflicted abortion in the corridor as she sneaks to the toilet and returns home on her own in the dead of night. As if this nightmarish experience were not enough, despite the foetal heartbeat having been detected at the hospital, Abigail's daughter is stillborn. Terence, waiting in the next room, is devastated and his earlier excitement immediately drains away. Significantly, the attending midwives, usually so professional, are equally distraught. Salvation comes when Dr Turner arrives to identify 'undiagnosed twins' and Terence, who has been sitting alone on the hallway floor, clearly articulates that he 'wants to be glad, but I don't know how'. The remaining third of the episode sees the Bissettes (ultimately successfully) attempt to come to terms with their sadness and reconcile the new life of Terence Jr with their feelings of guilt for his sister.

Of particular note in this episode is the continual presence of Terence. His participation in Abigail's pregnancy serves to undercut the aforementioned disreputable myths about West Indian men. Importantly, his participation is also atypical for the programme as, for the most part, the fathers in *Call the Midwife* are absent unless they are causing problems for the mother. The programme is, therefore, not only countering myths about West Indian men, but is positioning Terence's dedication to his family above the norm for the time.

The responses to *Call the Midwife* in the British press were frequently divided along gender lines, as often happens with programmes that deal with 'women's issues', with men often dismissing it as 'sentimental, nostalgic claptrap' or as sexist towards men.[16] Of note here is a particularly snide review by Sam Woolaston in the *Guardian* that mistakenly includes the publicity still of the Bissettes in its dismissal of the fourth series premiere. This episode provides ample opportunity to discuss the progressive ways in which the programme reasserts histories hitherto excluded from the national imaginary, yet the reviewer is more interested in dismissing the 'ladies with starched morals at Nonnatus House'. Similarly, the *Daily Mail*'s coverage of the episode is solely concerned with the technical slip of a microphone visible in a scene where the nuns comfort the grieving Abigail, even including a still of the scene, without engaging with the narrative, as underscored by writer Hugo Gye. Furthermore, the *Daily Telegraph*'s review of the Monique Hyde story reduces the complexity of the narrative to the following: 'When a black woman, who suffered prejudice from her racist neighbours, gave birth in an overcrowded tenement, her child was welcomed to Britain by the clucky midwives.' The opportunities for historical dialogue about race and racism that *Call the Midwife* enables are not taken up by the popular press and are left fallow.

Writing before the fourth series had aired, it is understandable that Louise Fitzgerald would criticise the lack of non-white characters in *Call the Midwife* as problematic 'for a show that is predicated on remembering, on representing women who have not traditionally remembered within the nation's cultural storytelling practices, this sort of social amnesia marks *Call the Midwife* as an extraordinarily and problematically white utopian account'.[17] However, as problematic as the white middle-class lens through which *Call the Midwife* tells its stories is, it is important to note the opportunities for engagement with the history of exclusion and demonisation in British history *and* media representations that the show does afford through the stories of Monique Hyde and those of its more progressive fourth series. One can only hope that it will continue to engage with cultural politics in such ways that also address issues of race and racial difference. The sixth series included an episode for Christmas 2016 shot in South Africa.

Cometh The Hour

Where *Call the Midwife* has frequently been dismissed as cosy, Sunday evening heritage programming, *The Hour* was greeted as 'quality' television with episode-by-episode review blogs appearing on the *Guardian* site and elsewhere. This can perhaps be explained by the fact that *The Hour*'s concerns are more macro than *Call the Midwife*'s focus on the quotidian and the soapy nature of its serialisation. The serial plots of *The Hour*'s two series address broad-scale issues: corruption at the heart of the British establishment and the cracks appearing in its hull from which the 1960s will eventually spill; the decline of the Empire, nuclear armament, police corruption; and the cloying to traditional notions of class and privilege. Furthermore, broadcasting on Tuesdays on BBC2, in a more serious and sophisticated timeslot than *Call The Midwife*, *The Hour* was presented as the British *Mad Men*, as was apparent from the majority of its promotional material and media coverage. Indeed, the show uses the world of television news similarly to unashamedly explore the social and cultural mores and discrimination of the era.

In a *Guardian* interview with Vanessa Thorpe, BBC's head of drama, Ben Stephenson, promised, '*The Hour* signals the confident new direction that BBC2 drama is taking. Viewers will witness the decade at its most exciting – from the ruthless sexual politics behind the polite social facade to the revelations that redefined the world for a new generation.'

Not all responded positively, however, with the *Daily Telegraph* dismissing what it felt 'appears to be less a story than an exercise in upbraiding the past for failing to live up to the politically correct ideals of the 21st century ... *The Hour* isn't content merely to portray this unpleasantness. It has to keep pointing at it and tutting.' Its representation of the internal workings of television news, a point of pride in promotional material, was dismissed by some who worked at that time: 'The devil is in the detail, and pretty well every detail is wrong.'

Unlike *Call the Midwife* and away from the generic pressures towards the cosiness of Sunday evening TV, *The Hour* positioned race and immigration somewhat to the forefront of its version of 1950s London. Initially, it appears that the macro nature of *The Hour*'s approach to the structural fault lines of 1950s Britain will enable a thorough examination of the racial politics, alongside the gender politics, of the era. In the first episode, once the opening narrative tide has settled, we follow the ostensible hero, Freddie Lyons, coming home from work to Notting Hill. The choice of this area for his home immediately evokes the racial fault lines characterised by the Notting Hill riots of 1958 which, coinciding with similar unrest in Nottingham, have become synonymous with the racial hostility of white Britons towards immigration. As he emerges from the underground, the tracking camera follows him as he passes a racially diverse group of people before stopping by a sign for The Windmill Hotel that expresses the then-common instruction 'No Coloured. No Irish. No Children'. Immediately, *The Hour* is visually establishing a very different London to *Call the Midwife*; one where division is more visible than unity. The visual is soon verbalised. When asked what his lead story would be at his interview for *The Hour* the next day, Freddie asserts that 'New Commonwealth immigration' would be his first priority given that '75,000 people are arriving every year from the colonies'. Freddie goes on argue that Martin Luther King has sparked debate about the race across the Atlantic, while 'we don't even challenge the fact that in every hotel window we still, without shame, say "No Coloured, No Irish"'.

The emphasis on immigration is continued in the second episode of the series. The first episode of the new programme (within the programme) appears to begin with an interview with a recently arrived West Indian man, Reginald Thompson (figure 3.6). Thompson has been filmed earlier that day attempting to find lodgings in the area around Victoria, only to be turned away while a white man is admitted to the same rooms. *The Hour* is here invoking the famous episode of the BBC's *Tonight* that followed Ben Bousquet on a similar fruitless search and grounding its representation of the past in the televisual record.[18] Freddie ends the taped segment with familiar line: 'If you're white, you're alright.' Instead of enabling Thompson to recount his experiences, the programme returns to the studio with an interview with a white 'expert on immigration' who agrees that the taped segment accurately shows the experiences of new immigrants to London. This further underlines the position of *The Hour* on the immigrant experience, but rather than use this opportunity to articulate a clear critique of the institutional racism that immigrants encounter on their arrival, this moment is instead used to demonstrate the professional ineptitude of the programme's dashing upper-class presenter, Hector Madden. Of course, this can be read as a comment on the fecklessness of the establishment in dealing with the hardships of immigrants, but it does seem to be a lost opportunity.

Following this initial engagement with immigration as a news story of value, the fictional *The Hour* becomes more concerned with the developing situation surrounding Nasser's seizing of the Suez Canal, although this does enable a clear anti-colonialist statement to be provided by 'Nasser's man in London'. The remainder of the first series only concerns itself with the representation of immigrants on a social level, especially as the characters of *The Hour* are also worldlier than the midwives. Their celebration for Freddie's birthday in the fourth episode spills over into a nightclub whose diversity is alien to the world of the East End. The 'Sunlight Club' that the characters frequent appears to be modelled on the real Sunset Club, a nightclub that showcased Caribbean culture and was frequented by middle-class whites.[19] The exoticism of the club is strongly juxtaposed with the grey domestic space that the establishment Hector lives in with which the scene shows through parallel editing. There is a harmony and joy to this integrated space, although the Caribbean waitress is somewhat objectified, and the show is not judgemental when Sissy, the spunky young office assistant, leaves with Sey, an incredibly polite Nigerian doctor-in-training. The programme's position is that immigration, integration and cultural hybridity are to be valued rather than feared and that segregation must be challenged.

The first series of *The Hour*, then, represents a Britain where race is a visible issue. Immigration is a topic that necessitates debate, but it is one factor among many that are subsumed to a general hotchpotch of factors threatening the power structures of society. A similar narrative dynamic characterises the second series where housing is again central to

The Hour's approach to immigration. Midway through the first episode Freddie delights Sissy by offering the upstairs flat in his house after she complains that Sey is threatening to move back to Nigeria because he's been 'thrown out three times now and rents doubled twice" That evening, as Sissy helps Sey move in, a local Teddy Boy (the character Norman), who is placing British Defence Union (BDU) leaflets that advertise a speech by Oswald Mosley on car windscreens, praises the car and asks if it belongs to her. She answers that it is her boyfriend's and he unashamedly says 'filthy nigger' as he walks away. *The Hour* thus succinctly addresses the colour bar and the very public presence of neo-fascists in a way rarely presented on screen.

At the beginning of the next episode, Freddie encourages Sey to come on to *The Hour* and speak of his experiences. Sey resists despite Freddie's entreaty that 'you're a coloured doctor, don't tell me you haven't had a white patient reluctant to be treated by you?' Their conversation takes place at a new interracial social club called The Chameleon which, as Freddie later tells the team gathered at a party at Hector's, 'offer[s] a positive view of immigration that's part of a brilliant anti-fascist initiative, but it's not a story if you don't also direct the camera at the other side'. Again, the programme is idealising spaces of social gathering and integration, but continues to note the personal reluctance of many to speak up, as well as the institutional resistance to spotlighting division. Hector and Bel resist Freddie's plan to broadcast a debate about immigration and the Rent Act because it would give Mosley's offensive views the airtime that he wants and, besides, the BBC refuses to broadcast fascist views. Freddie's response, that this refusal to engage gives hatred the space to fester and grow, is a text-book freedom of speech defence that contains an institutional critique of the BBC. After racist graffiti is written on Freddie's door, his new wife Camille has soot thrown at her in the street by the same Teddy Boy and is told 'now you fit in' as he jumps away making monkey noises. Sey witnesses her distress and is now determined to appear on *The Hour*. Freddie returns home and is apprised of the situation by an apparently sympathetic landlord, Norman Pike. After comforting Camille, he leaves the house to confront the Teddy Boy (Trevor) who, unlike the BBC at the time, *The Hour* allows to spew his received racist venom that embodies many of the stereotypes circulated in the anti-immigrant BDU propaganda. Ever the newsman, Freddie invites him to repeat his views on television. As with the juxtaposition of the reactions of Jenny Lee and Rita Bailey to Monique Hyde, the sophistication of the newly beatnik Freddie – he's been to America between series, read Kerouac and Ginsberg, and returned with a French wife – is in stark contrast to the ignorant Trevor. *The Hour* thereby privileges a progressive, anti-racist perspective.

The Hour performs a narrative pirouette in order to present the debate between Sey and Trevor to contemporary audiences, framing it as a demonstration for the BBC's board rather than as a broadcast. In reality, Hugh Carleton Greene, the director general of the BBC in the late 1950s had vowed that 'Mosley will only appear on the BBC over my dead body'. The directors gathered at the demonstration begin to immediately protest giving airtime to a fascist, given that they all fought a war to defeat such views. Notably, Bel presents an anachronistic neo-liberal argument about the ratings of their ITV competitor and the need for such a story. The fictional debate begins with Norman hiding his fascism behind the usual 'nationalist' veneer but his subsequent argument is clearly based on ignorance about 'unchecked immigrant community' taking British jobs and services. Freddie debunks his myths and states the patriotic aims and contributions of immigrants, redirecting the conversation to Sey's role as a doctor. Sey states that the open discussion and debate of this interview, and that Norman is free to espouse his views, is representative of the 'power of the British democratic system that is strong enough to fight this fever, to fight this rancid, toxic disease, and to come out of it so strong. That is the country where I want to live. That is where my home is.' As with the story of Monique Hyde and Rita Bailey, the power of dialogue and discussion leads to the overcoming of prejudice and ignorance. The board are impressed and, suitably chastised, Trevor reveals to Freddie that Norman Pike paid him to attack Camille.

The Hour thus ties the political fascism of Trevor to the exploitative tendencies of slum landlords, and Norman Pike becomes a Peter Rachman-like figure.[20] However, as with the first series of the show, the engagement with racism in the early episodes is subsumed by its broader conspiracy narrative in which its journalistic heroes uncover a scheme to profit from Britain's entry into the arms race. It is here that *The Hour* participates in a rather worrying trend across these three programmes to uncritically present southern European immigrants as villains. Behind this scheme is the inhuman Italian immigrant, Raphael Cilenti, who is also a major figure in Soho and who is blackmailing most of the London establishment, having lured them into 'honey traps' with dancing girls from his nightclub 'El Paradis'. Abi Morgan, the creator of *The Hour*, has said that she was drawn to the allure of Soho and was 'quite captivated by the kind of Reggie Krays of that time and the feeling of a sort of gangster underworld that was buying into wealth and money and the affectation of power'.[21] If the Krays were the inspiration for the second series' arc, then this is perhaps the most troubling aspect of the show. In reframing the very British underworld of 1950s London to be under the control of Cilenti, *The Hour* would appear to be playing into contemporary anxieties about asylum seekers and immigrants from outside the Commonwealth.

The perception that non-Commonwealth immigrants controlled organised crime in London also informs episodes of *Call the Midwife* and *The Bletchley Circle*. The second episode of the first series of *Call the Midwife* presents the story of an Irish girl, Mary, who is taken directly from Worth's memoir.[22] Having run away from home, isolated and alone, Mary is taken under the wing of the charismatic, reptilian pimp Zakir. This is the show's only representation of vice in the East End. *The Bletchley Circle* is set earlier in the decade than *The Hour* and *Call the Midwife*. It presents no stories of Commonwealth immigrants and therefore warrants only brief discussion here. This absence of diverse groups is perhaps understandable given that the rates of immigration were lower then and that the show ran for only seven episodes. However, it is noteworthy that its sole engagement with non-British natives is through the black market dealings of one of its main characters, Millie, which occupies its final two episodes. Millie is kidnapped by a gang led by the cold, Maltese 'Godmother' figure, Marta, as a consequence of the dishonest dealings of her supplier. It quickly becomes apparent that in addition to smuggling contraband into austerity London, the gang is responsible for the human trafficking of prostitutes from Eastern Europe, a problem at the forefront of contemporary concerns. The programme presents the gang as dangerously menacing but does not give voice to the political and social realities that might offer insight into their actions. Aside from their intention to reassert the place of women in British historical memory, these three shows together share an unquestioned presumption that immigrants who are not from the Commonwealth are a threat to the British way of life.

By way of a conclusion, I argue that these programmes work to deconstruct some of the myths that continue to persist about immigrants from the Commonwealth after the Second World War and the destructive racism that such myths engender. The early series of *Call the Midwife* are marked by the all-to-familiar omission of non-white faces and the show does create dichotomies between middle-class and working-class responses to immigration (as does *The Hour*). However, as the series have progressed, its cataloguing of the experiences of the Windrush generation, its positive and therefore revisionist representation of Black family life, and its depiction of the daily struggles of non-English-speaking immigrants, are markers of its progressive potential. Arguably, *The Hour* represents the most confrontational engagement seen in British television drama with the institutional racism of 1950s Britain, the limited role of television to correct the era's dominant myths and the roots of the era's neo-fascism. If the mosaic of cultural memory is best understood as 'a field of cultural negotiation through which different stories vie for a place in history', as Marita Sturken has suggested, then these representative examples go some way to creating a more inclusive and honest version of the past.[23] These programmes mark the beginning of a process, albeit practised through a predominantly white lens, and one can only hope to see more colour added to the national mosaic.

Figure 3.1 A fleeting exception to whiteness in *Call the Midwife* (BBC, tx. 29/1/12)

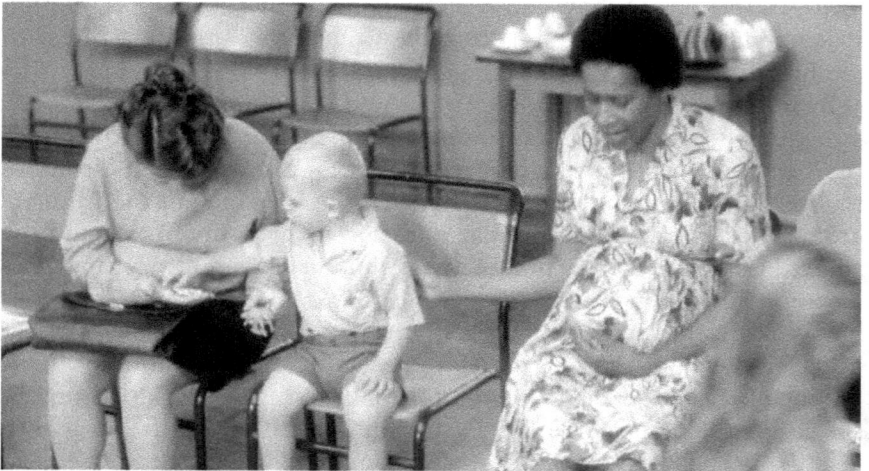

Figure 3.2 Another exception in which the presence of the 'Other' is seen in *Call the Midwife* (BBC, tx. 12/2/12)

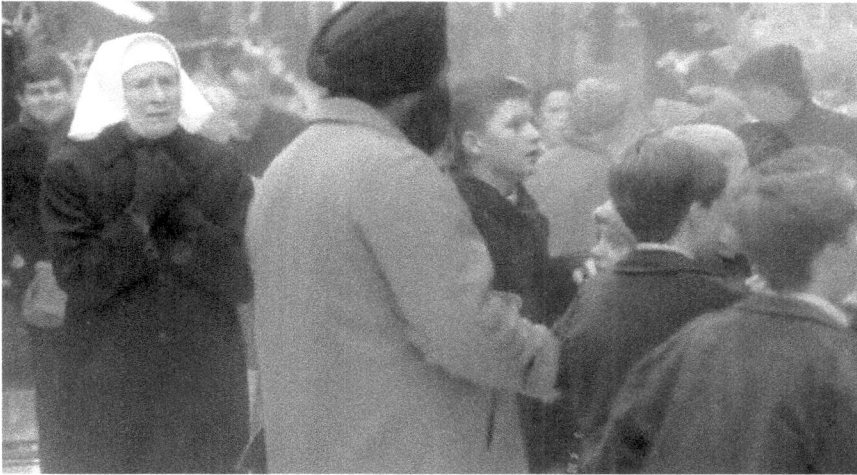

Figure 3.3 *Call the Midwife* Christmas episode and a diverse selection of characters (BBC, tx. 25/12/12)

Figure 3.4 Construction of ethnocentricity within the imagined community of *Call the Midwife* (BBC, tx. 10/2/13)

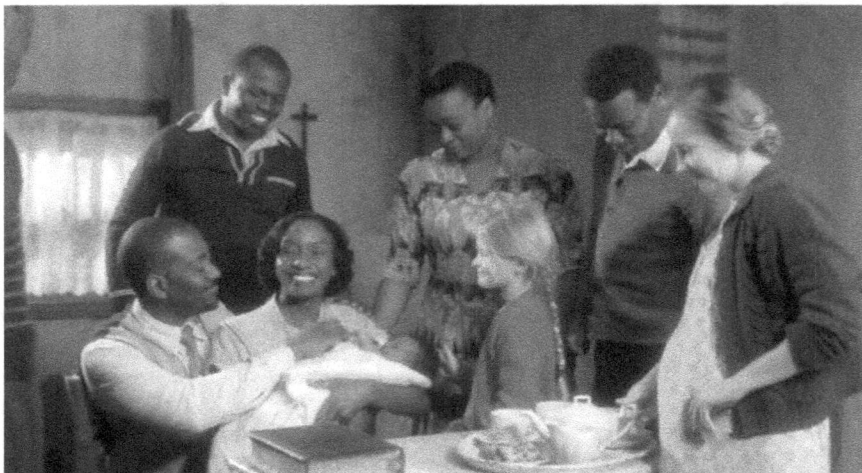

Figure 3.5 The innocent victimised and the ignorant victimiser are united in the closing montage of *Call the Midwife* (BBC, tx. 3/3/13)

Figure 3.6 *The Hour* recreates the BBC's coverage of racist housing practices in 1950s London with Zephryn Taitte (left) and Dominic West (BBC2, tx. 26/7/11)

Notes

1 Malik, Sarita, *Representing Black Britain: Black and Asian Images on Television* (London: Sage, 2002), p. 2.
2 *Ibid.*, p. 145.
3 Holdsworth, A., *Television, Memory and Nostalgia* (London: Palgrave, 2011), p. 103; Monk, Claire, 'The British Heritage-Film Debate Revisited', in Claire

Monk and Amy Sargeant (eds), *British Historical Cinema: The History, Heritage and Costume Film* (London: Routledge, 2002), p. 176.

4 Marcus, Daniel, *Happy Days and Wonder Years: The Fifties and the Sixties in Contemporary Cultural Politics* (New Brunswick, NJ: Rutgers University Press, 2004), pp. 19–25.

5 Waters, Chris, 'Dark Strangers in Our Midst: Discourses of Race and Nation in Britain, 1947–1963', *Journal of British Studies*, 36 (1997), p. 209.

6 *Ibid.*, pp. 211–12.

7 Julia Hallam, 'Power Plays: Gender, Genre and Lynda La Plante', in Jonathan Bignell, Stephen Lacey and Madeleine Macmurraugh-Kavanagh (eds), *British Television Drama: Past, Present and Future* (London: Palgrave, 2000), pp. 147–8.

8 Raeside, Julia, 'Is *Call the Midwife* Perfect Sunday Night Television?' *Guardian*, 26 January 2012, www.theguardian.com/tv-and-radio/tvandradioblog/2012/jan/26/call-the-midwife (accessed 29 May 2014).

9 See Worth, Jennifer, *Call the Midwife: A Memoir of Birth, Joy, and Hard Times* (London: Penguin, 2002).

10 See especially Thomas, Heidi, *The Life and Times of Call the Midwife: The Official Companion to Seasons One and Two* (New York: HarperCollins, 2012).

11 Corner, John, *Critical Ideas in Television Studies* (Oxford: Oxford University Press, 1999), p. 27.

12 Malik, *Representing Black Britain*, p. 176.

13 Worth, *Call the Midwife*, p. 151.

14 Fitzgerald, Louise, 'Taking a Pregnant Pause: Interrogating the Feminist Potential of Call the Midwife', in James Leggott and Julie Anne Taddeo (eds), *Upstairs and Downstairs: British Costume Drama Television from the Forsyth Saga to Downton Abbey* (Lanham, MD: Rowman & Littlefield, 2015), p 259.

15 Collins, Marcus, 'Pride and Prejudice: West Indian Men in Mid-Twentieth-Century Britain', *Journal of British Studies*, 40 (2001), p. 403.

16 Fitzgerald, 'Taking a Pregnant Pause', p. 250.

17 *Ibid.*, p. 249.

18 As highlighted in the 'Arrival' episode, *Windrush: A New Generation*, BBC2, 30 May 1998.

19 Phillips, Mike, and Trevor Phillips, *Windrush: The Irresistible Rise of Multi-Racial Britain* (London: HarperCollins, 1999), p. 94.

20 Perec 'Peter' Rachman (1919–62) was a landlord in the Notting Hill section of London during the 1950s and early 1960s. He was considered infamous for his mistreatment and extortion of tenants.

21 'Behind the Scenes of *The Hour*', *The Hour: Series 2*, Dir. Sandra Goldbacher, Catherine Morshead, Jamie Payne, Perf. Romola Garai, Dominic West, Ben Wishaw (Kudos Film & Television, 2012).

22 Worth, *Call the Midwife*, pp. 151–200.

23 Sturken, Marita, *Tangled Memories: The Vietnam War: the AIDS Epidemic, and the Politics of Remembering* (Berkeley: University of California Press, 1997), p. 1.

4

Black British drama, losses and gains: the case of *Shoot the Messenger*

Sarita Malik

Shoot the Messenger is a reflection of debates which are ongoing within the black community, and questions some of the stuff that black communities tell themselves and their children. It's like a fable. (Sharon Foster, writer, *Shoot the Messenger*)[1]

This chapter contributes to the range of debates around television drama and black representation presented in this volume. *Shoot the Messenger* (BBC2, 30 August 2006) was heavily promoted by the BBC as a 'bold' and 'thought-provoking' television drama.[2] The one-off 90-minute BBC Drama production focuses on the psychological journey of a Black schoolteacher, Joe Pascale (portrayed by David Oyelowo), accused of assaulting a Black male pupil.[3] This chapter discusses how stylistically, *Shoot the Messenger*'s (*STM*) non-realist techniques, non-linear form and overt constructedness depart from the traditional modes of social realism that have prevailed in Black British television drama. Moreover, the drama has an almost totally Black cast and was written and produced by two Black women, Sharon Foster and Ngozi Onwurah.[4] Screened at a 9 p.m. slot, the production attracted significant publicity before and after its airing. It was widely acclaimed at the 2006 Tribeca Film Festival, and Foster received the prestigious Dennis Potter Screenwriting Award in 2006 and BAFTA's Breakthrough Talent Award in 2007. All of this positions *STM* as radical British small-screen drama.

In *STM*, we witness Joe having a mental breakdown, which takes the form of a mounting loathing of Black people. Joe's piercing gaze and haunting to-camera iteration that 'everything bad that has ever happened to me has involved a black person' invites the viewer to participate not only in 'debates that are ongoing within the black community' but also a meta-discourse around the processes of racialisation that the text itself presents. For Joe, Black and specifically African Caribbean people begin to acquire a negative significance and the extremely caricatured Black characters that he encounters provide the ammunition for his self-hatred. These characters range from slack single mothers to domineering matriarchs and from manipulative community leaders to gangland killers. Joe's observation that 'we [Black men] go to prison and mental institutions', highlights a particular thematic concern around Black masculinity. Whether Joe is commenting on the destiny of Black men, and thus apparently accepting the 'grain of truth' contained within the stereotype, or on the structural inequalities underpinning the limited prospects faced by Black men, is never made entirely clear. Indeed, *STM* deliberately occupies a politically ambivalent space that requires the audience to actively negotiate the play's ideological orientations.

If *STM* refuses to be pinned down to any obvious moral position, so it also resists any clear-cut point of emotional identification. Joe is our lead protagonist and, crucially, the story is delivered through first-person narration and intermittent direct address to camera. At times, this is employed as a technique to encourage empathy with Joe. William Riggan in his typology of the unreliable narrator identifies the 'madman' as a first-person narrator whose fallibility as a spokesperson is derived from his mental illness. But Joe's mental fragility and sometimes contradictory politics also render him an unstable character and someone who, in fact, might be considered an 'unreliable narrator'.[5] As a result, there is a tension between the psychological realism of Joe's character and his wavering narrative authority. Joe's disdain for Black people, while intense in its delivery, also reveals flashes, at least tangentially, of compassion, connection and recognition. For Joe, Black people are a contaminating force in British society but he also refers to 'them' as 'we'. Through his romantic relationship with Heather (portrayed by Nikki Amuka Bird), a compassionate and politically conscious Black woman, Joe demonstrates both his ordinariness and humanity, confiding in her at one point, 'I feel depressed looking at the state of our lives … being Black feels like a curse' (figure 4.4).

The Black characters in *STM*, ranging from the God-fearing matriarch Mabel (portrayed by Jay Byrd) to the various insolent young Black people that Joe encounters as a schoolteacher and later as a job adviser, are mainly drawn as tabloid types. They are represented as feckless and amoral or as self-seeking with a sense of entitlement. The latter group is depicted in a climactic scene in which a gathering of local people at a community centre party blame the legacy of slavery for the current social disadvantage experienced by Black people. Considered in context, these racialised types may be identified as tapping into Blairite neo-liberal discourses prevalent at the time of *STM*'s making and airing. Such discourses derided so-called 'political correctness', attributed criminality to Black culture and denounced a growing 'blame culture' in British society.[6] In these ways, the text was potentially open to criticism for simply reproducing neo-conservative and hegemonic narratives of Black British identity and culture.

How then do we square this with my claim that *STM* may also be regarded as a piece of radical drama? Against the backdrop of a depoliticised multiculturalism, apparent since the early 2000s, there has been a growing preoccupation with personal, individualised screen dramas. I suggest that *STM* departs from this trend because the drama openly, if ambivalently, addresses a range of sociological concerns around social identity, inequality and difference through a focus on Black racial politics. Through Joe's schizophrenia, the important but rarely discussed issues of cultural representations of race and mental disorder are raised.

Predictably, given its controversial dramatic framework and stock characters, *STM* succeeded in eliciting powerful responses from both critics and viewers. These were primarily based around the issues of stereotyping and representation and their interpretation. For the African media campaign group, Ligali, *STM* constituted a 'flagship programme for racism' and was 'one of the most racist, demeaning and misrepresentative films ever broadcast and commissioned by the BBC'.[7] That these representations occurred and had been institutionally endorsed through commissioning and awards apparently intensified concerns about how these readings were negotiated by different racial audiences. For the *Guardian*'s best-known Black columnist, Joseph Harker, the play may have been 'professionally written, well directed, and well-acted by a predominantly Black cast' but this didn't 'come close to neutralising its relentlessly negative message'. The major point of contention for this discussion, therefore, is whether a drama that, at one level, appears to reinforce certain well-established media stereotypes of Black British life may also be interpreted as transgressive. Put simply, can a radical drama be conformist in some ways and subversive in others?

I want to propose that the major responses to *STM* have neglected its more complicated nuances and the ways in which these can help us understand the processes of racialisation in post-colonial settings. My reading suggests that, through its representation of mental illness, *STM* can in fact be interpreted as a radical critique of social inequality and the destructive effects of living with ethnicised social categories. I therefore want to nominate *STM as* a fascinating case study in both the histories of Black TV drama[8] and radical TV drama in Britain. Through critical cultural and textual analysis, involving attention to questions of authorship, form, themes and institutional context, this chapter aims to account for some of the concerns and responses previously identified but also offer an alternative reading of the text. I start with a broader contextualisation of the drama genre in its treatment of 'race' and reference an earlier BBC single play *Fable* (*The Wednesday Play*, 27 January 1965) written by the White playwright, John Hopkins. After setting up this relationship with *Fable*, I continue with a more focused discussion of *STM*. The aim is always to locate the 'radical' in *STM* and to consider its implications for, and within, a critical politics of 'race' and representation. Surprisingly, the production remains under-discussed in academic literature, perhaps because of its challenging formal properties and ambivalent ideological orientations, which make both its message and meaning especially tricky for critics to identify.[9]

Drama as radical space: the example of John Hopkins's *Fable*

Television functions as a privileged site in translating and organising the imagined needs and definitions of the nation. These needs and definitions – with the emphasis on translation – are especially important in relation to drama because it is here that we can speak most unequivocally about 'representation' rather than 'reflection'. Compared to other television genres the question of social construction, for example, how the nation and its various communities are conceived, becomes especially salient with drama. In broad terms, there is no pre-given reality to reproduce in dramatic form, only a set of choices to make about whom, how and what to represent. This offers some exciting possibilities of what 'race' and racial difference – marked in this discussion by 'blackness' – are made to signify, given that race and ethnicity are also understood to be social and political constructions and, therefore, ontologically unstable categories. Stuart Hall's work foregrounds the role of culture and cultural processes in determining how race is discursively constructed, so that 'race' is a 'floating signifier' whose meaning is never fixed,[10] So if we take 'race' as an 'open political category' as suggested by Gilroy,[11] albeit with powers of fixity within the politics of the state, our question may be posed in terms of what *STM* is saying about race through its representations.

Looking back at the early history of representations of Black characters or themes in British television drama, it is apparent that when a 'Black story' was to be produced it was up to the usually white, male and middle-class writer to fight the Black corner, and specifically in the mode of the newly emerging form of socially conscious drama of the 1950s and 1960s. John Elliot's *A Man From The Sun* (BBC, 1956), a live production featuring a range of Black British acting talent, was the first drama about the lives of Caribbean settlers in Britain, or what Elliot described as 'the clash between this mythical Britain and the actual grotty Britain, which West Indians would face when they got here'.[12] A few years later, Ted Willis's *Hot Summer Night* (ABC/ITV, 1959), featuring Lloyd Reckord, dramatised the impact of a Black presence in Britain.

While Black actors were beginning to be seen on screen during these decades, it was solely down to the creative vision of trusted white television writers such as John Elliott, Ted Willis and John Hopkins to script white-authorised representations of 'blackness'. A handful of early Black writers eventually began to see their work produced on television. These included Horace James (*Rainbow City*, BBC, 1967), Errol John (*Moon on a Rainbow Shawl*, ITV, 1960) and Barry Reckord (*You in Your Small Corner*, ITV, 1962). In the decades that followed, their successes paved the way for other writers such as Michael Abbensetts (*Black Christmas*, BBC, 1977; *Empire Road*, BBC, 1978–79). Black women writers, meanwhile, had a double struggle, obliged to challenge not just racial but gender hierarchies within the industry. Only a small number succeeded in doing so; Sylvia Wynter and Buchi Emecheta ('The Ju-Ju Landlord', *Crown Court*, ITV 1976; Nigeria: *A Kind of Marriage*, BBC, 1976) stand out. A new consciousness was emerging among Black cultural practitioners, stemming, as writer Mustapha Matura described it, 'from the intellectual realisation of our history: how you could perceive yourself had changed', but also about 'the political change, the metamorphosis happening to me and others around'.[13]

The 1980s and early 1990s brought new opportunities as part of a broader drive towards multiculturalism and anti-racism. This was a critical juncture in Black British culture, spawning not only a range of creative interventions in response to a history of marginalisation, but also attempts to find a unified public voice under the umbrella of 'political blackness'. Other notable writers included Rudy Narayan, Tunde Ikoli, Edgar White (*Black Silk*, BBC, 1985), Horace Ové (*The Garland*, BBC, 1981; *The Orchid House*, Channel 4, 1991), Caryl Phillips (*The Record*, Channel 4, 1985; *The Final Passage*, Channel 4, 1996), Michael Ellis (*South of the Border*, BBC, 1988) and Mike Phillips (*Bloodlines*, BBC, 1992). Each helped to transform conventional television treatments of Black-related issues amid a changing television drama marketplace in which the demise of single drama productions coincided with the rise of the series and soap operas from the late 1970s.[14]

As part of this discussion, I want to pay particular attention to *Fable* because it serves as a useful example of an early 'race drama' in which the ambivalence of the text mobilised a range of differing reactions. During the1960s, series such as *The Wednesday Play* (BBC1, 1964–70) provided an important outlet for new single dramas that could be topical, hard-hitting and popular. Although many of the plays remained within the prevailing discourses of ethical humanism, addressing moral issues such as homelessness, single mothers, race relations and abortion, they also succeeded in championing the need for new kinds of social and political legislation. Hopkins' *Fable* was made as a *Wednesday Play* and, like *STM*, it adopted a non-realist approach that departed from the prevailing tradition of social realism associated with 'ethnic' drama representations. Hopkins had written an episode of the police series *Z-Cars* (BBC1, 1962–78), 'A Place of Safety' (24 June 1964), focusing on police racism, which demonstrated his concern about the issue of institutional discrimination.

Although *Fable* made oblique reference to continuing repression in South Africa and the establishment of Bantustans by the South African government, it was set in a fantasy Britain where the balance of apartheid was reversed, so that the Black majority held political power while the White minority was subjugated. In envisaging a world in which the dominant racial power relations were transposed, *Fable* took viewers on an imaginative voyage in order to remind them that racial discrimination is based on social and conceptual, rather than biological, differences that have manifest themselves politically. For the Black actress, Carmen Munroe, who starred in it, 'it was actually very frightening ... because suddenly you were being asked to perform the sort of acts that were performed against you in real life'.[15]

At a time when Black characters were notable for their absence in 'serious' television drama, and with Whiteness posed as a social norm in terms of address, content and relations of looking, *Fable* unsettled otherwise taken-for-granted ideas of what Black and White ethnicities constituted (for example, by casting Whites as the murderers, pimps and prostitutes). In this sense, it served as a unique early illustration of television's capacity, through shifts in tone, format and characterisation, to re-imagine the typical ways of representing race and race relations. Like *STM*, *Fable* elicited a set of strong and mixed responses.[16] Despite Hopkins's anti-racist agenda, for some White British viewers the image of themselves on screen as subservient triggered fear not compassion. This was intensified at the time by broader anti-immigration sentiment and legislation. Thomas Baptiste, who appeared in *Fable* as liberal academic Mark Fellowes, who was part of 'the movement' which did not believe in the oppression of White people, received a letter after the broadcast warning: 'How dare you appear on our television screens, even as a friend or a liberal. Get back to your country! Hideous ape!'[17]

For Graham Murdock radical drama is a contestable term but one which might be identified by certain characteristics. This includes a critical interpretation of the present social order, an exposition of the gap between 'ideological promise and institutional performance', an investigation of social change and transformation and a challenge to conventional theatre practices and institutions.[18] The relevance of *Fable* is that, like *STM*, it may be seen to offer a complex and multi-layered 'critical interpretation of the present social order'. In *Fable* we are offered a bold critique of prevailing racialised power relations and structures. In *STM*, despite its seemingly hegemonic impulse, we are offered a critique of economic and political inequalities and their links with structural racism.[19]

Fable and *STM*, which aired over forty years apart, fictionalise the impact that ethnic social identities can have in different post-colonial contexts. Both adopt an innovative approach to realism and, partly owing to this, provoke real debate among their respective audiences. Put crudely, where the White-authored Fable unsettles White audience expectations concerning Black characterisation, *STM* sets a challenge for Black audiences, particularly for a drama authored by a Black writer. In both productions we find evidence of the playwright's sociological imagination at work and a provocative mode of address that, by design, serves to polarise viewers by asking them to negotiate the particular racial message or 'fable' in the text. The next section offers a closer textual reading of the useful provocation that *STM* provides.

Under the skin of *Shoot the Messenger*: a textual interpretation

Originally entitled *Fuck Black People!* the re-titled *STM* constitutes a risky enterprise that demonstrates many of the generic qualities identified by Murdock in his account of radical drama. As previously noted, the main responses to *STM* were centred on its stereotypical representations and their significance for viewers. However, my reading suggests that these stereotypical representations are necessary in order to demonstrate the impact of structural racism on cognitive states. Joe's degenerative mental condition materialises through his preoccupation with his own racial identity, marked simultaneously by recognition, shame and dis-identification (figure 4.1). These personal anxieties take the form of a public retreat from what he perceives Blackness to constitute and thus the play's extreme representations are always filtered through his racialised consciousness. Frantz Fanon argues in *Black Skin, White Masks*, 'the Negro makes himself inferior. But the truth is that he is made inferior'.[20] This idea is pertinent because it chimes with what Joe considers society to have 'done' to Black people; his own experience of feeling undermined and 'exhausted' by his Blackness is discussed openly with his girlfriend, Heather (figure 4.5).

I want to offer an alternative textual reading that avoids an over-dependence upon stereotyping theory and considerations of authorship (including authorial intentions) in favour of one that considers the role of power and social structures in shaping racialised categories and identities – and on which our lead character is obliged to draw. In the 2000s, work on the area of social divisions and mental health has noted the significance of research that foregrounds the psychic consequences of ethnic categorisations rather than ethnicity itself. Emphasis is also placed on the sociological processes that lead to the embodiment of social categories and the possible effects this has on the mental condition of those who are racially categorised. I suggest that *STM* can be read as a critique of social inequality and the destabilising impact of living with ethnicised social categories, as evidenced in the disproportionately high representation of ethnic minority groups in mental health units. Our anti-hero is entirely illustrative of such effects.

Joe opts for teaching over computer programming because it is 'what I am meant to be doing ... what I was put on this earth to do'. Our troubled protagonist is conscious of his racial identity and wider racial inequalities from the outset. An early scene jump-cuts to Joe recounting different headlines: 'Black Boys Failing', 'Gun Crime Goes up Again', 'Another Week, Another Death'. He describes becoming a teacher in this social context as 'like a call to arms'. The scene cuts to a local council education meeting where racial tensions proliferate around discussions of 'a racist conspiracy against black boys' and tabloid reports of Black under-achievement are 'yet another attempt to make the black community look bad'. We are privy to Joe's interpretation of the proceedings through a combination of diegetic and non-diegetic narration; though critical of this blame culture and its lack of solutions, he also opts to be a Black role model. He registers his social significance as a middle-class Black man, for working-class Black boys with limited choices beyond, it is said, self-destructive gang culture or glorification on the sports field.

As a Black male teacher in a 'failing', predominantly Black secondary school, Joe is positioned as an empathetic character with a moral social purpose but is also imbued with a weight of expectation from the 'Black community' about the value of his pedagogic practice, given the lack of Black male role models available. Like his creators, Foster and Onwurah, he utterly rejects such a representational burden. As his disposition is shown to wane, so too is his authority as our narrator. There is a murky element to Joe's apparently good intentions as he aims to 'force these boys to learn' through a self-devised system of 'enforced education' including detention plans that give a hint, perhaps, of his already unhinged condition. A nonchalant Black, male, year-nine student, Germal Forest (played by Charles Mnene), emerges as Joe's nemesis, accusing him of assault and so becoming the catalyst for Joe's, and eventually his own, undoing (figure 4.3). While we start to get a social account of institutional racism in how the media, school and legal system are shown to handle the subsequent legal case, what follows is a strong critique and caricature of the 'Black community' articulated through Joe's growing degenerative state.

The Black media, the baying public outside the court, and local councillors, are each shown to turn against Joe, and *his* ensuing critique becomes systematically cruel. Mirroring the opening credit sequence in which 'Fuck Teachers' was written on the school wall by multiracial youth, we now see a devastated Joe walking away with the school wall sprayed in red with the words 'Fuck Black people' in view. At this point within the text, prevailing racialised power structures are associated with the Black community and presented as a range of essentialist discourses and characterisations based on a Black culture of hypocrisy, blame politics and a sense of entitlement. For Joe, now, all Black people are the same. Black community leaders exploit 'their' communities for their own agendas, violence is intra-ethnic and Black single mothers and absent Black fathers are the norm. Joe's explicit positioning as our narrator from the first scene prior to the opening credit sequence sees him in medium close-up telling us how Black people are to blame for his misfortune.

Importantly, these representations and perceptions of Blackness are always filtered through Joe's disorientated paranoia; while listening to Miles Davis, even the jazz music is overlaid with the word 'traitor' and previous accusations of him being a 'house nigger' and 'a Ku Klux Klan man with a white face' reverberate in his mind. Joe is now conscious of himself only through how he thinks he is perceived. W. E. B. DuBois in *The Souls of Black Folk* describes this idea in terms of what he refers to as the 'peculiar sensation' of double consciousness:

> This sense of always looking at one's self through the eyes of others, of measuring one's soul by the tape of the world that looks on in amused contempt and pity. One ever feels his twoness – an American, a Negro; two souls, two thoughts, two unreconciled strivings; two warring ideals in one dark body.[21]

When the Black people Joe encounters turn their back on him, we see how he deliberately and increasingly alienates himself from society and how the 'warring ideals' come to possess him. The tense mood music is overlaid with 'everything bad that has ever happened to me', and linguistic motifs and *mise-en-scène*, including dim lighting in a disordered room, reflect the change in atmosphere. Unable to pay the rent and looking unkempt, Joe starts to live a life between cardboard city, psychiatric institutions and hostels. In the psychiatric ward, he is fixated with Black people and asks to be moved to a ward with White people because 'I just don't do well around them [Black people]'. On the streets he refuses charitable donations from Black passers-by. His 'twoness', to use DuBois' term, is presented here as a schizophrenic condition marked by an acute paranoia and reversal of more commonplace articulations of extreme, far-right White racism. The surreal image of a congregation of church Evangelists emerges from the river Thames and he confides: 'They're not giving up. The Black people. They always find me.'

There is a particularly dark segment in which Joe witnesses a 'Black on Black' gun killing through flashbacks overlaid with Jay Z's pessimistic rap anthem '99 Problems'. When he sees Mabel (Jay Byrd), an elderly black woman, struggling with bags in the heavy rain, he offers to help her but then runs away when she invites him in. He later accepts her compassion and, in a rather surreal turn of events, spends Christmas with her and her family – but also talks himself, and us by means of direct rhetorical questioning to camera, into the idea that she is trying to kill him. Mabel's family includes her daughter, Sherlene (portrayed by Sharon Duncan-Brewster), and four grandchildren with four different fathers. Joe, showing condescension as much about class as race, ridicules their ascribed names and spellings, 'Kaylon' and 'Shanequa', and pours scorn on Sherlene who, he suggests, 'probably gave more thought to their names than who should father them'. Mabel represents in-community racism when she says, 'black people too t'ief', and 'anything too Black is no good … because we're cursed'. A scene in a wig shop introduces the issue of Black beauty and style and an account of a politics of Black aesthetics that can be related to Eurocentric ideals of beauty. We later see the effects of such beauty ideals on Heather, who is deemed ugly by the Black community because of her dark skin and knotty hair. The psychological-social dimension of racial categories and coding remains the underlying idea running through the text (figure 4.6).

Fanon uses psychoanalytic theory to explicate how feelings of dependency and inferiority can be engendered in the mind of the Black subject who experiences the white world. Imitative behaviour, Fanon argues, is even more marked in upwardly mobile and educated Black people, such as Joe, who can afford to acquire status symbols. The questioning of Joe's authenticity as a 'Black man' is allegorised through his paranoid schizophrenia and inner voice, to which we are privy. After being suspended, Joe recounts the headteacher's words while looking at his own gloomy reflection in the mirror, indicating the dualistic character of his racialised identity, accentuated now by his loss of social capital. The black and white chess pieces, with which he plays, seen in close-up, again symbolise the racial power struggle that consume hims, and particularly the issue of slavery for which he later actually uses the metaphor of chess. Joe's schizophrenia is mirrored stylistically in the construction of the text. Within the text, he sits both on the inside and outside of the drama – he is our central protagonist 'inside' the production but his to-camera delivery also suggests his distance from it. While the *loci* of Joe's paranoia are the Black community, his ethnicity – and indeed narrative authority – is revealed to be unstable and always in a state of negotiation because it is filtered through the experience of mental illness.

Amid the bleak version of denigrated social life that Joe experiences, a degree of redemption is offered by Mabel, by the church, and later by Heather. Largely thanks to Heather, the closing scenes see Joe accumulating a certain amount of social capital including employment at a Job Centre where, in a reversal of fortune, he meets a regretful and troubled Germal. In fact, an oblique critique of the impact on structural racism is apparent here; without Joe's pedagogic guidance following his suspension, Germal has failed like so many of his Black male peers – the political case being made here for more social diversity in education roles. But the theme of slavery constantly bubbles beneath the narrative surface with numerous references to either its melancholic effects or the need to relegate it to the past. In a climactic scene at the community centre party, Joe suggests that we should 'Get over slavery' and eventually utters an out-loud 'Fuck Black people'. This leads to his break-up with an outraged Heather but also acts as a form of catharsis for him.

Now working in the psychiatric hospital where he had previously spent two months, he discovers that Germal has been admitted with police intervention, thus fulfilling his depressing prophecy of the pervasiveness of mental disorder in the Black community. Through a mutual apology, first from Germal to Joe and then vice versa, we are offered a sense of reinstated calm and bonding between these two Black men. Joe's apology to Germal for letting him down and for not recognising the fear within is a major admission, and Joe resumes his teaching career, wins his appeal against suspension and is reunited with Heather. But although Joe's mental state has improved, and he dresses smartly in a suit, the political ambiguities within the text still linger and Joe suggests to us that this is far from the 'happy ending' required by audiences of this particular narrative drama. With a direct provocation to the camera – and in turn to the audience who are likely to have taken offence at 'his' script – Joe calmly states: 'It's not the end is it? I'm not taking back everything I said. You didn't like the way I said it? So shoot me.'

Problems in the text

One of the struggles within *STM*, which has led to the offence rightly prophesied by Joe in this closing scene, is the subtlety of its critique, particularly as set against the gaudy stereotypes at hand. Joe's positioning of Black people as *the* problem threatens to undermine any potentially transgressive position. But actually it is always the white-led prejudice within state institutions, for example, the press and the education, legal and health systems, that is the implicit underlying agenda and that arguably provokes Joe's mental illness. On the surface, though, any hope of transformation is left with the Black characters themselves, regardless of broader socio-political circumstances. It is precisely through the marginalisation of Whiteness in the text that a depressing portrait of metropolitan space emerges. In spite of the way that it is first set up to deal with these issues, through the stylistic techniques employed, flashbacks, non-linear narrative, surreal encounters, the drama constructs an abstract view of the social structures that affect urban psychosis. The drama is not anchored in any identifiable geographical space and is thus abstracted from the social world. In this sense, we are presented with an over-dramatisation and stylisation that refuses to overtly connect Joe's interpretation of Blackness with 'real' structural issues. So, for example, the shooting script of the production tells us that it is set in an 'inner city' space, but few visual signifiers in the production demonstrate this or help us ground the story in relation to empirical reality.[22]

Furthermore, the emotional and psychological realism of the play is undercut by its departure from social-realist style. Comic asides, direct-to-camera address, the use of ironic music, for example, the playing of 'Rule Britannia' in the White-led school and flashbacks, are all techniques that work against a realistic reading of the text as a socially conscious drama. The mediating effects of the screen are laid bare through the device of direct address. The shooting script tells us that Joe 'catches us looking at him' (figure 4.2). From the outset, Joe provokes us into a response about the racialised politics under scrutiny here; inadvertently asking us to make a judgement about him and his dis-identification as a Black man. He teases us with his knowing looks to camera, more usually associated with the comedy genre, and his whispers – 'I know what you're thinking' – appear to address us personally by inviting us to question our own racialised politics. Of course, contemporary audiences are now accustomed to this particular mode of direct address because of its prevalence in hybrid forms such as docu-soaps and mockumentaries such as *The Office* (BBC2, 2001–3). While not a particularly radical narrative convention today, the significance of the use of direct address is that we are made aware of how we are reflected and implicated in the meanings that the text produces.

Ien Ang draws the distinction between connotative and denotative levels of identification experienced by audiences in their viewing of soap opera whereby they might find certain aspects of the drama realistic on a connotative level in spite of the unrealistic denotative basis of the form.[23] We are aware of the mediating, denotative effects but are also invited to recognise – through the mobilisation of common stereotypes – the connotations of Blackness presented here. Adding to the play's self-consciousness is Joe's self-narration and therefore our awareness of his utter subjectivity. While direct address can indicate persuasive intentions – and this is certainly Joe's ploy here – the effect of the artifice is to undermine his narrative authority. Baggaley, in his work on the psychology of the television image, suggests that the 'unusual intensity' of the speaker's eye-contact with the viewer can weaken, rather than heighten, the speaker's credibility.[24] These stylised elements in the text provide the means whereby *STM* draws attention to its own constructedness and, in so doing, requires us to negotiate actively, and certainly not passively to accept, the stereotypes that are being presented. As it is assembled as an open text, it is impossible to attempt a textually deterministic view of *STM* as fixing audiences in any particular way, because the viewer is left unanchored in any one emotional reality. The ambiguous political lens can be regarded as both a strength and a weakness because it produces an anxiety within the text that both upholds and muddles its radical potential.

Psychological realism is also undermined by the generic shifts between drama and comedy. Joe's tone slips from wryness to exasperation, and many of his observations about Black social life, which are delivered as witty asides to the camera, seem better suited to the comedy – and specifically ethnic comedy – form, a genre that has always been more at ease with presenting racialised stereotypes. When Reece, a Black student, tells him he is unable to carry out detention because he has football practice, Joe whispers to us: 'We've got enough black footballers ... and Thierry Henry he ain't.' In the midst of a heated discussion about slavery and any positive effects, he says: 'At least they took us somewhere sunny!'

Aspects of the narrative development also lack dramatic coherence. Signs of Joe's breakdown seem more or less apparent, and his brief foray into church life lacks credibility. His relationship with Heather seems antithetical to his repugnance of Black people, especially because it starts at the height of his inner chaos. Stephen Harper rightly draws attention to the film's failure to address the intersections of class and race, and to the way it invites audiences to resolve the debates it raises, while refusing clearly to 'disavow Joe's racial and class hatred'. Drummond suggests that such ambiguity can also be seen as radical because it deliberately challenges the audience's identifications with the camera and the character.

The upshot is that viewers are left disorientated and devoid of any particular emotional position to which they are safely directed, especially in the hands of Joe. Again, Riggan's typology of the unreliable narrator identifies the 'madman' as a first-person narrator whose fallibility as a spokesperson is derived from their mental illness. In the crudest sense, Joe can be considered a 'madman' and his authority is therefore undermined. To this extent, the criticisms of the drama as 'racist', inevitably influenced by a legacy of representational politics and marginalisation, do not treat it on its own terms or consider the destabilised position from which our first-person narrator, or messenger, speaks. It is Joe's mental illness that is the real story here and yet there is a limited engagement with his psychological profile in the popular critical responses as acknowledged in academic discussion such as Harper and Cross. What is certain is that the world crafted here is based entirely on Joe's interpretation. It is not, as many of the evaluations of the production suggest, a statement from Foster about what Black people constitute per se nor an attempt at literal truth.

Shoot the Messenger in context

I have been suggesting that *STM*'s devices of unstable narration, irony and stylistic abstraction add to the difficulty of reading the text as a 'reflection' of reality. This makes the debates around stereotyping especially superfluous by directly challenging the major theoretical impulse of the well-rehearsed 1980s 'burden of representation' debate.[25] This burden has commonly been applied to fictional treatments of Black life, highlighting how 'Black cultural representations' have been expected to solve all such problems and match up with a particular version of reality, in line with the values and beliefs of that group, against which all representations can be tested. This impulse has had an important bearing on way that Black screen drama has been received, acclaimed and analysed, typically in relation to the dualistic framework of good and bad, positive and negative.

'Radical-ness' – vis-à-vis the aims of traditional identity politics to 'correct' so-called misrepresentations – has become a dominant trope (but not always an achievement) of Black television drama. Paradoxically, the representational impulse at work here has facilitated a revised normative politics around the basis of Black British drama and expectations of the Black writer/producer (for example, having to align themselves unambiguously with the 'Black community'). In so doing, an essentialising concept of ethnicity has been reconfigured. It is, of course, important to recognise the basis for the criticisms about stereotyping, reception and authorship levelled at *STM*, and to situate these within a historical screen context of marginalisation, racialisation (with race and racism as the prevailing themes) and politicisation. At the same time, these concerns have generated an ideological politics of expectation hinged around the function and motivations of Black drama and its producers, something we can identify as a continuing representational burden.

With this legacy in mind, *STM* does not provide an easy basis for accepting it as radical Black British drama because, on a certain level, it flaunts a politics that fixes the 'crisis of Blackness' within Black communities themselves. *STM* lays itself open to the criticism that it rehearses well-versed clichés of Black culture, and that it therefore capitalises on traditional racialised pathologies that project difference and unassimilability on to the Black subject. In an early discussion of Black artistic practice, Neal links the Black Arts movement to the Black Power movement and suggests that it is 'radically opposed to any concept of the artist that alienates him from his community'.[26] *STM* clearly challenges this alignment of artistic and political affiliations with simple notions of 'community'. Through its apparently deliberate provocation, extreme characterisation and ideological positioning, which foreground the oppressive rather than facilitating character of racial identity, *STM* recklessly disrupts clear-cut expectations that Black artists need to align themselves with, rather than alienate, 'their' community. Foster's production meddles with this idea and, in so doing, also makes the case for a post-structuralist imperative that transcends the rhetoric of 'stereotypes' and 'positive' and 'negative' images.

In fact, *STM* endorses the view that 'typing' has to be recognised as an inevitable and necessary system of representation. As with *Fable*, the basis on which its 'positive' and 'negative' characterisations are constituted is also uncertain. For example, Germal is an alienated Black youth but only with reference to a state that offers him limited opportunities; Mabel is a 'good Christian' but she, herself, demonstrates hypocrisy and racism. This is not to suggest that stereotypes can be identified any more easily in social-realist texts, but *STM's* non-realist aesthetic does obstruct any simple reading of the text.

In conclusion, I consider briefly the political and economic value of *STM* as 'radical drama' and its status as a 'media event' in relation to twenty-first century socio-political and institutional shifts. For Roly Keating, the BBC2 Channel Controller under whom the film was commissioned, quoted in an article in the *Guardian*, on 8 December 2005,

STM is a landmark piece, comparable to John Osborne's *Look Back in Anger* (1956), with the potential to speak to a 'generation of black Britons', even though the question of what exactly it is 'saying' is not broached. Keating also suggested that as audiences for television drama decline, one strategy for broadcasters is to back more 'strongly authored, contemporary dramas' such as *STM*.

In this way, Keating's comments place a renewed emphasis, reminiscent of the early single-play era out of which *Fable* emerged, on the agency of the writer as author of the single drama production. Thinking contextually, *STM* emerges from a period (the mid-2000) overwhelmed by public debates around 'institutional racism' and 'hideous Whiteness' in the media, which help to make sense of the significance of how interpretations of a play are created out of a wider sense of institutional lack and/or bias. Thus, for one viewer, the founder of the independent film production company, riceNpeas – Ishmahil Blagrove Jr – *STM* provided evidence of Black writers who feel they need to assassinate their community to get commissioned, invoking, in this way, more general ideas about continuing institutional discrimination.

A review of *STM*'s publicity suggests that the controversy around the film was utilised by the BBC as a marketing manoeuvre and also as evidence of its own concern at the time with the issue of impartiality.[27] 'Race rows' are now a prominent theme in mediatised debates, apparent in the sensationalist meta-discourses of race, such as those around 2007's *Celebrity Big Brother* on Channel 4. The question of what 'racism' is – from the football pitch to the talent show – is now played out in the public sphere. For all its potential co-option into this broader expedient agenda, the various interpretations of *STM* themselves demonstrate that racism is context-specific, polysemic and experienced in different ways.

Even before its television screening, the production was already mired in controversy by virtue of an early theatrical preview in a London cinema. It was here that the film first drew intense criticism from some members of the audience for contributing to the problematisation of the Black British community in the British media. *STM*'s writer, Sharon Foster, was at the theatrical screening and later stated that she loved the 'pandemonium' that the film had created. Heightening the controversy, the writer and producer have both insisted that *STM* marks a watershed in Black screen representation precisely *because of* the 'authenticity' of its racialised stereotypes. For Foster, the public outrage was 'an authentication of what I had written. It was like real life following drama.'[28] This claim of 'authenticity' from the writer inevitably creates a dilemma for audiences, unsettling the basis on which we validate a text if we register the author's intentions rather than reading it on its own terms.

It may be useful in this instance to think about the writer as only one aspect of a broader industrial process that shapes the text. This reading recognises *STM*'s radical and transformative potential. The drama's ambiguous orientations, stylistic innovations, the critical work it demands of its viewers, and ultimately the heterogeneous interpretations that the production makes possible – essentially through the theme of Black mental illness – all cement its radical credentials.

Figure 4.1 *Shoot the Messenger*, David Oyelowo and the controversial way in which issues of race are represented in the text (BBC Films, tx. 30/10/06)

Figure 4.2 The mediating effects of the screen are laid bare through the device of direct address from *Shoot the Messenger* (BBC Films, tx. 30/10/06)

Figure 4.3 Charles Mnene as David Oyelowo's nemesis in *Shoot the Messenger* (BBC Films, tx. 30/10/06)

Figure 4.4 Visual representation of Joe's often depressed state from *Shoot the Messenger* (BBC Films, tx. 30/10/06)

Figure 4.5 Oyelowo's Joe and Heather (Nikki Amuka Bird) from *Shoot the Messenger* (BBC Films, tx. 30/10/06)

Figure 4.6 The wig shop, Black style, and the Eurocentric beauty of *Shoot the Messenger* (BBC Films, tx. 30/10/06)

Notes

1 This chapter has been previously published as 'Locating the "radical" in *Shoot the Messenger*', *Journal of British Cinema and Television*, 10:1 (2013), pp. 187–205. Quoted in 'Shoot the Messenger', www.bbc.co.uk/drama/shootthemessenger/ (accessed 15 May 2012).

2 As noted by Jane Tranter, BBC Controller of Drama Commissioning in an interview.

3 The term 'Black' within this chapter refers to people of African or African Caribbean descent.

4 Foster's first television drama was *Babyfather* (BBC, 2001–2) based around the rites of passage of four Black men experiencing fatherhood, love and friendship. Onwurah is the writer and director of another controversial production, *Welcome to the Terrordome* (1995).

5 Riggan, William, *Picaros, Madmen, Naifs, and Clowns: The Unreliable First-Person Narrator* (Norman, OK: University of Oklahoma Press, 1982).

6 *STM*'s airing also occurred around the time of the bicentenary of the abolition of slavery and shortly before Tony Blair's public statement of 'deep sorrow': 'Blair "Sorrow" Over Slave Trade', BBC News website, 27 November 2006, http://news.bbc.co.uk/1/hi/6185176.stm (accessed 15 May 2012).

7 Quoted in 'BBC Accused of Making Perfect "BNP Propaganda" Drama', MailOnline, 20 August 2006, www.dailymail.co.uk/news/article-401496/BBC-accused-making-perfect-BNP-propaganda-drama.html (accessed 15 May 2012).

8 The term 'Black drama' is used here to refer to fictional treatments that are either authored by Black people and/or focus on issues related to Black lives and experiences.

9 Two important exceptions here are Phillip Drummond's 2007 analysis of *STM* and *Yasmin* in relation to the question of intercultural identities, and Stephen Harper's 2008 review of *STM*. See Drummond, P. 'Intercultural Identities in British Film and Television: Shoot the Messenger and Yasmin'. Paper presented to The Realist Impulse: Contemporary Film-making in Britain conference, St Anne's College, Oxford, 12 July 2007; and Harper, S., 'Shoot the Messenger', *Scope: An Online Journal of Film and TV Studies*, 11 June 2008, http://news.bbc.co.uk/1/hi/entertainment/5274198.stm (last accessed 10 May 2012).

10 Hall, Stuart, 'The Whites of their Eyes: Racist Ideologies and the Media', in Hugh Mackay and Tim O'Sullivan (eds), *The Media Reader* (London: BFI, 1990).

11 Gilroy, Paul, *'There Ain't No Black in the Union Jack': the Cultural Politics of Race and Nation* (London: Hutchinson, 1997).

12 Pines, Jim (ed.), *Black and White in Colour: Black People in British Television since 1936* (London: BFI, 1992), p. 86.

13 Matura quoted in McMillan, Michael, 'Ter Speak in Yer Mudder Tongue: An Interview with playwright Mustafa Matura', in Kwesi Owusu (ed.), *Black British Culture and Society: A Text Reader* (London and New York: Routledge, 2000), p. 275.

14 Cooke, Lez, *British Television Drama: A History* (London: BFI, 2003), p. 191.

15 Pines, *Black and White in Colour*, p. 58.

16 'Fable', BBC Audience Research Report, 12 February 1965, BBCWAC T5/1349.

17 Pines, *Black and White in Colour*, p. 67.

18 Murdock, Graham, 'Radical Drama, Radical Theatre', *Media, Culture and Society*, 2 (1980), p. 151.

19 Later productions such as Mustapha Matura's *Black Silk* (BBC, 1985) have exposed racial bigotry within institutions while others, such as Lennie James' *Storm Damage* (BBC2, 2000) and Ronan Bennett's *Top Boy* (Channel 4, 2011), have criticised structural inequalities.

20 Fanon, Franz, *Black Skin, White Masks* (New York: Grove Publishers, 1994), p. 115.

21 DuBois, W. E. B., *The Souls of Black Folk* (Minneola, NY: Dover Publications, 1994), p. 3.

22 The shooting script of *STM* is available from the BBC TV Drama website, www. bbc.co.uk/writersroom/scripts/shoot-the-messenger (accessed 17 May 2012).

23 Ang, Ien, *Desperately Seeking the Audience* (Routledge, 2006). Anonymous, '*Luther* Creator Preparing Big-screen Version of the Idris Elba Drama', *Radio Times*, 22 March 2012.

24 Baggaley, Jon, *Psychology of the Television Image* (Ann Arbor, MI: Saxon House, 1980), p. 30.

25 Mercer, K., *Welcome to the Jungle: New Positions in Black Cultural Studies* (Routledge, 1994).

26 Neal, Larry, *Visions of a Liberated Future: Black Arts Movement Writings* (New York: Thunder's Mouth Press, 1989), p. 15.

27 In the 2007 BBC Trust session 'Saying the Unsayable', Foster discussed responses to *STM*.

28 Quoted in 'Edgy New Film Tests Opinion', BBC News website, 24 August 2006, http://news.bbc.co.uk/1/hi/entertainment/5274198.stm (accessed 10 May 2012).

5

The iconic ghetto on British television: Black representation and *Top Boy*

Kehinde Andrews

Top Boy is an eight-part British drama, which ran over two series in 2011 and 2013. The show follows the rise of Dushane up the ranks of drug dealers on the fictional Summerhouse estate in London. Alongside his story is an ensemble cast of characters and narratives that explore life on the estate. The focus on drugs and gangs in the inner city led to the show inevitably being dubbed the 'British answer to the *Wire*'.[1] Like the *Wire*, the show was written by a white writer (Ronan Bennett) and based on his impressions of life on the estates. The show was generally well received both critically and commercially, presenting a mostly neglected section of life in the UK.

Top Boy is notable in the British context because it is one of the very few series with a majority black cast ever to air. Most of the small number that have been made are comedies with the only exceptions on the publicly funded BBC being: *Empire Road* (1978–79), extensively covered by Darrell Newton in 2011;[2] the television programmes *Babyfather* (2001–2) and *Undercover* (2016). ITV has never run a majority black drama, whereas Channel 4 aired *Dubplate Drama* (2005–9) before *Top Boy*. This context is important because it speaks to the absence of any sustained representation of black life. In the rare instances that shows with black majority casts do emerge, they are essential to analyse. Each allows for a detailed examination of representational discourse through the constant presence of black characters. This is particularly important because television is a 'primary contributor to common knowledge, to the widely shared pool of information and perspectives from which people shape their perceptions of self, world and citizenship'.[3] Channel 4's production of black majority dramas is instructive because although they have a public service remit, they are a commercial broadcaster and therefore necessarily more framed by popular discourse. It is no coincidence that both Dubplate Drama and *Top Boy* draw on recognisable stereotypical tropes of black representation, in this case that of the 'iconic ghetto'.[4]

The chapter explores the importance of the concept of the iconic ghetto, examining its discursive importance in reproducing racism. It has particular resonance, given that the majority of black people live in concentrated urban centres, and therefore how they are represented to the broader to society through the media has major consequences. I develop a critical discourse analysis of *Top Boy* to understand how the iconic ghetto is reproduced throughout the show. My study involved watching and re-watching the series to pull out the discursive themes. From this analysis the basis of the iconic ghetto portrayed throughout the show became apparent and is captured in the number of themes explored, including the proliferation of poverty, crime and violence agency; a lack of female agency and, ultimately, blame cast on black communities for the problems the show exaggerates.

The 'iconic' ghetto

The 'iconic ghetto' is a concept from African American sociologist Professor Elijah Anderson who argues that the Black ghetto has a particular significance, given the history of racism in America. In the post-slavery society of the South, the system of Jim Crow enforced residential segregation of African Americans.[5] During the great migration of African Americans into the North in the early twentieth century, black people found that northern cities were no less segregated than in the south. African Americans were forced to live in particular areas through white flight and the red-lining of districts that were demarked as black neighbourhoods.[6] Across America these historic patterns of segregation have left a lasting legacy, creating large areas that are predominantly African American. In fact, the public school system in America is more segregated today than it was in 1956, demonstrating that racial segregation is just as endemic in contemporary society.[7]

The concept of the iconic ghetto goes beyond the idea of racial segregation; African Americans were (and continue to be) forced to live separately in conditions of poverty and disadvantage. Anderson explains how deviance is key to ideas of the ghetto, which become represented in the popular imaginary as:

> where 'the black people live,' symbolizing an impoverished, crime-prone, drug-infested, and violent area of the city. Aided by the mass media and

popular culture, this image of the ghetto has achieved an iconic status, and serves as a powerful source of stereotype, prejudice, and discrimination.[8]

For Anderson, the imagery of the ghetto is so powerful it becomes iconic and a symbol that black people carry with them wherever they go. He argues that all African Americans have provisional status because they have to prove they are not 'ghetto' to be accepted in mainstream spaces. The power of this iconic ghetto can have deadly consequences when it becomes a taken for granted reading of Blackness.

In February 2012 an African American teenager was walking back through the gated community where he was visiting after going to the local store to buy some Skittles. Trayvon Martin was seen by the over-zealous neighbourhood watchman George Zimmerman, and identified as a suspicious person in the white, privileged space. Being a young, black male and dressed in a hoodie signified all the hallmarks of the iconic ghetto. His provisional status led Zimmerman to follow, confront and ultimately shoot an unarmed teenager to death. The fact that the police took so long to charge Zimmerman and that he was eventually acquitted speaks to the power of the iconic ghetto. The image of the ghetto and all it stood for was enough to cast a reasonable doubt that Zimmerman was lying when he said he felt threatened for his life by an unarmed teenager.

Alongside the discriminatory and potentially deadly consequences of the iconic ghetto, it is a concept that is central to progressive movements for social change. The Black Power movement in particular embraced the image of the ghetto, with Malcolm X proclaiming during a 1963 speech that he was a 'field negro', one of the masses who caught hell in the ghettoes of America.[9] The Black Panthers aimed to recruit the 'bad nigger off the block' who understood and would fight racism to the death.[10] This orientation of the iconic ghetto in politics has also played out in popular culture such as Hip Hop, where the political roots of the genre have defined authenticity in an orientation to the 'street' or the ghetto.[11]

Detached from the political roots of ghetto authenticity, black popular culture has been criticised for reinforcing the negative role that the iconic ghetto can play in social life. Gangsta Rap, in particular has been challenged for its hypermasculine, hypersexualised representation of Blackness, rooted in criminality and the ghetto.[12] The excessive stereotypical negativity of Gangsta Rap has been compared to the black and white minstrel shows of the past that paraded caricatured images of Blackness.[13] Anderson argues that popular culture is a key mechanism for transmitting the idea of the iconic ghetto and when black artists produce such negative images, they are colluding in its dissemination.

Whether for discriminatory ends, or efforts to create a politics of liberation, the ghetto has an iconic role in shaping the representation of African American life.

The 'iconic ghetto' in Britain

The UK is not subject to the same kind of residential segregation as in the USA, although there are patterns of concentration of ethnic minorities in particular locations, based on discrimination. Mass migration of those minorities from the colonies only began in earnest after the Second World War when, owing to the loss of millions of men, Britain was in desperate need of workers. During this period of migration, ethnic minorities were only invited to the urban centres for work.[14] This historical settlement is mirrored in residential patterns today. Sunak and Rajeswaran explain that half of all ethnic minorities in the UK live in London, Birmingham or Manchester. For black communities this is even more acute with half of the demographic living in London, according to the 2011 census. As cities dominate the popular imagination it is easy to forget that outside urban centres, the vast majority of the population is white. The West Midlands serves as a good example because it includes one the most diverse metropolitan areas in the country, centred on the city of Birmingham. According to the 2011 census the city itself was 53.1 per cent white, while the conurbation as a whole was 66 per cent white. However, more people in the West Midlands live outside the conurbation of Birmingham and 92.6 per cent of them are white.[15]

Not only were the children of the colonies funnelled into the urban centres, but they were also restricted to particular inner-city locations.[16] As in the USA, this was done through a combination of housing policy, white flight and discrimination. Rex and Moore, in one of their classic studies of Birmingham, gave the example of the city council's plans in 1953 to open a boarding house for Caribbean men in the then affluent area of Northfield. When the residents learned of the plan they quickly protested and had the boarding house moved to the migrant zone of Handsworth. The historical legacy of these policies is that ethnic minorities are concentrated within the inner cities of the country.[17]

In a direct parallel to the US experience, the ethnic minority areas of settlement were defined by their deprivation and poorer housing stock.[18] Economic racism meant that minorities were confined in low-paid sectors of work, and their children faced (and continue to face) high level of unemployment. This economic discrimination has meant that while white people have found success and moved out of the inner city, ethnic minority communities have largely been restricted to living in deprived inner-city areas.[19] Institutional racism in the criminal justice system allows for these communities to be defined as problems and over-policed. Stop and search, arrest rates and police patrols are all disproportionately high in the dark inner-city communities.[20] The impact of the concentration in the deprived inner city is the same as the iconic ghetto in the USA.

Perhaps the most detailed examination of the impact of the iconic ghetto in Britain is the study *Policing the Crisis* by the Centre for Contemporary Cultural Studies (CCCS) in 1978. This foundational study focused on how mugging became the basis of a moral panic in the 1970s. There is actually no such crime as 'mugging', which in legal terms is robbery. However, the CCCS highlighted how the media, police and the courts all colluded to create a new category, which signified a violent disorder running rampant in the ethnic minority dominated inner city. This quote in the book, which was taken from the *Sun* newspaper, perfectly captures the centrality of the iconic ghetto in the creation of the moral panic of mugging:

> Handsworth, that sprawling Birmingham slum where the three muggers grew up is a violent playground ... Paul Storey, son of a mixed marriage, tried drugs, then theft – and finally violence in a bid to find excitement in his squalid environment. Paul's mother, 40-year-old Mrs Ethel Saunders, said 'What chance do young people have in a lousy area like this?'[21]

The racially coded category of mugging was important because it was treated differently from other comparable crimes. Judges sentenced those guilty of so-called muggings to harsher sentences, resulting in high levels of racial discrimination. In the criminal justice system this disparity in sentencing for ethnic minorities continues, demonstrating the enduring power of the iconic ghetto.

Analysis of *Top Boy*

As one of the handful of black majority cast shows, *Top Boy* has an important role in framing how black communities are portrayed on British television. The critical discourse analysis carried out on both series of the show demonstrates the extent to which the idea of the iconic ghetto permeated the representations in the series. This section outlines how the key features of the iconic ghetto are reproduced in the show. From the opening scene of the first episode it is clear that the visuals of the estate, the ghetto, are as much a part of the show as any of the characters. The first six shots are of the soaring tower blocks of the fictional Summerhouse estate that introduce us to and frame the rest of the action (figure 5.1 and 5.2). From these shots we can see the expanse and magnitude of the estate. The first character we see is Ra'Nell (portrayed by Malcolm Kamulete), a teenage boy who negotiates life on the estate throughout the series. In the opening shots he stands looking out over the estate as we are brought in to life in Summerhouse (figure 5.3).

The introduction to each episode reinforces this message of location. There is no theme tune, just an aerial shot that pans from one part of the estate to the next as it gets dark and we end up with a shot of the estate with the city of London in the background. Discursively, this opening shot creates the image of distance between the estate and the affluent world of the city. As the camera pans across the estate we see the tower blocks, hear the police sirens and then finish with the city in the distance: another world that those on the estate have no access to.

Watching *Top Boy* you are constantly reminded of the location of the story. The aerial shots of the estate are a persistent feature and used as the glue to connect the various narratives that are all part of the story of the estate. In a sense, the story is really one of the estate, rather than of the characters that inhabit it. Almost all of the action takes part in the estate, with much of it being outdoors, in the visual concrete jungle. Even for those scenes shot indoors, inhabitants remain framed by the estate. The tower blocks have no curtains in *Top Boy*, yet have large windows to help frame the action within the dilapidated buildings (figure 5.4).

The continuous visual reinforcement of the estate creates its own world, something outside of ordinary experience. The market is particularly important in shaping the exotic nature of the estate. In the first episode, the first scene is in the outdoor market. In one scene audiences see a Caribbean food store, a reggae stall, a Vietnamese fishmonger, and a stall with the cured head of an unidentifiable animal (figure 5.5). This market represents the exotic cultural space of the estate and is often used as a location throughout the show. This domain is also home to numerous young people and their raucous activities. As an example, in the second series we witness youngsters sitting around playing a British version of the 'dozens', where they are trading barbs in rhyme. Again, this seemingly reinforces the vastly different lifestyles these characters experience on the estate.

Throughout *Top Boy* we are introduced to all of the key signifiers of the ghetto: the tower blocks, the market, the basketball courts, the abandoned yards, the crack den, the whorehouse, the gym, the murals, the graffiti and the subway walks. This is more than just where the characters live, the estate is the narrative and shapes the characters. In the second series, the main character Dushane explains his connection to the area: 'I was born and bred in Summerhouse, 26 years old. I ain't nothing to be except this.' Leaving the estate is always seen as a big step discursively in *Top Boy*. Very little action takes places outside Summerhouse and when it does attention is drawn to it. For instance, Ra'Nell's mother, Lisa (portrayed by Sharon Duncan-Brewster) is sectioned and locked in an institution, away from her child. Her absence is a key part of the story and her struggle to return to life on the estate.

The other time in the first series when the story leaves the estate is when Dushane and Sully (Kane Robinson) set up a temporary drugs operation in a suburb of London. They take some of the younger kids from the estate to sell the drugs, including RaNell's friend, Gem (Giacomo Mancini). When he is in the car Sully asks him, 'You ever been to the country?' On the car ride we see the buildings change as they leave the estate and go out of the city. There is a sunny optimism in these shots as Gem looks out the window, excited about his adventure. This is very short lived because, when they arrive, the cottage turns out to be a rundown, crack den and Chantelle (Letitia Wright), a teenage dealer, complains, 'This place is dirty, man.' Even when they leave, the characters take the ghetto with them.

In the second series, Michael (portrayed by Xavien Russell) who is a 12-year-old member of Dushane's crew, is sent to do a drug deal with a middle-class white man. Again, we see the shots of the changing architectural landscape and Michael's awe on the journey. The contrast could not be drawn more sharply between the estate and the affluent area of the deal, where we see trees for one of the few times in the show. Once Michael is let into the middle-class man's house we can see the wealth but he is completely taken by the amount of books, exclaiming 'Jeez, blood you got a lot of books', and mentioning this again when he gets back to the estate. This distinction of the books is an important one for how the estate is constructed as a separate space. It is not just different, *Top Boy* represents the ideal type of Anderson's iconic ghetto, the outsider image of the 'ghetto as impoverished, chaotic, lawless, drug-infested, and ruled by violence'.[22]

Representations of poverty, drugs and violence

Yuen explains how the domination of negative stereotypes of black communities on screen forces actors into 'playing ghetto'.[23] This applies to all the characters in *Top Boy* who portray roles that embody the iconic ghetto. Ra'Nell is rare in *Top Boy* as he only commits one crime, helping Heather, a pregnant friend of his mother to start a cannabis farm so she can secure the funds to escape the estate. She wishes leave because 'I ain't bringing up my kids round here no way ... There are places believe it or not where you can let your kid out at night, and you don't have to worry about them being stabbed or picked on by the police.' Heather's description of Summerhouse perfectly captures the representation of the estate in *Top Boy*.

Poverty is a clear theme that runs throughout, constantly reinforced by shots of the tower blocks. In series two, we see extreme poverty in the character of Jason (portrayed by Ricky Smarts), a child who is introduced running round the estate stealing whatever he can lay his hands on. At one point he steals from Michael, and one of the crew comments that 'he stinks'. Later in the show we get to see where he lives, a completely neglected and disgusting hovel he shares with his crack addicted mother and her abusive partner. Sully makes a connection with him, taking him under his wing because – as we learn – he had a similar upbringing.

Every episode comes with a warning of violence, and it does not disappoint. Violence is a feature of daily life with beatings, stabbings and shootings commonplace in the narrative. A plethora of characters are murdered, in myriad ways, across the two series. Some particularly memorable moments of extreme violence emphasise its continuing background presence on the estate. In order to make a deal with a drugs boss, Bobby Raikes, we see Dushane and Sully cut two of a man's fingers off in the first series. In series two, while doing an errand for a Vietnamese drug dealer, Gem witnesses a man having his arm chopped off with cleaver. In series two we are also introduced to Rafe (portrayed by Daniel Green), the brother of Sully's cousin, who he kidnapped to make some money. Rafe is the embodiment of the pure violence of the 'bad nigger' that haunts the psyche of whiteness.[24] Dushane warns Sully not to cross him, asking, 'Have you heard those stories about Rafe and the brother he tortured in Finsbury Park? When they found him his eyes were cut out.' We later see Rafe shoot Sully's friend in the head at point blank range, in the middle of the street.

The connection between violence and the estate is clear, but goes even further. Being violent to those 'on road', who are engaged in crime is seen as acceptable. Violence comes with the territory, where you have to accept it happening to you and be willing to dole it out. When Sully accidentally kills Kamale's cousin (Kamale is portrayed by Tayo Jarrett), who has stolen their drugs, Sully shrugs it off with, 'We knew this was gonna happen sooner or later.' Dushane responds: 'I would have preferred to be someone who fucking deserved it', because Kamale's cousin was not on road. However, while this may be Dushane's code it is certainly not the case in *Top Boy*.

There are very few people in the show who are not to some extent on road, engaging in illegal activity. This demonstrates the level to which criminal activity is naturalised in the narrative and becomes synonymous with life on the estate. Most of the characters whose hands are completely clean are white and work in statutory services like the police or the hospital. The only black male characters who are not (or no longer) caught up on road are: Lee, Lisa's friend who helps Ra'Nell when she is in hospital; Kamale's cousin and; Dushane's brother. These three have something in common, however, in that they are all victims of violence. Kamale's cousin and Lee are both killed by Sully; while Dushane's brother is burned in the chest with an iron in retaliation for Dushane losing the drug boss's money. The message for black men here is that they are never free from the violence of the ghetto no matter what their current status. Anderson talks of the 'nigger moment' as something that always lurks as a possibility for black people who achieved status in white society.[25] The nigger moment is that 'acute moment of disrespect' where a black person realises that they can never fully be part of the white space, because someone has insulted them in a way that it makes that clear racism is alive and well. In *Top Boy* the nigger moment is not at the hands of whites – it is the violence from the ghetto catching up on them and reminding them they can never escape the iconic ghetto.

Violence is also strongly connected to agency in the narrative. The show essentially chronicles Dushane's rise towards the top of the drug food chain. To climb the career progression ladder he has to engage in ever-increasing levels of violence. In series one, to work with the big boss he and Sully have to chop off a man's finger. After Kamale steals their drugs again he kidnaps his cousin and Sully accidentally kills him. They manage to get the drugs back by storming into Kamale's girl's house, attacking one of his boys with a machete and kidnapping Kamale. To get him to talk they bury Kamale alive until he gives up the information. Dushane's own personal violence continues to escalate, he has his lieutenant Dris (portrayed by Shone Romulus) shoot Kamale while he walks away. When they go to retrieve the drugs they find out that Lee Green (Cyrus Desir) has been betraying them. To seal his place as top boy on the estate Dushane has to commit his own solo premeditated murder. He shoots the unarmed Bobby Raikes, a white drugs enforcer, and frames him for the murders that Sully committed. Dushane's eventual undoing comes about when he encounters the Albanians who take the violence to another level, being prepared to murder anyone in their way, including the 12-year-old Michael. In *Top Boy* violence is ubiquitous and is synonymous with power.

Lack of female agency

The power of violence in the narrative underscores that men have a dominant role on the estate. Violence is used against women in the show to demonstrate this power. Very early in the first episode, Chantelle is hit in the face when the drug stash is stolen from Dushane's crew. Later in the series Dris punches a white teacher in the face when she tries to prevent him forcing Gem off the school grounds. It is made clear that when women interfere in the affairs of men they will be controlled through violence. The threat of violence clearly hangs over the women in the show, who are careful not to cross the men. When Ra'Nell is viciously beaten by Vincent, the Vietnamese drug runner, his mother Lisa goes to confront the perpetrator. However, she reconsiders when she sees him in his shop shouting at and pushing around one of his workers. Instead, she goes to Dushane and asks him to 'have a word' with Vincent. In the scene where Dushane and Dris are confronting Vincent, the father of Gem – who Ra'Nell was trying to protect – turns up with a knife and stabs Vincent in the leg. In the discourse of *Top Boy* the women demur, while the men solve problems with violence.

There are relatively few female characters across either series of the *Top Boy*. In series one this is particularly marked, especially in relation to black women. The series features prominent or semi-prominent roles for Lisa, Chantelle, a teenage drug dealer and Heather (portrayed by Kierston Wareing), who is white. Heather is the only one who displays any agency, deciding to grow a cannabis so that she can escape the estate. However, she is dependent on Vincent to get the equipment and to sell the cannabis. Being heavily pregnant, and therefore burdened by motherhood, she asks for Ra'Nell's help, who ends up taking care of the crop and also getting a better price for her drugs from Dushane. At the end of the series her agency has entirely disappeared as she sits out the culmination of her storyline in hospital.

Lisa, Ra'Nell's mother is the most present throughout the show. However, her character is a case study of removing agency from black women. Lisa suffers from mental health problems and we are introduced to her struggling to get out of bed when Ra'Nell tries to wake her up in the morning. In the next scene featuring her, Lisa has an episode where she becomes paranoid and collapses. She is then sectioned in a mental hospital and lies about having a son so that they do not take him into care. She is presented as entirely helpless throughout most of the first series and does not actually speak until after the first commercial break in the second episode. This is the overwhelmed black woman, unable to cope with raising a son without the father around. Her first substantive conversation in the show involves her asking whether Ra'Nell's father asks about her, and what he is up to. Throughout the show Lisa relies on men to take care of important aspects of her life. Lee, who is a former road man turned physiotherapist looks after Ra'Nell while she is in hospital and also helps her back to health through his training regime. When she comes out of hospital Ra'Nell assumes the role of the man in the house, at one point telling his mother: 'watch TV. I'll be back in a bit.' In the second series Ra'Nell is explicit about how much power he sees his mother having on the estate. He tells her, 'You don't know nothing about the road' and when she says she will sort the problem he shouts, 'You're just a woman, how you gonna do that?'

As the show progresses Lisa gains more of a voice in the finale of the first series telling Dushane to leave her son alone. In the second series, her mental health issues appear to be under control and she is working as a hairdresser. She is much more vocal, particularly in challenging the gentrification of the estate. However, her most vocal moments are within the comfort of the hairdressing salon. It is here in this female dominated *liminal* space that she really has voice. When she steps outside it to confront Vincent about him beating her son, she shrinks noticeably and has to turn to Dushane. The salon also closes in the show, taking away an avenue for her agency.

Chantelle is, on the face of it, a strong female character who is involved in dealing. She befriends Gem, shows him how to carry drugs and evade police detection, and comforts him after his dog is hung by Dris. However, she only ever appears in scenes with boys or men and her actions are therefore framed by, or in relation to, the male characters. While she is friends with Gem, she is helpless in protecting him when Sully incorrectly identifies him as a snitch, and actually leads Dris and the others to the spot where they kill his dog. Chantelle's street smarts are also used to diminish her femininity. She dresses very much like one of the boys and at the same time is used to represent the hyper-sexualisation of teenage girls on the estate. At one point she is teasing a boy because as she says, 'man's be telling me you're a virgin, what's up with that?' His response is that he is saving himself but gets his 'thing sucked blatant', as well as the occasional 'smelly finger'. She then goes on to laugh at him for being a 'bocat', a man who gives oral sex to women. In the patriarchal world of *Top Boy* clear lines are being drawn between men and women, or rather boys and girls, in relation to sex.

The hyper-sexualisation of black women is used to underpin the controlling image of the 'Jezebel' to represent black womanhood in the media.[26] Chantelle is not generally represented as hyper-sexual but this scene underscores the importance of the idea as a means to diminish black female agency. When women's power becomes defined by sex, this assigns agency to the men they are sleeping with.

There a very few female characters in the show but a number turn up solely in the context of sex. For example, in series one we are introduced to the mother of Sully's daughter when he visits to take a present for his child. She manages to utter two sentences before putting a movie on for her daughter to watch while she takes Sully into her bedroom, and we never hear from her again. There is also the prostitute in series two who gives Dushane and Sully access to the Albanian's warehouse. However, she never speaks and her only other active role in the show is to give Sully oral sex. Such examples are littered across the show but the most glaring would be the relationship between Dushane and Rhianna.

In series two Dushane is picked up and questioned by the police for the murder of Kamale. His solicitor is Rhianna (portrayed by Lorraine Burroughs), a black woman who he is initially a little sceptical of until she shows she is tough in the interview room. She is presented as a woman with power and agency, dealing firmly with the police, with her tagline being 'now move on'. However, when we see this successful black woman for a second time she has agreed to go for a drink with the drug-dealing, criminal Dushane. The third time we see her, she is now completely sexualised, the embodiment of the Jezebel, drinking with Dushane in a club in a scene that inevitably leads to a lingering sex scene between the two of them (figure 5.6). At this point she has spoken a few lines of dialogue, which is all it took for her to sleep with her criminal client.

It also transpires that not only is she unable to control herself sexually but she is also planning to convince Dushane to let her launder his drug money into property developments. She is drawn into further criminal activity when she helps Dushane intimidate a witness to his kidnapping of Kamale, by passing messages to Kayla that Dushane has taken her son. Ultimately, she decides that Dushane is too much for her to handle, but only after being tempted and committing a serious criminal offence. Apparently, even when black people are successful they are still attracted by the lure of the iconic ghetto.

White agency

The power of the iconic ghetto is that it does more than simply represent a set of stereotypes of black people for mainstream society. Black people actually become defined by the icon, its codes and rules in a way that binds their beings and fates to the ghetto. There can be no black agency because the ghetto dictates the lives of the black characters.

Black people do not just live in the ghetto, they *are* ghetto, defined by conditions of poverty, violence and deviance. The iconic ghetto is a discursive tool of whiteness and is therefore defined by white agency. White agency is the ability to produce and disseminate the icon in the first instance, but also in the way the narratives from the ghetto are told. Even though the iconic ghetto is inhabited overwhelmingly by black people, their agency is removed and white agency is embedded in how the stories are told.

One of the ways we can see white agency play out in the show is in the characters' freedom to leave the estate. *Top Boy* makes it clear that leaving is a desirable outcome, to escape the conditions of poverty and violence, and the only characters who are able to do so are white. Heather, the pregnant woman with the cannabis farm, raises the money to buy a flat outside the estate. When the fish and chip shop that Gem's father runs is closed following gentrification of the area, they decide to move almost immediately. While Gem is conflicted at first, after he gets into trouble with Vincent, he is just as eager to flee. This is in direct contrast to Lisa and Ra'Nell who, faced with the same dilemma in relation to the hairdressing salon and after Ra'Nell's beating from Vincent, never discussed whether they should leave the estate. The black characters who live on the estate belong to it in a way the white characters do not, though is a distinction regarding those who are out of the ghetto.

Dushane's brother lives in a nice flat off the estate and after being attacked as a result of his brother's actions, bans Dushane from ever 'setting foot' in his house again. After Dushane kidnaps Kayla's daughter, Rhianna is appalled and refuses to work him on the money laundering scheme. She tells him 'you and me, we're not the same' as she walks away from him. A clear barrier is erected between the black people in the ghetto and the very few that we see outside it. Once assigned to the ghetto you become part of it and are unable to traverse its boundaries. These boundaries are also maintained by the black characters who have managed to escape, and have to distance themselves from the ghetto to prove their status in mainstream society.

Though the majority of the characters in *Top Boy* are black and the show charts Dushane's rise through the ranks of the drug world, there is always a white man above him. The story of the first series is Dushane ascent to become 'Top Boy' of Summerhouse. However, at the end of the series he still answers to, and receives his drugs, from the white big boss Joe. Throughout his rise, Dushane relies on white characters for his drugs and expansion, to escalate his levels of violence, and to provide the guns to take his organisation to the next level.

In the second series, Dushane's relationship with Joe is represented as a partnership, with the two of them going in together for a major drug deal. However, it is clear who is the junior partner in the relationship. In the second scene of series two, Joe takes Dushane out to a dock where they are awaiting news of a major drug shipment. Joe is the one in control, receiving and relaying the information, and at one point telling Dushane to wait in the car while he goes and talks to another white man about the drugs, saying, 'You stay here, it's illegal for a black man to be within five miles of a marina.' This joke works to locate boundaries around Dushane and his role in the drug world, specifically confining him to the estate. In terms of agency, it is also Joe who decides to go to the eventual exchange by himself after Dushane gets embroiled with the police for the murder of Kamale. Joe is killed during that pick-up, at which point Dushane is now the one in charge, leading the effort to get the money and drugs back from the Albanian gangsters who stole it. Even here, though, his agency is severely limited.

Dushane and his crew hatch a plan to retrieve the drugs from the Albanians that ultimately proves successful. However, after initial scenes of celebration the show ends with the Albanians tracking down Dushane and waiting in his apartment after they have killed one of his crew. As Dushane is walking across the estate, Michael, who has been hiding in Dushane's apartment runs out on the balcony to warn his mentor. The Albanians throw Michael over the balcony and begin shooting at Dushane, the show concluding with him hiding under a bridge and having no idea what to do next. This ending is the ultimate reinforcement of white agency in the narrative. Throughout the series we very rarely see the faces of any of the Albanians. They appear sparingly in the show: killing Joe, when they are robbed by Dushane's crew, and in the climactic scenes. This lack of individualisation of the Albanians presents them as the ultimate, almost omnipotent force of the drug world. After being robbed they very quickly find out who did it, where he lived and then institute their judgement with an extremely violent decisiveness. The pretence of Dushane ever becoming Top Boy in this world is shattered in the conclusion to the show, when the ultimate forces of Whiteness are brought to bear on him and his associates.

Absence of the police

In series one of *Top Boy* the police are noticeably absent – being barely present in the narrative. We are made aware that they are constantly in the background and can interrupt life, for example when they prevent drug sales while they are canvassing for information on the murder of Kamale's cousin. However, the police are not a central feature in the story or action. Black communities consistently complain about police harassment and though all of the negative signifiers of the ghetto are littered across *Top Boy* there is not a single stop and search. The *Guardian* newspaper ran a community panel of residents in a similar estate to the one which *Top Boy* is set and the unanimous verdict for the first series was it was unrealistic in that the police were not a constant feature. One of the participants in the panel remarked:

> 'Where's the feds, man? You think you can stand around on the street like that and no police come? Tsssk,' he said, sucking his teeth in disgust. 'Every day you get stopped and searched by feds. You can't even stand on a street corner round this estate. I'm out? I don't stop, I don't stop.'

Writer Ronan Bennett has spoken about his intention to represent life on the estate and the amount of work he did in researching the sub-culture of drug dealing. He interviewed a number of people involved in dealing in order to 'familiarise' himself 'with that world and get to know its nuances'.[27] Effort was made to get the language right and parts of the script; the stories of violence and even the name of one of the gangs 'London Fields' are all taken directly from real life. He explained that one of the aims of the show was 'to enter that world from the ground up, from the point of view those involved in it. We wanted to give the viewer a visceral appreciation of what that world is like.'[28] The absence of the police from the first series of *Top Boy* seriously damages the credibility of the show's aims to represent life on the estate.

From the very beginning of series two the background role for the police is reversed. Two of the first characters we see are detectives driving up to the site where they have discovered Kamale's body. Evading the police by stopping the investigation into the murder of Kamale is a large part of the narrative in series two. The police are represented as being among the few people who can bring down Dushane's crew, and he worries throughout about getting caught. The police represent a significant source of agency in the show and it cannot be a coincidence that they are all white in *Top Boy*.

One of the mechanisms for demonstrating the power of the police is how they interrupt daily life. Both Dushane and Dris are picked up without warning by a number of armed police officers bursting on to an otherwise ordinary scenes to arrest them for killing Kamale. Dris is picked up after one of the few occasions we see him not engaged in criminal activity. He has just got his daughter ready for school, dropped her off and is talking to a fellow parent when the police ambush him. Dushane is picked up after sending Michael on an errand; his arrest takes place as he is walking down the street and he is confronted and taken by surprise by a combination of undercover officers and armed units. The arbitrary nature and locations of these arrests underscore the power of the police to invade the protective environment of the estate. The police must have been aware of their movements, followed them undetected and struck with complete authority. There is no chase, no inkling that they can evade capture.

In series two Dushane, Sully and Dris all have to go with the police and we see Dushane being processed, his fingerprints taken and his personal belongings taken from him. This again reinforces the power of the police. Large amounts of the action in the second series take place in the police interview room as Dushane, Michael and Kayla all face questioning at various times. The crucible of the interview room is enough to break down Michael and Kayla. Michael gives the police information about the killing of Kamale and names Dushane, Sully and Dris as the perpetrators of Kamale's kidnap, while Kayla is ready to give up Dushane after pressure from the police. Dushane, however, is never fazed during his interview and actually controls Kayla from outside the interview room by kidnapping her son and having Rhianna relay the information to her. Though the police are displayed as powerful with the likely prospect being Dushane's downfall, he ultimately overcomes their reach through his power base of the estate. The police may control the interview room but his roots on the estate means his reach extends beyond theirs. Dushane and the rest of the drug world is presented as being above the law and there are never any repercussions from the police.

The police are represented as white agents, with significant powers, but ultimately unable to prevent the criminality on the estate. Discursively, this is important to the construction of the iconic ghetto. When the police do feature in the second series they are portrayed in a largely positive light, justly seeking to solve the murder of Kamale. By displaying high levels of violent crime and drugs, *Top Boy* presents a pro-police image of life on the estate, and that they are necessary to combat the evils of the ghetto. The iconic ghetto stands as a testament to all that is wrong with the black community and the futility of the police's efforts reinforces the depth of deviance and depravity that permeates the estate. Even when the police *are* centrally involved in the second series they are very rarely actually *on* the estate. They swoop in to make arrests but are mostly featured at the station, in the interview room. The estate is left as a space relatively untouched by the police, a separate ecosystem with its own life and codes. To show how entrenched the police, and police harassment, are within the estate would ruin the picture of the iconic ghetto. To do so would raise questions of culpability of the police and other institutions in maintaining the conditions of deprivation on the estate.

In fact, there is no social commentary on the role of public institutions at all in the show. The local school features occasionally as a location, mostly where we see children skipping class or being accosted by drug dealers. The most memorable school-related scene is when Dris punches a female teacher in the face because she tries to prevent him taking Gem off the premises. However, schooling has been subject to high levels of criticism in Britain, in the same way as the police. The absence of any critique of public institutions is important because it works to present the problems of the estate as those produced by its inhabitants. Children on the estate appear to act and move around with no parental control or responsibility; Ra'Nell spends most of the first series looking after himself and then his mother. If black people generally have little agency, they are constructed as agents in their own downfall on the estate. The police, schools, hospitals are doing what they can but are unable to impact on the pervasiveness of the iconic ghetto.[29]

Conclusion

By analysing *Top Boy* it is clear that the show represents all of the hallmarks of the iconic ghetto on British television. The relentless image of crime and poverty on the estate discursively bind the black community to the ghetto. Those few black people who have 'escaped', still find themselves caught up by the workings of the estate and struggle to erect solid boundaries to keep themselves from being caught up by the 'road'. The show is important because it is one of the few black majority cast shows in the history of British television. As such, it offers a glimpse into the prevailing discourses around black communities. The show was written, directed and produced by white people, for a mainstream, largely white audience. It stands as testament not only to the discourses that the people who made it were drawing on, but also those they thought would resonate with the mainstream public.

Top Boy is also important because of the role of the media in shaping how black communities are understood. Britain is only diverse in the major cities, and even in these cities there are high levels of ethnic concentration. As a result, the majority of the British public have very little interaction with black people and therefore the media must play a key role in how black people are understood. *Top Boy* adds to the image of the iconic ghetto, through the show itself and the advertising around it. The analysis has demonstrated the levels to which the show reproduces the idea of black communities being defined by poverty, crime and violence. The impression the show leaves is of communities living outside the law and governed by the violent drug world. As we saw with the tragedy of Trayvon Martin in the USA, when Blackness symbolises the 'ghetto', the consequences can be deadly. British television needs to do much more to expand the narratives of Blackness available on screen.

Figure 5.1 *Top Boy's* Summerhouse estate as 'iconic ghetto' (Channel 4, tx. 24/10/11)

Figure 5.2 Life on the Summerhouse estate, its story, and the *Top Boy* characters who inhabit it (Channel 4, tx. 24/10/11)

Figure 5.3 Ra'Nell (Malcolm Kamulete), and the Summerhouse estate in *Top Boy* (Channel 4, tx. 24/10/11)

Figure 5.4 Ra'Nell talks to Lee (Cyrus Desir), with the estate framing the scene in the background in *Top Boy* (Channel 4, tx. 24/10/11)

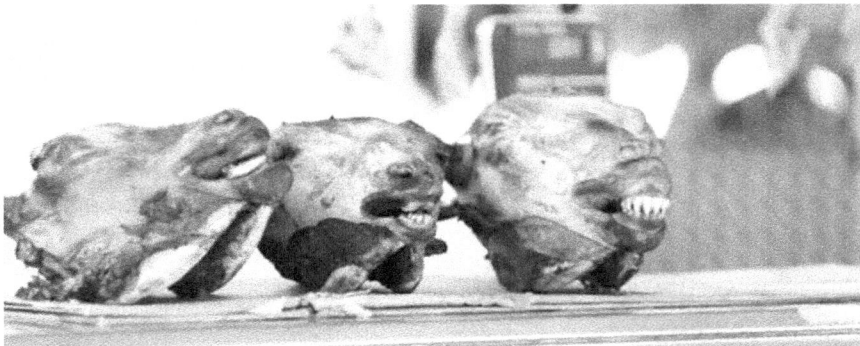

Figure 5.5 *Top Boy*'s marketplace as cultural signifier, with its 'ethnic' sounds, foods and stalls (Channel 4, tx. 24/10/11)

Figure 5.6 Rhianna (Lorraine Burroughs), as a successful Black female solicitor later seduced by her criminal client in *Top Boy* (Channel 4, tx. 20/8/13)

Notes

1 Hughes, S., 'TV review: *Top Boy*, Channel 4 – Britain's Answer to The Wire is So Much More than Guns and Gangs', *Independent*, 21 August 2013.
2 Newton, Darrell, *Paving the Empire Road: BBC Television and Black Britons* (Manchester: Manchester University Press, 2011).
3 Gripsrud, J. (ed.), *Television and Common Knowledge* (London: Routledge, 1999), p. 2.
4 Anderson, E., 'The Iconic Ghetto', *The ANNALS of the American Academy of Political and Social Science*, 642:1 (2012), p. 8.
5 Massey, S., and Denton, N. A., *American Apartheid: Segregation and the Making of the Underclass* (Cambridge, MA: Harvard University Press, 1993).
6 Harrison, A. (ed.), *Black Exodus: The Great Migration from the American South* (Jackson, MS: University Press of Mississippi, 1992).
7 Orfield, G., *Reviving the goal of an Integrated Society: A 21st Century Challenge* (Los Angeles, CA: The Civil Rights Project/Proyecto Derechos Civiles at UCLA, 2009), p. 7.
8 Anderson, 'The Iconic Ghetto', p. 8.
9 X, M., 'Message to the Grassroots', Speech at the Northern Negro Grassroots Leadership Conference, Detroit, 1963.

10 Seale, B., *Seize the Time: The Story of the Black Panther Party* (New York: Random House, 1970), p. 8.

11 Andrews, K., 'From the "Bad Nigger" to the "Good Nigga": An Unintended Legacy of Black Radicalism', *Race & Class*, 55:3 (2014), p. 24.

12 Kubrin, C., 'Gangstas, Thugs, and Hustlas: Identity and the Code of the Street in Rap Music', *Social Problems*, 52 (2005), p. 365.

13 LaGrone, K. L., 'From Minstrelsy to Gangsta Rap: the "Nigger" as a Commodity for Popular American Entertainment', *Journal of African American Studies*, 5:2 (2000), p. 120.

14 Phillips, D., 'Ethnic and Racial Segregation: A Critical Perspective', *Geography Compass*, 1:5 (2007), pp. 1138–59.

15 Sunak, R., and Rajeswaran, S., *A Portrait of Modern Britain* (London: The Policy Exchange, 2014), pp. 6–7.

16 Phillips, D., and Harrison, M., 'Constructing an Integrated Society: Historical Lessons for Tackling Black and Minority Ethnic Housing Segregation in Britain', *Housing Studies*, 25:2 (2010), p. 228.

17 Rex. J., and Moore, R., *Race, Community and Conflict: A Study of Sparkbrook* (Oxford University Press, 1971), p. 31.

18 Kalra, V. S., and Kapoor, N., 'Interrogating Segregation, Integration and the Community Cohesion Agenda', *Journal of Ethnic and Migration Studies*, 35:9 (2009), p. 408.

19 Phillips and Harrison, 'Constructing an Integrated Society', p. 226.

20 Andrews, K., 'Black is a Country: Building Solidarity across Borders', *World Policy Journal*, 33:1 (2016), pp. 15–19.

21 Centre for Contemporary Cultural Studies. *Policing the Crisis: Mugging, the State and Law and Order* (London: Macmillan, 1978), p. 96.

22 Anderson, 'The Iconic Ghetto', p. 9.

23 Yuen, Nancy Wang, 'Playing "Ghetto": Black Actors, Stereotypes, and Authenticity', in Darnell Hunt and Ana-Christina Ramon, eds, *Black Los Angeles: American Dreams and Racial Realities* (New York: New York University Press, 2010), p. 232.

24 Andrews, 'From the "Bad Nigger" to the "Good Nigga"', p. 22.

25 Anderson, Elijah, *The Cosmopolitan Canopy: Race and Civility in Everyday Life* (New York: W. W. Norton & Company, 2012), p. 249.

26 Hill Collins, P., *Black Feminist Thought: Knowledge, Consciousness, and the Politics of Empowerment* (London: Routledge, 2000), p. 81.

27 Interview with *Top Boy* writer, Ronan Bennett, Channel 4, www.channel4.com/programmes/top-boy/videos/all/writer-ronan-bennett/3403220113001 (accessed 30 March 2017).

28 Interview with *Top Boy* writer, Ronan Bennett, Front Row, BBC Radio 4, 24 April 2012.

29 Graham, M., and Robinson, G., '"The Silent Catastrophe": Institutional Racism in the British Educational System and the Underachievement of Black Boys', *Journal of Black Studies*, 34:5 (2004), pp. 653–71.

6

Imperial fictions: *Doctor Who,* post-racial slavery and other liberal humanist fantasies

Susana Loza

> Science fiction often talks about race by not talking about race, makes real aliens, has hidden race dialogues. Even though it is a literature that talks a lot about underclasses or oppressed classes, it does so from a privileged if somewhat generic white space. (Isiah Lavender III, *Race in American Science Fiction*)[1]

In *Framing Monsters: Fantasy Film and Social Alienation,* Joshua Bellin claims that fantasy texts 'frame social reality: They provoke a perspective, provide a context, [and] produce a way of seeing.' Mass-produced fantasies 'give image to historically determinate anxieties, wishes, and needs, they simultaneously function by stimulating, endorsing, broadcasting the very anxieties, wishes, and needs to which they give image'.[2] Speculative fantasies, like all science fiction imaginings, are socially embedded and reflective of their time.[3] Although they attempt to show us future worlds and alternative realities, fantasy texts have much more to say about our contemporary moment.[4]

In the fragmented media landscape of today, television remains a pivotal site where such imaginings occur, 'where the nation is imagined and imagines itself'.[5] As the countless Twitter hashtags dedicated to popular television shows testify, television still 'saturates our leisure time, our conversations, and perceptions of each other and of self'.[6] The ardent discussions on social media attest to television's role in the 'articulation, construction, and contestation of racialized identities'.[7] In the introduction to *The Persistence of Whiteness: Race and Contemporary Hollywood Cinema,* Daniel Bernardi observes: 'We learn about other people, other cultures, ourselves by watching Hollywood films over and over again – all too often without questioning what we see.'[8] Television clearly serves the same pedagogical function. We do not escape the clutches of ideology when we watch television uncritically but, in fact, fall deeper into its embrace. This is especially true of science fiction and fantasy television shows, which are often dismissed or lauded as 'pure, innocent diversions',[9] but like all mass-produced texts invite and incite 'the discourses, beliefs, and practices of racism characteristic of that culture'.[10]

The hugely popular BBC television programme *Doctor Who* (BBC1 1963–89; 2005–) has been fabricating and exporting British racial fears and fantasies across the globe for more than half a century. *Doctor Who* is the 'longest running science fiction television series in the world, is watched in over fifty countries and routinely garners millions of viewers for each episode'.[11] Launched in 1963 amid the turmoil of decolonial struggles in Africa, South Asia and the Caribbean, *Doctor Who* is a product of the dying days of empire.[12] As Lindy Orthia elaborates in the introduction to *Doctor Who & Race*, the serial

> emerged from and continues to dwell in the post-empire period British history, a potent time when formerly colonized people were migrating to Britain in larger numbers than ever before as well as reclaiming their cultural heritage and political independence elsewhere in the world, transforming conceptions of Britishness, the meaning of 'race' on the global stage, and the ways in which the western media understand and deal with racism.[13]

From its inception, *Doctor Who* has envisioned itself as an anti-imperialist, post-colonial, and multicultural antidote to entrenched British ethnocentrism. Whovian scholars, like Charles (2007), Clark (2013), Fly (2013), and Orthia (2013), suggest the serial's ontological and ideological perspective is more accurately described as liberal humanist and colourblind Universalist. This perspective is embodied by the show's protagonist, 'the Doctor', a sardonic white male alien who could easily be mistaken for a traditional Western hero.

Doctor Who centres on the galactic misadventures of the Doctor, a Time Lord who journeys through space and time in a ship called the TARDIS. One or more Earthlings typically accompany him on these jaunts. The Doctor looks suspiciously like a human but he has two hearts and his body is able to regenerate if fatally injured. This plot device has allowed the show to continue for over half a century with different actors playing the lead role, (thus far) all of them have been heterosexual white men.[14] Although the Doctor is ostensibly an alien, he behaves like a quintessentially British dandy; he adores tea, the European aristocracy and fashion. His costumes – Edwardian frock-coats, Victorian vests, smoking jackets, cricket whites and Bohemian garb – visually 'recall the period of the height of British imperial power'. In terms of political disposition, the Doctor epitomises colonial liberalism. He is an objective, emotionally detached, saviour-explorer who thirsts for knowledge and technical mastery.[15] The Doctor eagerly embraces the 'imperialist Enlightenment ideal of objectivity'.[16] As one Whovian expert wryly comments, the Doctor 'possesses near-omniscience and near-omnipotence that scientists and imperialists can only aspire to, but like them his tools are Western science and Western morality'.[17] Another fan-scholar suggests that the Doctor epitomises 'triumphant western humanism, with all its arrogance, self-proclaimed superiority and blindness'. One might say that the Doctor possesses what science fiction scholar John Rieder calls the colonial gaze, a gaze that 'distributes knowledge and power to the subject who looks, while denying or minimizing access to power for its object, the one looked at'.[18]

The liberal humanist whiteness of *Doctor Who* is most clearly laid bare in episodes that thematise the sins of European imperialism: slavery, genocide and dispossession. In such episodes it becomes evident that the show is framed and filtered through the Doctor's cosmopolitan, colonial and colourblind gaze and thus tells stories 'from an uncontested White British viewpoint',[19] not from the perspective of the subjugated and enslaved. In the tenth version of *Doctor Who*, the most sustained engagement with slavery occurs in the three episodes – 'The Impossible Planet' (2006), 'Satan Pit' (2006) and 'Planet of the Ood' (2008), which feature the Ood: an alien species described as born to serve.

Utilising an interdisciplinary amalgam of critical ethnic studies, media studies, cultural studies and post-colonial theory, this chapter considers how the 2005 reboot of *Doctor Who* utilises deracialised and decontextualised slavery allegories to absolve white guilt over the transatlantic slave trade; express and contain xenophobic anxieties about post-colonial British multiculture; reinforce black racial stereotypes, and bolster white privilege by demanding that viewers adopt the series' colourblind liberal humanist standpoint. In *The Racial Contract*, Charles Mills asserts that 'white misunderstanding, misrepresentation, evasion, and self-deception on matters related to race are among the most pervasive mental phenomena of the past few hundred years, a cognitive and moral economy psychically required for conquest, colonization, and enslavement'.[20] By closely examining the imperial fictions and post-racial slavery parables of *Doctor Who*, I hope to illuminate the programme's 'structural opacities', how its colourblind universalism sustains and nourishes the boundaries of contemporary whiteness and colonial consciousness, and the fraught place of race in multicultural and, ostensibly, post-colonial Britain.

Savage and servile: rabid rebels, natural slaves, and taming the Ood

Although 'The Impossible Planet' and 'Satan Pit' allude to the existence of natural slave races 'born to serve', this popular colonial theory – which justified the subjugation and enslavement of Africans and indigenous New World peoples – is the central theme of 'Planet of the Ood', the third episode in which the tentacle-faced pale grey aliens appear. In this episode, the historical horrors of British imperialism are transposed onto Cthulhu-like cephalopods and projected into the year 4,126, the era known as the Second Great and Bountiful Human Empire. 'The Planet of the Ood' opens with a brief commercial that establishes the servile nature of the aliens. As glimmering galaxies glide by, we hear the following dialogue:

> NARRATOR: The Ood. They came from distant world. They voyaged across the stars, all with one purpose.
> OOD: Do you take milk and sugar?
> NARRATOR: To serve.

In the advertisement's closing shot, the camera zooms in on a cheerful Ood expectantly holding a teapot aloft. Tea and sugar are products suffused with colonial import. These freighted commodities symbolise the apex of British mercantilism. Tea invokes The East India Company and its role in growing and maintaining the British Empire in the Indian subcontinent. Sugar recalls the Caribbean plantations in which Caribbean Indians and then Africans toiled and died to sweeten the coffers of British slaveholders. This short scene suggests that the Ood are surrogates for the South Asians, Caribbean Indians and Africans colonised by the British. In the future, space ships may have replaced slave ships but European imperialism churns on. The parallels between Ood oppression and African enslavement intensify as the episode unfolds (figure 6.4).

Like the Africans enslaved by the British, the captured Ood are treated like mere livestock. They are chained, whipped, bred, branded, imported and exported. Like the Africans whose bodies were broken through a brutal process called 'seasoning', the Ood are maimed and rendered mute through 'processing'. Much like the Africans forced into chattel slavery, the Ood are dehumanised and animalised, and a process Aimé Césaire (1972) called 'thingification'. Thingification is fundamental to the workings of colonialism. It is how colonialism creates unequal classes, how it cements racial hierarchy, how it decides which beings can be sacrificed and subjugated.[21] The edifice of colonialism is erected on relations of domination and submission. It requires thingification. It thrives on zombification. The lobotomised Ood 'represents the ultimate imperialist dream – a slave labourer that is truly a thing, unthinking, un-aspiring, and non-threatening'.[22] And just as the bloody slave revolts throughout the Americas exposed the docile labourer as a self-serving fiction of exploitative Europeans, the rebellion of the Ood suggests that slaves are not 'born to serve' but ideologically manufactured for imperial purposes. Let us consider a few examples of how slavery and conquest are discursively produced in 'Planet of the Ood'.

In 'The Ood as Slave Race: Colonial Continuity in the Second Great and Bountiful Human Empire', Eric Foss emphasises how *Doctor Who* echoes previous justifications for imperial conquest. 'Just as the public records of early European explorers and conquerors emphasized the importance of "civilizing mission" and described native populations as natural-born slaves',[23] Klineman Halpen (portrayed by Tim McInnerny), the industrious CEO of Ood Operations, plays up the naturalness of having Ood servants and claims that they 'rescued' the Ood from a life of savagery (figure 6.1). For example, he angrily avers that 'The Ood were nothing without us, just animals roaming around on the ice!' Halpen's mapping of species characteristics onto biological differences, the conversion of savagery and civilisation into permanent and fixed conditions, clearly echoes how Westerners used science to cement a racial hierarchy. In this white supremacist worldview, rationality is reserved for the West and the 'dangerous irrational non-Western and the colonial savages and heathens could therefore be excluded. They were primitives, children of a lesser god, requiring management and control, and in some cases, outright extinction.'[24]

The same imperial logic animates Halpen's racist dismissal of the Ood as lowly beasts. His insistence that the Ood are a natural labouring class, suited only for performing the dirty work of civilisation, expresses 'a nostalgia for lost authority and for a pliable, completely subordinate proletariat that is one of the central fantasies of imperialism'.[25] Halpen clearly sees the Ood as primitive beings, as chattel to be corralled, savages to be domesticated. As Francis Jennings notes in *The Invasion of America: Indians, Colonialism, and the Can of Conquest*, the British devised the term 'savage' to indelibly mark the inferiority of non-Westerners: 'The savage was prey, cattle, pet, or vermin – he was never citizen.'[26] This inherent inferiority meant that there could be no justification for resistance to European invasion. By labelling the Ood as 'animals roaming the ice', Halpen not only justifies the enslavement of the Ood but the conquest of their planet as well.

Halpen's virulent racism toward to the Ood can be contrasted with the benevolent, yet equally lethal, racism of his chief marketing officer, Solana Mercurio (portrayed by Ayesha Dharker) (figure 6.2). During her sales pitch to the young, male and multiracial gathering of would-be slave-owners, Mercurio repeatedly emphasises how well the Ood are treated: 'We like to think of the Ood as our trusted friends. We keep the Ood healthy, safe, and educated" She insists: 'We don't just breed the Ood. We make them better. Because at heart, what is an Ood, but a reflection of us? If your Ood is happy, then you'll be happy, too.' Ood Operations thus cunningly neutralises the prospective buyer's guilt by suggesting that slavery is truly good for the Ood because they lack the mental capacity to properly care for themselves. As quoted by Davis, the aliens are offered as proof that Aristotle was right when he proclaimed: 'From the hour of their birth, some are marked out for subjection, others for rule.'[27]

Ood Operations' professed desire to make the Ood 'better' through breeding and education replicates the white supremacist logic of scientific racism, the Western discourse that self-servingly carved up the world into enlightened Europeans and dangerous Others that must be remoulded in their image, by force if necessary.[28] The naturalistic and scientific arguments that Halpen and Mercurio 'make about slavery, suggest that far from overcoming the problems of the past, the Second Great and Bountiful Human Empire has simply outsourced them'.[29]

The Doctor (portrayed by David Tennant) and Donna Noble (Catherine Tate) do not see the Ood as dangerous Others that must be reformed but rather as 'harmless', 'completely benign' and 'peaceful' creatures. Towards the end of the episode, Noble angrily confronts Halpen for lobotomising the Ood. She explodes: 'You idiot! They're born with their brains in their hands. Don't you see, that makes them peaceful? They've got to be, because a creature like that would have to trust anyone it meets.' Noble's depiction of the Ood as docile amicable beings invokes the spectre of the 'noble savage'. The term, which can be traced to seventeenth-century French literature, personified 'European discontent with modernity. As European colonialism gained momentum, Africans and indigenous New World peoples were said to possess the noble qualities of harmony with nature, generosity, childlike complicity, happiness under duress, and a natural innate moral compass.'[30] Noble's impassioned defence of the Ood recycles similar stereotypes and is equally patronising and unintentionally derogatory as the imperialist rhetoric deployed by Halpen and Mercurio. The humans are united in their belief that the aliens are savages who need saving. The only difference is that Halpen and Mercurio seek to rescue the Ood from themselves and Noble seeks to rescue them from her fellow humans.

Saviourism is a powerful imperial fiction woven through 'Planet of the Ood', as is the supposed 'unruliness' of the subject race, their inability to be tamed and racially contained.

The imagined savagery of the Other is a durable, if morally dubious, rationale for enslavement and conquest but it is just one of the racial technologies in imperialism's arsenal. Colonisers, past and present, have also embraced the language of madness and monstrosity to justify the persecution and execution of subject populations because of the supposed 'absence of sufficient 'rationality' – in other words, stupidity, foreignness or a dangerous criminal psychology. In *Toward a Political Philosophy of Race*, Falguni Sheth utilises the term, the 'unruly', to illuminate how this kind of difference is racially weaponised. Consequently, rationality – or its absence – becomes a weapon with which to deem a group as insufficiently rational, and hence 'dangerous, unruly, mad, or even evil'.[31] Sheth's analysis differentiates 'racial' markers – skin type, phenotype, physical differences – from signifiers of 'unruly' behaviours. The former, she suggests, 'are not the ground of race, but the marks ascribed to a group that has already become (or is on the way to becoming) outcasted'. The unruly provides the ground for 'classifying, distinguishing, separating, and dividing'. It 'signifies the threatening aspect of the strange; it is threatening because it will not melt away into some comfortable, familiar, configuration but continues to be conspicuous, like a protruding excrescence'.[32] The racialisation of the Octopus-faced Ood by the human citizens of the Second Great and Bountiful Human Empire in *Doctor Who* illustrates how unruliness is politically manufactured and discursively maintained.

In *Law and Imperialism: Criminality and Constitution in Colonial India and Victorian England*, Preeti Nijhar reminds us that the 'social construction of the non-Western as dangerous and primitive was designed to mask and displace Western anxieties'.[33] Fear about the unruliness of the colonised was a manifestation of this anxiety – a concern that was eased by representing them as dangerous savages in need of discipline and enlightenment. The grey-skinned Cthulhu-like Ood are conspicuously marked as physically different from their human captors and their alien-ness is the ground upon which their mental inferiority is inscribed. Unlike the Doctor who can pass as human and, perhaps more importantly, shares that species' possessive individualism and taste for galactic imperialism, the colourless crustacean-faced aliens communicate telepathically, travel in herds and think collectively. For the human capitalists that exploit the Ood, the tentacles and translucent skin serve as convenient biological signposts for the aliens' most subversive behaviour: their intense communalism.

'Planet of the Ood' thematises the coloniser's problematic conflation of 'unruly' behaviour (collectivism) with racialised biological defect (madness). In the first moments of the episode, we learn that several Ood have become infected with red-eye, a contagious disease that transforms the once-faithful servants into rabid rebels. The infected aliens have been gleefully slaughtering their human masters. Instead of seeing this as a slave rebellion, Ood Operations treats it as a disease that can be cured through containment. The cruelty of the human colonisers, the thingification of the Ood and the callousness of capitalism is encapsulated in the following exchange between Commander Kess (portrayed by Roger Griffiths), Ood Operations' head of security (figure 6.5), and Halpen:

KESS: We've contained it, sir. Fenced them in. But the red eye seems to be permanent this time. It's not fading. Worse than that, sir, there's more of them going rabid. In my opinion, sir, I think we've lost them. The entire batch [is] contaminated.

HALPEN: What's causing it? Why now? What's changed? How many Ood in total?

KESS: I'd say about two thousand, sir.

HALPEN: We can write them off. That's what insurance is for. We've plenty more on the breeding farms. Let's start again. Fetch the canisters. No survivors.

KESS: My pleasure, sir. You lot. Canisters.

In *Race in American Science Fiction*, Isiah Lavender III observes that contagion is a common trope in science fiction narratives because it captures the 'xenophobia, territoriality, raw hostility', and racial alienation that frequently accompany colonial relations.[34] Contagion narratives treat race as a dangerous and infectious biological agent and symbolise white fear of being contaminated by the racial Other.[35] These science fiction scenarios typically culminate with the dominant class attempting to 'contain' the threat of racial difference by animalising and annihilating the unruly Other. 'Planet of the Ood' clearly follows this familiar imperial formula. The Ood are chattel; animals to be shipped and sold. They are bred in batches and corralled for their own good. They are unruly things that can be guiltlessly gassed and easily replaced. While most of 'Planet of the Ood' focuses on how the mad aliens are infected by a mutinous desire to rebel against their human rulers, the episode culminates with an exploration of another kind of contagion: the racial contamination of Halpen by Sigma Ood.

Throughout 'Planet of the Ood', the tentacle-faced aliens are represented as meek, effete, and humble servants, a representation of the colonial Other that echoes Orientalist representations of Indians in British literature in the nineteenth century surveyed by Radhika Mohanram in *Imperial White: Race, Diaspora, and the British Empire*.[36] Much like his British ancestors, Halpen's white Western heteromasculinity hinges on the racialisation and feminisation of the colonised. This is why Halpen is particularly devastated by the betrayal of his personal valet, Sigma Ood (portrayed by Paul Kasey), for it proves that the boundaries between master and servant, civilised and savage, masculine and feminine, are not natural divisions but hierarchical social constructions. At the end of the episode, it is revealed that the hair tonic that Sigma Ood has been anxiously pressing upon the balding Halpen for five years is actually a toxic elixir that slowly and inexorably converts humans into Oodkind. For Halpen, the only thing worse than being poisoned by his trusted valet is realising that he has become the sullied Other.

The fact that Halpen's transformation from human Self to alien Other is due to contamination by an elixir composed from liquefied Ood biological material invokes the 'one-drop rule', which asserts that 'one drop' of black blood compromises white racial purity. This racial convention was an integral part of the cultural politics of race in imperialist and xenophobic Britain in which foreign blood was 'viewed as not only a potent pollutant but also a fundamental element in assembling an essentialised racial identity' for both whites and non-whites.[37] The one-drop rule has been debunked but the threat of contamination clearly lingers; its pivotal place in 'Planet of the Ood' speaks to Britain's unresolved anxieties about the transition from a homogenous nation to a heterogeneous multiculture. While the episode ostensibly critiques the brutality and inhumanity of slavery, its suturing of a contagious virus associated with animals gone mad (rabies) to a species that has been subjugated (the Ood) has the unfortunate consequence of bolstering the association of rebellion with insanity and difference with disease. Ultimately, Halpen's horror at becoming Oodkind reinforces white fears that racial others are treacherous, tainted and to be avoided at all costs.

Neo-liberal multiculturalism: The Whoniverse, multiracial white supremacy and the imperial future

Race is a social construct. Fluid and fixed, it morphs and mutates, fades and flames. *Doctor Who* has – and continues to – enthusiastically embrace the values of liberal humanist whiteness but the place of race in the Whoniverse has undeniably shifted since the 1960s. While the original series was resolutely monochromatic, the reboot is awash with colour. The more contemporary versions of the show, according to Lindy Orthia in 2010, represent 'Earth's past as a place of happy and benign diversity. Depression-era New York contains mixed-race shanty towns led by a black man, while black women populate the streets and royal courts of Victorian England and Enlightenment France.'[38] The 1920s, 1940s, 1950s, even slavery-era Elizabethan England, are inhabited by well-to-do people of colour. These multicultural tableaux establish 'human diversity as an unremarkable and timeless fact'. The reinvented *Doctor Who* is a post-racial world in which humans differ in colour but are 'united in all other respects'.

The appropriate metaphor for this brave new realm, opines Whovian scholar-fan Lindy Orthia, 'comes from *Doctor Who*'s most famous food-stuff: humanity is so many colored jelly babies inside a colorless (white) paper bag'.[39] But, as Eduardo Bonilla-Silva and Austin Ashe caution in 'The End of Racism? Colorblind Racism and Popular Media', audiences should not settle for symbolic inclusion within the neo-liberal white supremacist imaginary. It is not sufficient that the reboot incorporates more people of colour 'because the issue that matters most is how [they] are represented and what kind of racial messages are conveyed'.[40] Instead of prematurely celebrating the cosmopolitan and colourblind visions of the latest iteration of *Doctor Who*, we must remember that the symbolic inclusion of diversely hued humans does not 'necessarily challenge the logic and the structure of an unequal racial order'.[41] In fact, the multi-racial cosmopolitanism of the revamped series often bolsters the white supremacist imperialist status quo by obscuring the lingering effects of racism and colonialism on screen and in real life.[42] *Doctor Who*'s sani-tised representations of past, present and future erase the material reali-ties of a post-colonial world profoundly 'shaped by exploitative trade practices, diasporic trauma and racist discrimination'.[43]

Since I have already documented how contemporary *Doctor Who* obscures the racist past of British slavery, I would like to conclude by turning my attention to the pivotal role that people of colour play in operating the forty-second-century's imperial machinery and how the serial's multicultural futurism masks the racial inequities of the neo-liberal present.

Much like the actual British Empire, which strategically incorporated neocolonial subjects to reinforce racial hierarchy, the Second Great and Bountiful Human Empire maintains its brutal dominion by assimilating the formerly subjugated and placing them in positions of power over the enslaved. The Second Great and Bountiful Human Empire repre-sents what happens when white supremacy and colonialism morph and commingle. Its cosmopolitan colonialism is the logical culmination of what contemporary critical race scholars have variously dubbed the new racism (Eduardo Bonilla-Silva), neo-liberal multiculturalism (Jodi

Melamed), multiculturalist white supremacy (Dylan Rodriguez) and multiracial white supremacy (Falguni Sheth). This brand of racism is reproduced through 'practices that are subtle, institutional, and apparently nonracial'.[44] It eschews traditional white supremacy's reliance on phenotype and innovates 'new ways of fixing human capacities to naturalize inequality'. It deploys 'economic, ideological, cultural, and religious distinctions to produce lesser personhoods, laying these new categories of privilege and stigma across conventional racial categories, fracturing them into differential status groups'.[45] This is a system of power that invites in 'people of color in order to wage institutional, legal, political assaults on other black, brown, and poor people'. It realises that having people of colour in positions of authority opens 'new possibilities for history's slaves, savages, and colonized to more fully identify with the same nation-building project that requires the neutralization, domestication, and strategic elimination of declared aliens, enemies, and criminals'. Multiracial white supremacy does not abolish the colour-line; it redefines it. The Second Great and Bountiful Human Empire is the fruition of these neo-liberal and neocolonial logics.

It is a colonial system that maintains a strict hierarchy of species difference in which biology dictates whether one is free or unfree. Like its imperial predecessor, the future British Empire utilises specious science to justify its enslavement and exploitation of an alien race. In the forty-second century, humans of all hues are virulently *speciesist* signalling that racism, the technology of creating and maintaining lesser personhoods, has not been vanquished but simply redirected to Other bodies, while universal speciesism also suggests that racial prejudice is innately human and that whites should thus not be blamed for past or present racism. But, perhaps, the best proof that the Second Great and Bountiful Human Empire is the apex of colourblind colonialism is that the descendants of the formerly enslaved (Zachary Cross Flane played by Shaun Parkes, and Roger Griffiths' Commander Kess) and colonised (Ronny Jhutti as Danny Bartock, and Ayesha Dharker's Solana Mercurio) vehemently defend the conquest of the Ood as natural and necessary, thus shoring up imperial racism while seeming to break with these supposedly defunct racial formations. In the multiracial white supremacist imperialist future envisioned by *Doctor Who*, people of colour have mutated from neocolonial collaborators to wily agents of empire (figure 6.6).

The first indication that the phenotype of British colonialism has changed in the forty-second century is that the first slavery apologist we encounter is not the sneering white capitalist patriarch who profits so handsomely from the galactic slave trade but rather the brown middle-class bureaucrat tasked with managing the aliens. It is Danny Bartock, the ethics officer for Sanctuary Base Six, who nonchalantly informs an incredulous Rose Tyler (portrayed by Billie Piper) that the Ood are born to serve humans and are essentially livestock ('they're basically a herd race. Like cattle'). He vehemently swears, 'The Ood offer themselves. If you don't give them orders, they just wither away and die.' Bartock also implies that British colonisation is the only thing keeping these feeble-minded creatures alive when he contemptuously proclaims: 'They're so stupid, they don't even tell us when they're ill!' English actor Ronny Jhutti, as Bartock, was born to Punjabi parents but raised in London, and has been typecast for most of his acting career as a Muslim and/or racialised immigrant of South Asian descent.[46]

His appearance as Bartock is one of the few occasions when Jhutti plays a character not explicitly marked as Indian, Pakistani or Arab via his name. Jhutti is not the only actor of colour featured in 'The Impossible Planet' and 'Satan Pit'. Flane is the captain of the doomed expedition and a representative of the Torchwood Archive. The Torchwood Archive is the latest incarnation of the Torchwood Institute, an organisation founded in 1879 to protect the British Empire (later Great Britain) from extraterrestrial threat and to secure alien technology and material resources for Britain ('Torchwood Institute'). The reason that Captain Flane and his crew are orbiting the impossible planet is because it contains a power source that would 'revolutionize modern science' and 'fuel the Empire'.

The casting of Jhutti and Parkes in such prominent roles on Nu Who demonstrates the BBC's commitment to colourblind casting – a commitment that the network recently reaffirmed: 'Reflecting the diversity of the UK is a duty of the BBC, and casting on *Doctor Who* is colourblind. It is always about the best actors for the roles.' But, one must ask does casting 'history's slaves, savages, and colonized' as the defenders of British Empire challenge the racial status quo? Or does compelling the subaltern to retroactively defend their own subjugation simply incite white supremacist imperialist amnesia? One cannot help but be struck by the tragic absurdity of having a brown man bemoan the white man's burden (to a sceptical English Rose no less!) and having a black man proudly represent the rapacious interests of British imperialism. In 'Impossible Planet' and 'Satan Pit', we see glimmers of the neocolonial past and glimpses of the neo-liberal multiculturalism yet to come, a multiracial white supremacy more fully realised in the 'Planet of the Ood'.

'Planet of the Ood' presents us with a cosmopolitan vision of a new racial order. A neo-liberal multicultural order in which 'privileged and stigmatized racial formations no longer mesh perfectly with a color line.

Instead, new categories of privilege and stigma determined by ideological, economic, and cultural criteria overlay older, conventional racial categories, so that traditionally recognized racial identities – black, Asian, white, or Arab/Muslim – can now occupy both sides of the privilege/stigma opposition.'[47] In 'Planet of the Ood', we encounter white victims (Doctor Ryder played by Adrian Rawlins), villains (Tim McInnerny as Klineman Halpen), and crusaders (Donna Noble played by Catherine Tate); enslaved aliens fighting for their freedom (the Ood) and liberal humanist aliens with saviour complexes (the Doctor); a cunning South Asian slave dealer (Solana Mercurio) who sells subjugated aliens to black/brown/white buyers eager to establish their bourgeois bona fides; and a multiracial mercenary army helmed by a ruthless black slave-driver (Commander Kess). Solana Mercurio and Commander Kess, in particular, reflect the complexities of an emergent racial order in which people of colour are allowed to occupy positions of power so long as they follow the white supremacist script.

Like Danny Bartock and Zachary Cross Flane, Solana Mercurio and Commander Kess are ambiguously raced, if not colourblind characters. Solana Mercurio, the Head of Marketing and Galactic Liaison for Ood Operations, is played by Ayesha Dharker – a British Indian actress who typically appears in roles ethnically designated as South Asian and/or Muslim.[48] Much like Bartock, Mercurio emphasises the naturalness of slavery ('The Ood are happy to serve') and the benevolence of the slave-owners ('we keep the Ood healthy, safe, and educated'). During her sales pitch to a racially diverse group of investors, Mercurio enthusiastically proclaims: 'We don't just breed the Ood. We make them better!' But, as the Doctor and Noble subsequently learn, Ood Operations is not improving the Ood; they are enchaining and enslaving the aliens. When an outraged Donna asks what people would think if they knew the aliens were treated as chattel slaves, an exasperated Mercurio exclaims: 'Don't be so stupid! Of course people know … they don't ask. Same thing'. As Foss points out, the tacit acceptance of the oppression of the Ood and/or wilful misunderstanding of their plight closely parallels the actions of empires on earth in the nineteenth century.[49]

When the Doctor presses Mercurio to confess what the corporation does to render the aliens compliant, she stubbornly replies: 'That's nothing to do with me.' Undeterred, the Doctor pleads: 'Come with me … you can't agree with all this. You know this place better than me. You could help.' A temporarily guilt-stricken Mercurio tells the time-travellers where they can find Ood Conversion, the complex where the aliens are lobotomised. But, just as the Doctor and Donna prepare to run away, Mercurio reports their location to Commander Kess's military guard and her boss Mr Halpen. Mercurio's willingness to sell – and sell out – the slaves that took her place in the colonial hierarchy reveals her complicity with biopower and her self-subjection – or, in the language of neo-liberalism, her self-governance and active participation in another being's bondage. Her capitulation to colonial capitalism preserves her place in the multiracial white supremacist hierarchy and verifies that 'neoliberal governance operates through rather than against the agency of its subjects'.[50] Mercurio's commitment to the imperial futurity of Ood Operations is the mechanism of her own subjection and ultimately proves her undoing (she is electrocuted by a rebel Ood for her betrayal). Commander Kess faces a similarly gruesome fate for his dedication to post-racial imperialism (he is caged and gassed by the rebel aliens).

Lavender III observed that science fiction transmits 'assumptions of racism even in stories that are ostensibly envisioning a future where race has become irrelevant'.[51] 'Planet of the Ood' constructs a post-racial future in which people of colour are willing agents of empire. But, the manner in which they have been incorporated into the imperial edifice, makes it clear that race and racism linger behind the multicultural facade. The canny inclusion of the Black British Commander Kess, as part of the apparatus of enslavement, is particularly instructive. Kess is the head of the Ood Sphere's multiracial security forces. The integration of people of colour into Ood Operations' corporate army is open to various interpretations. On the one hand, since, like a prison guard, a soldier-for-hire has power over others without having authority or prestige, this may be seen as proof that racialised minorities remain trapped in menial jobs and undesirable positions. On the other hand, this can be taken as evidence that people of colour have been thoroughly assimilated by the imperial system of domination and exploitation that once victimised them. Eric Greene suggests 'that we learn to enslave by being enslaved, that oppression is the surest teacher of oppression'.[52] If so, Commander Kess, the merciless overseer of the subjugated aliens learned the lessons of his enslaved ancestors all too well. In the course of the episode, we witness Kess whip, chain, beat, kill and gas the Ood. All with a fiendish smile plastered to his face.

In the cruel, complicit Kess, British culture sees its own racist practices mirrored back in monstrous form. Unfortunately, the depiction of Kess as a bloodthirsty sadist also reinvigorates the tired trope of African savagery. *Doctor Who*'s strategic role reversal also obscures the white supremacist roots of British slavery. Putting a Black soldier in charge of the slavery apparatus not only deracialises the imperial past, but also suggests that the condition of Blacks and Black–White relationships have so improved that Blacks see no problem being part of the master class and have no difficulty in participating in the subjugation of another race. In the post-racial alchemy of *Doctor Who*, the historical crimes and burdens of the White slave master, which should be borne by the despicable Halpen, are transmuted to the brutish Black overseer, Kess.[53] In a truly neo-liberal multiculturalist twist, the series implies that Blacks – not Whites – are the ones truly responsible for the sins of slavery. The question we need to ask is: who is served by these representations? Whose economic, political, cultural and psychological interests are served by the serial's revival of the white saviour (the Doctor, Noble and Dr Ryder), the disloyal and scheming Indian (Mercurio), the vicious Black brute (Kess), the loyal lackey of colour (Bartock and Flane), and the treacherous slave (Sigma Ood)? Who is invested in the resurrection of the racist tropes of colonialism? Who profits from the expansion of white supremacy to a select few people of colour?

In *The Racial Contract*, Charles Mills reminds us that 'racism as an ideology needs to be understood as aiming at the minds of nonwhites as well as whites, inculcating subjugation'.[54] The ultimate triumph of a white supremacist education is that it makes it seem that people of colour willingly align themselves with a system that racially devalues them. Science fiction television is a key space in which such indoctrination occurs. Although *Doctor Who*'s Ood episodes ostensibly take place on a distant planet in a far-off future, they must be understood as a commentary on contemporary racial relations. By foregrounding 'racial differences in order to celebrate multicultural assimilation while simultaneously denying the significant social, economic, and political realities and inequalities' that defined racial relations in the past and the present, *Doctor Who* sustains and supports the colonial logic of white supremacy. The installation of the formerly enslaved (Zachary Cross Flane and Commander Kess) and colonised (Solana Mercurio and Danny Bartock) as key agents in the British galactic slave trade is particularly problematic.

Putting people of coluor at the centre of a historically white supremacist institution obscures the racist roots of British imperialism and bondage; it denies the historic culpability of whites in the colonisation of Africans and Indians. The multiculturalist white supremacy of the Forty-second Century Bountiful Empire thus entails, at best, a diversifying of management for a colonial apparatus of repression and enslavement (figure 6.3). The apparatus may look different but it has not changed at its core; it is still driven by the imperial desire to conquer and subjugate in the name of racial capitalism. The ascendancy of people of colour as managers and agents of the Second British Bountiful Empire marks the obsolescence of 'classical white supremacy as a model of dominance based on white bodily monopoly, and celebrates the emergence of a sophisticated, flexible, 'diverse' (or neoliberal) white supremacy'. Cosmopolitan colonialism is the logical culmination of contemporary neo-liberal multiculturalism.

Recovering from the trauma of transatlantic slavery requires acknowledging the racism of the imperial past in the present and refusing to imagine future worlds that replicate such colonial hierarchies. It requires letting go of imperial fictions and post-racial fantasies. In *Re-Forming the Past: History, The Fantastic, and The Postmodern Slave Narrative*, Timothy Spaulding argues that we need new narratives about slavery, speculative narratives that 'reveal the complexities embedded within the slave experience and obscured by traditional historical accounts'; fantastic fictions 'designed to reshape our view of slavery and its impact on our cultural condition'; fictions 'designed to intrude upon history as a means to re-form it'.[55] Although *Doctor Who* claims to be anti-imperialist, post-colonial and multicultural, the long-running serial often operates as 'a paradigm of ideological and ontological conservatism'.[56] It does not re-form the imperialist past; it reifies it. David Higgins once opined that science fiction's emergence from – and ongoing entanglement with – imperialism means that it not only performs the dreamwork of empire but also produces rich imaginative possibilities for empire's antithesis'.[57] While the Ood episodes testify to how the reincarnation of *Doctor Who* performs the dreamwork of multiracial white supremacist neo-liberal empire, I hold out hope that a popular science fiction television programme might some day reshape how we remember British imperialism and perhaps even remind us why there can be no racial reconciliation without reparations for the sins of slavery.

Figure 6.1 Tim McInnerny as CEO Halpen of Ood Operations, with his enslaved alien valet, played by Paul Kasey in *Doctor Who* (BBC, tx. 9/5/08)

Figure 6.2 Ayesha Dharker as Solana Mercurio emphasising the naturalness of slavery in *Doctor Who* (BBC, tx. 9/5/08)

Figure 6.3 BAME citizens demonstrate loyalty to the multiculturalist white supremacy of the 42nd Century Bountiful Empire in *Doctor Who* (BBC, tx. 9/5/08)

Figure 6.4 Space ships as slave ships, the captured Ood and the Tri-Galactic trade in *Doctor Who* (BBC, tx. 9/5/08)

Figure 6.5 Roger Griffiths as Commander Kess obscures the white supremacist roots of British slavery and reinvigorates the tired trope of African savagery in *Doctor Who* (BBC, tx. 9/5/08)

Figure 6.6 Ronny Jhutti as a middle-class bureaucrat Danny Bartock tasked with managing the Ood aliens in the 42nd century in *Doctor Who* (BBC, tx. 9/5/08)

Notes

1. Lavender III, Isiah, *Race in American Science Fiction* (Bloomington, IN: Indiana University Press, 2011), p. 7.

2 Bellin, Joshua David, *Framing Monsters: Fantasy Film and Social Alienation* (Carbondale, IL: Southern Illinois University Press, 2005), p. 9.
3 Balfe, Myles, 'Incredible Geographies? Orientalism and Genre Fantasy', *Social & Cultural Geography*, 5:1 (2004), p. 75.
4 Nishime, Leilani, 'Aliens: Narrating US Global Identity through Transnational Adoption and Interracial Marriage in Battlestar Galactica', *Critical Studies in Media Communication*, 28:5 (2011), pp. 450.
5 Malik, Sarita, *Representing Black Britain: Black and Asian Images on Television* (London: Sage, 2002), p. 2.
6 Bernardi, Daniel (ed.), 'Introduction: Race and Contemporary Hollywood Cinema', in Daniel Bernardi (ed.), *The Persistence of Whiteness: Race and Contemporary Hollywood Cinema* (London: Routledge, 2008), p. xvi.
7 Nilsen, Sarah, and Turner, Sarah E., 'Introduction', in Sarah Nilsen and Sarah E. Turner (eds), *The Colorblind Screen: Television in Post-Racial America* (New York: New York University Press, 2014), p. 4.
8 Bernardi, 'Introduction: Race and Contemporary Hollywood Cinema', p. xvi.
9 Bellin, *Framing Monsters*, p. 5.
10 *Ibid.*, p. 12.
11 Orthia, Lindy A., '"Sociopathetic Abscess" or "Yawning Chasm"? The Absent Postcolonial Transition in Doctor Who', *The Journal of Commonwealth Literature*, 45:2 (2010), p. 4.
12 Charles, Alec, 'The Ideology of Anachronism: Television, History, and the Nature of Time', in David Butler (ed.), *Time and Relative Dissertations in Space: Critical Perspectives on 'Doctor Who.'* (Manchester: Manchester University Press, 2007), p. 115.
13 Orthia, '"Sociopathetic Abscess" or "Yawning Chasm"', p. 4.
14 *Ibid.*, p. 209.
15 Charles, 'The Ideology of Anachronism', p. 117.
16 Fly, Fire, 'The White Doctor', in Lindy Orthia (ed.), *Doctor Who & Race* (Bristol: Intellect Ltd, 2013), p. 19.
17 Orthia, '"Sociopathetic Abscess" or "Yawning Chasm"', pp. 217–18.
18 Clark, Phenderson Djèlí, '*Doctor Who* (?) – Racey-Wacey-Timey-Wimey', *The Musings of a Disgruntled Haradrim*, blogpost, 3 June 2013.
19 Malik, *Representing Black Britain*, p. 146.
20 Mills, Charles Wade, *The Racial Contract* (New York: Cornell University Press, 1997), p. 19.
21 Mavhunga, Clapperton Chakanetsa, 'Vermin Beings, On Pestiferous Animals and Human Game', *Social Text*, 29:1 (2011), p. 154.
22 Bishop, Kyle William, *American Zombie Gothic: The Rise and Fall (and Rise) of the Walking Dead in Popular Culture* (Jefferson, NC: McFarland, 2010), p. 71.
23 Foss, Eric, 'The Ood as a Slave Race: Colonial Continuity in the Second Great and Bountiful Human Empire', in Orthia (ed.), *Doctor Who & Race*, p. 112.
24 Nijhar, Preeti, *Law and Imperialism: Criminality and Constitution in Colonial India and Victorian England* (London and New York: Routledge, 2015), p. 75.

25 Brantlinger, Patrick, 'Victorians and Africans: The Genealogy of the Myth of the Dark Continent', *Critical Inquiry*, 12:1 (1985), p. 181.

26 Jennings, Frances, *The Invasion of America: Indians, Colonialism, and the Cant of Conquest* (Williamsburg, VA: The University of North Carolina Press, 2010), p. 59.

27 Davis, David Brion, *Inhuman Bondage: The Rise and fall of Slavery in the New World* (Oxford: Oxford University Press, 2006), p. 55.

28 Nijhar, *Law and Imperialism*, p. 75.

29 Foss, 'The Ood as a Slave Race', p. 112.

30 Hughey, Matthew, *The White Savior Film: Content, Critics, and Consumption* (Philadelphia: Temple University Press, 2014), p. 64.

31 Sheth, Falguni, *Toward a Political Philosophy of Race* (Albany: State University of New York Press), 2009, p. 9.

32 *Ibid.*, 70.

33 Nijhar, *Law and Imperialism*, p. 73.

34 Lavender III, Isiah, *Race in American Science Fiction* (Bloomington, IN: Indiana University Press, 2011), p. 156.

35 *Ibid.*, 119.

36 Mohanram, Radhika, *Imperial White: Race, Diaspora, and the British Empire* (Minneapolis: University of Minnesota Press), 2007.

37 Nama, Adilifu, *Black Space: Imagining Race in Science Fiction Film* (Austin: University of Texas Press), 2008, p. 43.

38 Orthia, '"Sociopathetic Abscess" or "Yawning Chasm"', p. 214.

39 *Ibid.*, p. 215.

40 Bonilla-Silva, Eduardo, and Ashe, Austin, 'The End of Racism? Colorblind Racism and Popular Media', in Sarah Nilsen and Sarah E. Turner (eds), *The Colorblind Screen: Television in Post-Racial America* (New York: New York University Press), 2014, p. 73.

41 Doane, Ashley, 'Shades of Colorblindness: Rethinking Racial Ideology in the United States', in Nilsen and Turner (eds), *The Colorblind Screen*, p. 19.

42 Bonilla-Silva and Ashe, 'The End of Racism', p. 69.

43 Orthia, '"Sociopathetic Abscess" or "Yawning Chasm"', p. 207.

44 Bonilla-Silva and Ashe, 'The End of Racism', p. 3.

45 Melamed, Jodi, *Represent and Destroy: Rationalizing Violence in the New Racial Capitalism* (Minneapolis: University of Minnesota Press, 2011), p. 14.

46 Prior to his 2006 turn as Danny Bartock in *Doctor Who*, Ronny Jhutti appeared as Sohail Karim in *EastEnders* (TV series; 1988–90), Rashid in *Family Pride* (TV series; 1991), Raja in *Siren Spirits* (TV mini-series; 1994), Asif in *Moving Story* (TV series; 1994–95), Wasim in *Wing and Prayer* (TV series; 1997), Sandip in *Melody's Her 2nd Name* (Film; 2000), Jeet Singh in *The Residents* (TV series; 2001), Hussan in *Where the Heart Is* (TV series; 2001), Rikki Mahmood in *The Bill* (TV Series; 1992–2001), Sunil Desai in *Red Cap* (TV movie; 2001), Jay 'Ajay' Verma in *Always and Everyone* (TV series; 2001–2), Remi Kuluwitharana in *Cutting It* (TV series; 2003), Rafiq Ali in *M.I.T.: Murder Investigation Team* (TV series; 2003), Pallav Veer/Ashok Kumar in *Holby City*

(TV series; 1999–2004), Salim in *Chosen* (TV series; 2004), Imran in *Meet the Magoons* (TV series; 2005), Ronny Bhutto in *Judge John Deed* (TV series; 2006), and Zubin in *Banglatown Banquet* (TV movie; 2006). (Ronny Jhutti IMDb Profile, IMDb, (www.imdb.com/name/nm0422588/)

47 Melamed, *Represent and Destroy*, p. 2.
48 Prior to her 2008 appearance as Solana Mercurio in *Doctor Who*, Ayesha Dharker starred as Amrita H. Pal in *City of Joy* (Film; 1992), Kuhu Vrundavan in *Saaz* (Film; 1997), Malli in *The Terrorist* (Film; 1998), Leela in *Split Wide Open* (Film; 1999), Leela G. Ramseyor in *The Mystic Masseur* (Film; 2001), Mrs Daljeet Kumar in *Anita & Me* (Film; 2002), Sunni Khadir in *Cutting It* (TV series; 2003), Mina Patel/Meena Chauhan in *Doctors* (TV series; 2001–3), Chila in *Life Isn't All Ha Hee* (TV series; 2005), Hameeda in *The Mistress of Spices* (Film; 2005), Asha in *Outsourced* (Film; 2006), Farah Hamid in *Bodies* (TV series; 2006), Opama Menon in *Loins of Punjab Presents* (Film; 2007), and Tara Mandal in *Coronation Street* (TV series; 2008–9). (Ayesha Dharker IMDb Profile, IMDb, www.imdb.com/name/nm0223499/)
49 Foss, 'The Ood as a Slave Race', p. 116.
50 Elliott, Jane, 'Suffering Agency: Imagining Neoliberal Personhood in North America and Britain', *Social Text*, 31:2 (2013), p. 87.
51 Lavender III, *Race in American Science Fiction*, p. 20.
52 Greene, Eric, *Planet of the Apes as American Myth: Race, Politics, and Popular Culture* (Middletown, CT: Wesleyan Publishing, 1998), pp. 100–1.
53 Guerrero, Ed, *Framing Blackness: The African American Image in Film* (Philadelphia: Temple University Press, 1993), p. 54.
54 Mills, Charles Wade, *The Racial Contract* (New York: Cornell University Press, 1997), p. 98.
55 Spaulding, Timothy A., *Re-Forming the Past: History, the Fantastic, and the Postmodern Slave Narrative* (Columbus, OH: Ohio State University Press, 2005), p. 4.
56 Charles, Alec, 'The Ideology of Anachronism: Television, History, and the Nature of Time', in David Butler (ed.), *Time and Relative Dissertations in Space: Critical Perspectives on 'Doctor Who'* (Manchester: Manchester University Press, 2007), pp. 120–1.
57 Higgins, David M., 'Toward a Cosmopolitan Science Fiction', *American Literature*, 88:2 (2011), p. 333.

7

Myth of a multicultural England in BBC's *Luther*

Nicole M. Jackson

In his January 2016 speech to Parliament, actor Idris Elba asserted that the 'British Empire gave birth to the multicultural miracle that is modern Britain', while noting that the diversity of contemporary Britain is absent from the popular media. Elba discussed the limited roles available to Black actors in the UK, asserting that since 'I never saw myself or my culture on TV, I stopped watching TV. I decided to just go out and become TV.' To gain roles 'I had to transform the way [the] industry saw me. I had to climb out of the box.'[1] Elba challenges his audience to support the diversification of British television by providing roles for Black, Asian and minority ethnic (BAME) actors and supporting programmes that better reflected the various and complex realities of British life. However, Elba's own show (*Luther*), for all it attempts, does not rise to the standard he sets.

BBC1's detective show *Luther*, which is often lauded for its groundbreaking cinematography, Elba's acting and, in some quarters, its healthy representation of race, is just as flawed as the larger British television industry from which it emerged. *Luther*'s diversity is a representation of modern British multiculturalism's reliance on the (sometimes compulsory) assimilation of non-white people (immigrant or British-born) as a means to uphold the presumptive whiteness of Britain's national character. But for Elba *Luther* would be just as white (if not more so) than any other show on British television. The popular image of a multicultural Britain is not challenged by one Black man. Rather, multicultural Britain can allow space for 'the other' so long as the other strives to mimic British cultural norms and, most importantly, remains a statistical minority. Thus, the sprinkling of Black and Asian actors throughout *Luther* does not challenge the (white) status quo of the detective genre or British television.

This chapter critiques the representation of BAME characters in *Luther* in the historical context of racism within the British police forces, particularly the Metropolitan Police Service (the Met). Using social and cultural historical methodologies informed by British cultural and media studies, this chapter argues that, even though *Luther* has been lauded for its positive representations of race, the show actually conforms to a multicultural paradigm, which has matured from the 1980s, that privileges assimilation, the tokenisation of racialised 'others' and masks the continued marginalisation of Black Britons.

On 4 May 2010, *Luther* premiered on BBC1 to mixed reviews. Anchored by Elba playing the titular John Luther, the show was a new twist on a comfortable English television standard: the detective series. In the *Telegraph* review of the first episode, Serena Davies praises Elba's acting, but highlights *Luther*'s lack of originality. 'It is formulaic ... Its "big idea" is that we know the killer from the start of each episode – something Columbo did for decades ... His team think he's unreliable but keep him on because of his brilliant criminal intuition.'[2] In fact, *Luther* stepped on to a crowded field of similar detective shows already on the air: *Above Suspicion* (ITV, 2009), *Agatha Christie's Poirot* (ITV, 1989), *Ashes to Ashes* (BBC1, 2008), *The Bill* (ITV, 1984), *Foyle's War* (ITV, 2002), *Inspector George Gently* (BBC1, 2007), *Law & Order: UK* (ITV, 2009), *Lewis* (ITV, 2006) and *Midsomer Murders* (ITV, 1997).

Among all of the detective shows cluttering English airwaves, John Luther was one of only a small handful of fictional Black detectives and he was the only prominent Black lead. Luther's (and Elba's) race did not emerge as part of the narrative surrounding the UK premiere, as none of the initial reviews mentioned it as part of the show's appeal. However, as the American debut loomed, bolstered by Elba's critically and popularly acclaimed stint on *The Wire*, BBC America touted the show as a 'bold new look at the crime genre'.[3] If, as Davies asserts, *Luther* dipped into an oft-tapped well of inspiration, what exactly was new? It seems clear, in the light of the differences between media discussions in the USA and UK, that the biggest difference was race. Even though the British media seems to have ignored Elba's blackness, as *Luther* was the only detective show on the BBC (or British television networks in general) with a Black lead, American media latched on to this. Part of the reason why the British media ignored the significance of race in Elba's casting, this chapter argues, was related to a particular expression of colourblind multiculturalism.[4]

Neil Cross, the show's creator and sole writer, has affirmed that John was not written with race in mind and Elba's subsequent casting did not change his characterisation. In a 2012 interview, Cross said that

John 'was cast as a character, purely and simply'; one of the aspects that attracted Idris to the role. 'I have no knowledge or expertise or right to try to tackle in some way the experience of being a black man in modern Britain'. Cross's assertion reflects an element of *Luther*'s production that has often garnered praise. The show's colourblind casting and 'raceless' storytelling obscures the fact that race matters, even if only in its absence. And like the criminal element with which Luther is obsessed, the spectre of race in a modern British context lives just at the edges of one's vision, colouring perception and reality. Luther's blackness and the diversity of modern London are marginalised, mirroring a historical process that has masked the importance of assimilation in defining multicultural Britain. Especially when considering the police, it is important to note that this myth has been built on a history of recurring conflicts between Black communities and the police.

Black British history is replete with tensions between various Black communities and local police forces. In the 1920 British police enforced racially discriminatory immigration laws, most notably The Special Restriction (Coloured Alien Seamen's) Order of 1925, to separate Black and Asian seamen from their families and homes in England. In the aftermath of the First World War, Black residents faced violent, racist attacks as they attempted to settle in the UK. Even in this instance when the police acted to protect Black residents, it only enforced their foreignness, strengthening the idea that they did not belong. And most famously, in August 1958 when teddy boys rampaged throughout Notting Hill and Nottingham attacking West Indians the police were often slow to respond and did little to protect Black residents, many of whom were actually citizens of the United Kingdom and Colonies (CUKCs) and thus legal residents in the metropole. These few instances belie a pattern that had long since strained relations between police and Black communities. In this historical context, the representation of a Black police officer, let alone a high-ranking Black detective, takes on high representational weight. However, the importance of a character like John Luther, and the stakes of the show's representation of race, takes on even more significance when understood in the light of the death of Stephen Lawrence.

On the evening of 22 April 1993 in Plumstead, 18-year-old Stephen Lawrence was stabbed by a group of white teenagers while waiting at a bus stop with his friend Duwayne Brooks. While the Black community immediately decried the attack as racially motivated, as one of the assailants was heard to have said 'What, what, nigger', the police were less certain. The initial police investigation was fraught. In her memoir, *And Still I Rise: Seeking Justice for Stephen*, Stephen's mother Doreen Lawrence asserts that the police treated the family poorly. They were suspicious of Stephen and his friends, at one point insinuating that Stephen and Duwayne were casing houses to rob that night. She also notes that they withheld information from the family and lied outright that they were investigating Stephen's murder at times when they were not. 'The police did nothing for over a week ... They dragged their feet, mishandled witnesses, slowed things down ... Like everything else in the case during this early and crucial phase, the behaviour of certain policemen was murky, careless and indifferent.'[5] Lawrence asserts that Stephen's murder shattered the normalcy that had defined her family life. 'Two lives ended one chilly night in April ... One was the life of my eldest son ... The second life that ended was the life I thought was mine.'[6] Compounding the grief of losing a child was the mishandling of the investigation, which shattered her perception of the country where she had lived since 1962. The alienation that Doreen Lawrence describes is an amplified sentiment that, for some, had become a fixed understanding of British police forces; that they did not exist to protect or serve Black people.

On 31 July 1997, Home Secretary Jack Straw appointed Sir William Macpherson to investigate the police handling of Stephen's case. In the final report, the Macpherson committee deemed the Met 'institutionally racist', asserting that there had been a miscarriage of justice in the initial investigation. The committee described the first police investigation as 'palpably flawed' and worried that 'the underlying causes of that failure are more troublesome and potentially more sinister'.[7] While focusing specifically on the Lawrence family's complaints against the Met, the committee found that these concerns were echoed broadly throughout various ethnic communities. Most importantly, the Macpherson report acknowledges that the Met had long failed to provide justice and protection to Black people as part of the communities they were meant to serve, giving official recognition to a fairly widespread grievance. The Macpherson report provides a useful framework to understand the absences around race in *Luther* and the stakes of such erasure.

Luther's executive Producer Phillippa Giles asserted in a 2011 interview that, with regard to race: 'He [Elba] said he wanted to try to reflect the country. We've tried really hard. We didn't achieve that.' Despite Giles's assertion that the show had failed in this regard, journalist Alyssa Rosenberg pronounces *Luther* a 'fresh ... approach to race' and suggests that it is 'full of interracial relationships that range from the emotionally and sexually intimate, to the professionally bracing'.[8] However, what little diversity actually exists on the show almost completely centres on Luther's character. The programme *Luther* does not contribute significantly to the representation of BAME characters on television. John is the lone Black detective in the first and fourth series (figure 7.1). His wife, Zoe (Indira Varma), is the only prominent Asian character in the entire show and she only appears in series one (figure 7.2). In the second and third series, Erin Gray (Nikki Amuka-Bird) joins John at the Met and is the only other prominent Black character in the entire series run. This very limited representation of BAME characters on the show begs a number of questions about racial and ethnic diversity in contemporary London and in the Metropolitan Police Service.

In the *Stephen Lawrence Inquiry*, a central critique levied against the Met was that its personnel did not reflect the communities it served. The Macpherson committee made seventy recommendations to combat institutional racism in the police forces; seventh on the list was 'that the Home Secretary and Police Authorities should seek to ensure that the membership of police authorities reflects so far as possible the cultural and ethnic mix of the communities which those authorities serve'.[9] The report's authors believed that because the population of police offic-ers was (intentionally) much whiter than its environs, an adversarial dynamic was fostered between police officers and BAME communities. Thus, Macpherson recommended that the Met increase the number of BAME officers assuming that a more diverse police force would improve community relations. This was not, however, a new suggestion.

In the aftermath of the Brixton riots of April 1981, a committee led by Lord Leslie Scarman was tasked with investigating the cause of the disorders. The chief complaint made by the Black community members who gave evidence to the inquiry was the pervasive harassment by local police. In the final report, published in November 1981, Lord Scarman disavowed accusations that the police were institutionally racist, which made Sir William's statement eighteen years later so important, but he did concede that policing methods exacerbated various economic and political problems in the area. One of these mistakes, according to Scarman, was a lack of racial diversity in the Met's personnel:

> There is widespread agreement that the composition of our police forces must reflect the make-up of the society they serve. In one important respect at least, it does not do so: in the police, as in other important areas of society, the ethnic minorities are very significantly under-represented. The number of black officers serving in the Metropolitan Police on 6 October 1981 was 132, 0.5 per cent of the total strength of the force: on the same date, there were only 326 black officers in the police of England and Wales (0.3 per cent of the total strength).[10]

With so few Black officers Lord Scarman conceded that it would not be difficult for BAME residents to feel alienated from the police, neither would it be such a stretch for officers to view people of colour as outsiders (to the police force and potentially the nation). Thus Lord Scarman recommended that Black officers be specifically recruited and suggested that the Met train the ranks to 'prepare them for policing a multiracial society'.[11] That the *Stephen Lawrence Inquiry* makes roughly the same recommendation almost two decades later indicates a failure in this arena, which has not been corrected at the time of writing.

According to data from the Ministry of Justice's report on race in the criminal justice system, it is clear that Black officers remain under-represented in the British police. In 2010, when *Luther* was first broadcast, BAME officers comprised 4.8 per cent of the police officers in England and Wales. This was slightly up from the five-year average (2007–11), which was 3.9 per cent. Of this percentage only one per cent identified as Black, a figure that had remained consistent each year.[12] In late 2015, *Luther* aired a fourth series of two episodes. In this storyline, the fictional police force was even whiter than previous seasons. However, in reality 'there were 6,979 Minority Ethnic police officers in the 43 forces' throughout England and Wales in March 2015.[13] This represents an almost 4 per cent increase from the previous years and a 5.5 per cent increase since 2006. The Met had the largest proportion of BAME officers. However, in the highest ranks (DCI or above) Black officers totalled just 3 per cent, while the lowest ranking had 6 per cent – the highest percentage. Even though the real ranks are overwhelmingly white, in the fictional world of *Luther* this trend is exacerbated.[14] Even though John often stands out in a sea of white colleagues, *Luther* essentially ignores his hypervisibility and its potential effects on the show's central character – something that actual Black officers have attempted to address.

What became the National Black Police Association (NBPA) emerged in 1990 after the loss of Black staff from the service [reached an] alarming level. Black personnel created 'a black support network', which, in September 1994, led the London police commissioner to launch the Metropolitan Black Police Association. 'From its inception the NBPA has sought to highlight issues facing BAME staff in the Police Service, helping those in need of support.' The Association's annual conference report publishes statistical information about Black officers in the ranks, recruitment strategies, profiles of exceptional officers and local forces, and reports on past and future initiatives.[15] From this data, one can assume that a real-life counterpart to the fictional John Luther, of whatever rank, would likely have experienced instances of racism on the job, from the public as well as fellow officers. He or she would most likely have a hard time accessing the necessary courses needed for advancement, and would have been among the very few Black officers, especially as they ascended in the ranks. This last point is conveyed, unintentionally, in the television show.

Besides the BAME characters mentioned, actors of colour may be found in the background, mostly as extras, however, because most of the victims, criminals and witnesses are white. The only other significant Black character appears in the first two episodes of series three. John is investigating the murder of a white 'cyber activist', who previously caused a mixed-race girl to commit suicide through cyber bullying (figure 7.6). After interviewing the girl's family, John deduces that her Black father (portrayed by Lucian Msamati) committed the murder in revenge. John is reluctant to give the case his full attention for a variety of reasons, one of which is that he, on some level, believes that the murder is justified. This is not completely out of character, as John has shown himself to be sympathetic in cases such as these. However, the investigation features a haunting scene, where the father breaks down crying in his kitchen at having to talk about his daughter's suicide. When he slumps to the floor, John follows, his face etched in pain. While this particular scene is moving, this brief list is hardly representative of a show putting forth a 'fresh … approach to race … full of interracial relationships that range from the emotionally and sexually intimate, to the professionally bracing'.[16]

Throughout the series John is never shown to have a community outside of the workplace. With the exception of his ex-wife Zoe, John is a man without connections and any that he does have after series one are always with his white colleagues. In the first series he describes a troubled relationship with his father and makes a passing reference to his mother in series four, but it is unclear if they are alive. There is a brief mention of his grandmother in the prequel novel *Luther: The Calling* and in the third series John tells his love interest Mary Day (portrayed by Sienna Guillory) that his last name came from his grandfather who chose it 'for love'. But there is no mention of siblings or any extended family. This depiction of a black British man without, or maybe outside of, his community deserves further attention.

Lord Scarman's report on the Brixton disorders expended considerable attention on the state of the Black (in particular West Indian) family in England. Lord Scarman asserted that West Indian family models disintegrated upon immigration as 'black people had to do without the support of the extended network of kin which is a feature of traditional West Indian society'.[17] He continued, 'the role of the man was at best supportive, but seldom dominant. At worst, he was an absentee of little or no significance … Mothers, who in the West Indies formed the focus of the family, became in many cases wage earners who were absent from the family home.'[18]

These assertions, based on generalisations and a gross misreading of Black family structures, effectively blame Black parents for Black youth criminality. Pathologising Black British families has become the centre of a narrative wherein Black (immigrant) families and communities can be understood as facing almost insurmountable obstacles to assimilation and the promise of acceptance in the national (read: white) community. Thus, by divorcing Black people from their (Black) communities and families, one can lay the foundation for a particular kind of multicultural community that does not challenge the country's perceived whiteness.

In some ways John's characterisation escapes popular stereotypes of Black men in British detective procedurals where most Black actors tend to play criminals. John also avoids the somewhat problematic formula that had previously defined the representation of Black police officers, namely that, 'When black police officers *do* figure prominently, it is usually because "race" is a theme in a particular episode or else they have been drafted in to deal with a problem in the black community.'[19]

However, in *Luther* the pendulum has swung too far in the opposite direction. As Karen Ross notes in her study of Black television viewers, this group suspects that Black characters often suffer from 'a lack of "cultural" authenticity'. This is a complicated frustration. Either Black characters are 'never properly integrated into the [white] community they inhabit', or they are presented with 'no ornament or decoration or picture which suggest the personality of its incumbent, no signs of a provenance (or even contemporary reality) deriving from a place other than the normative cultural environment of white Britain'.[20] The latter scenario is the perfect description of *Luther*'s depiction of John.

Throughout the series, John's lack of Black family and community is palpable. In a 2014 BAFTA speech, actor-comedian Lenny Henry made this comment on *Luther*:

> Idris plays the title role – an intellectual, troubled, maverick cop who has no black friends or family. Not at all. Have you seen this? He never has any black mates. You never see him talking to his Uncle Festus or whatever his name is? He's never down Jerk City having a curry goat and rice with his bredrens. You never see Luther with black people, what's going on?[21]

While Henry makes a joke of the omission, he actually offers a serious critique that should not be ignored. Ross asserts that Black viewers 'argued that black minority characters are rarely shown with other members of their family so they are never allowed to develop as fully rounded characters'.[22] But John is not a minority character; thus this relative isolation from family and community is a curious omission.

Paul Gilroy argues that a significant feature of Conservative politics in the early 1980s required assimilation as the 'price of admission to the colour-blind form of citizenship'. He continues: 'Blacks are being invited to forsake all that marks them out as culturally distinct before real Britishness can be guaranteed'.[23] This was a central theme in Lord Scarman's response to the Brixton riots and became a function of Margaret Thatcher's immigration policy at the same time. For Black people to become fully integrated, and 'accepted', in society they had to shed all of their 'foreign' cultural markers, which John Luther has ostensibly done. And yet even that does not seem to have been enough.

The audience often sees John like this: his back sloped, hunched in a small car; his large frame balancing on short, flimsy office furniture; his body slumped casually in a chair, masking his height as he brings himself down to his suspect's eye level. He is, in these moments, the definition of someone who does not belong. In series four, this is also demonstrated in a number of sequences where John is shown to be in two places at once, visually representing the split nature of his character. Sometimes John uses this as an illusion to manipulate the perceptions of those around him, but it is also an allusion to the ways in which John (black, tall, powerful) is out of place. The racial boundaries of the nation make gestures towards the inclusion of those who assimilate culturally, although one can argue that this acceptance is always conditional. Gilroy posits that

> 'Race' is bounded on all sides by the sea. The effect of this ideological operation is visible the way that the word 'immigrant' became synonymous with the word 'black' during the 1970s. It is still felt today as black settlers and their British-born children are denied automatic national membership on the basis of their 'race'.[24]

The boundaries to which Gilroy refers are heavily policed and, historically, the Met has been a mechanism supporting exclusion.

In response to repeated conflicts between the police and Black youth in the 1970s, Cecil Gutzmore argues that the Notting Hill riots of 1976 stemmed from police attacks on Black cultural forms such as music, dress and speech specifically performed by Black youth. Gutzmore suggests that police considered Black youth to be inherently delinquent, which made the simple act of walking down the street 'jauntily' an invitation for police intervention.[25] Black newspapers reported repeated clashes between police and Black youth occurring outside dance clubs, at concerts and anywhere youth congregated in large numbers. These clashes were fomented by the use of a criminal ordinance that reinforced city streets as boundaries of social citizenship.

The 1824 Vagrancy Act was developed in the aftermath of the Napoleonic War to address the problem of former soldiers and tramps flooding into London. The ordinance expanded the local constable's power to remove vagrants from the city's streets and stop them from harassing 'productive' members of society, thus criminalising homelessness. Eventually, the Act fell into disuse and was all but forgotten by the turn of the twentieth century. It was revived, Black activists argued, to harass Black youth in public spaces. Section IV, colloquially known as 'sus' (suspicion), became the focal point of Black community ire. The code was a preventative measure to deter street crime, specifically pick-pocketing and car theft, and criminalised the 'intent to commit an arrestable offence and [gave] the police power to arrest [a] 'suspected' person or reputed thief loitering in public places with intent to commit crimes'.[26] Anti-sus activists argued that the law unfairly targeted Black youth and, as a police officer's word was the only evidence necessary to prosecute and convict a defendant in a magistrates' court, arrest was tantamount to conviction.[27]

Through sus, police officers became gatekeepers of English citizenry. The ability to harass Black youth on the streets defined who did, and did not, belong in these public spaces (and, on a larger frame, in the nation). These sus arrests were a significant feature in the series of events that led to the Brixton riots and only in this context does John's isolation become most clear. Presented with very little family or a Black community to belong to, and a police environment where he is a statistical anomaly, John is a perpetual outsider. To present him without a Black family or community is to buy into the assimilatory promise of multicultural England, while ignoring the cost of such 'inclusion'.

In the first series, John's relationship with his estranged wife Zoe provides an interesting contrast to his work relationships. On the one hand their interactions are usually full of tension as a result of their crumbling marriage. However, Zoe also represents a part of his personality, and his past, which might best be sublimated so that he can perform his job well. And yet he clings to her, and only through this relationship does the audience get a glimpse of an unassimilated John.

Zoe understands that John's compulsion is not about the job per se, but stems from his worldview. In the second episode of the first series,

Alice confronts Zoe in an attempt to understand John's motivations. 'Why do you think he does it?' Alice questions. In return, Zoe asks:

ZOE: Why does who do what?
ALICE: John. His job. It takes such a toll. Why does he put himself through it? What do you think compels him to do it?
ZOE: Duty?
ALICE: To What?
ZOE: The dead. He believes – one life is all we have. Life. And love. Whoever takes life steals everything.
ALICE: And you agree?
ZOE: I don't know. I think if he'd read a different book by a different author at the right time in his life, he'd have been a different man. He'd have been happier as a priest than ...
ALICE: Than what?
ZOE: Than what he is.

The audience mostly sees John in a context where his job is the defining feature of his identity, whereas Zoe, in the television show and the novel, is a window through which the viewer can see John as a man – flawed, brilliant and vulnerable – but still a man as opposed to just a 'copper'.

Especially in this first series, Zoe is the only person who seems to understand him fully. While the audience learns more about John over time, usually mirrored in Alice's growing understanding of him, it is clear that no one will ever know him as well as Zoe did. It is only as the first series progresses and through the prequel novel that it becomes clear that the John the audience encounters has been stripped of everything he was before. He has been divorced from his own history. And what glimpses one gets of that history illustrate that there is more to the man that the job requires or allows.

The only sustained glimpse of John's personal history emerges in the first series as well. The plot of the second episode concerns a sniper targeting police officers to free his imprisoned father. John mentions his own father sporadically throughout the episode as he attempts to understand his suspect, Owen. In these moments, the audience learns that his father was a soldier 'First Armoured Division, Seventh Armoured Brigade. So Germany, mostly – Canada, for a bit. Year in Cyprus.' The suspect's father, Terry Lynch responds, 'I bet he was a right hard bastard.' And Luther gives a singular detailed description of his relationship with a blood relative:

Well, it was tough for him. Here I am, big boy, eager to please, trying to care about what he cared about – the army, sport. But no, nothing there.

He wanted me to box. I wanted to write lyrics, read books, go out with girls. In the end I gave up trying to make him proud because I knew it was never going to happen.

This glimpse into the person John was before becoming a police officer is tantalising, but ultimately undeveloped. The audience never learns more about who he is outside of his vocation, what he is like without the burden of his job or how he fitted into a family unit. And after the first series, when John's friend and fellow detective Ian Reed (played by Steven Mackintosh) kills Zoe, John becomes a man without family. While the absence of familial relations certainly feeds into a characterisation of John as an isolated genius, and makes sense in the context of his own emotional fragility as a result of his job, it also strips him of a racial and cultural identity. And, in the aggressively whitewashed London of *Luther* there is only one place for him to turn for such connection (figure 7.5).

DS Erin Gray is introduced in the first episode of the second series. There are a number of significant women in *Luther*, but Erin is one of only two women of colour in the main cast. She is also the only Black female character (figure 7.3). Erin is presented as efficient, ambitious and ethical. These traits are made clear in the first episode of the second series. While investigating a public murder, John instructs Justin and Erin to confiscate mobile phones from the crowd. Erin challenges the directive: 'On what grounds, legally?' John replies, 'Find grounds.' After John walks away Justin explains, 'When he says "confiscate" what he means is appeal to the owners of the phones, okay?' Erin's response encapsulates her characterisation over the rest of the series, 'Fine, but that's not what he said, is it?'

The overarching crux of John and Erin's relationship is that Erin's morality and desire to follow procedure clashes with John's moral ambiguity (figure 7.4). The two, while working towards the same goal, are never travelling along the same path. While Justin and Zoe can see the best in John's intentions, that understanding has developed over time. Erin and John never manage to achieve this level of intimacy. Almost right up until her final scene, it is made clear that Erin does not understand John and it is ambiguous as to whether he fully understands her. Participants in Ross's study discussed the lack of intimacy between black men and women in British television:

> In most mainstream shows, and especially in entertainment genres, black minority characters most usually have white partners ... While it might seem rather distasteful to interrogate and criticize black minority characterizations to this degree of detail, black minority viewers see such casting

strategies as deliberate rather than accidental devices which contribute to their subordination through privileging 'whiteness' as the ultimate goal.[28]

Ross critiques this focus by her participants to some degree, arguing that the representation of interracial couples actually mirrors trends in the wider culture. However, she misses the fact that intimate relationships between Black men and women do not always have to be sexual or romantic to be significant. Rather, especially when facing an oppressive or isolating system Black people might turn to one another for comfort in their similar, if not shared, experience.

Erin leaves the Serious and Serial crime division at the end of the second series as a result of her friction with John. John has become entangled with a group of criminals while trying to rescue an at-risk girl, Jenny Jones (played by Aimee-Ffion Edwards). He is blackmailed into locating a witness under police protection and, with time running out, he pulls a fire alarm to get everyone out of the precinct so that he can access the information from DSU Schenk's (Dermot Crowley) computer, which Erin witnesses. Believing that he is corrupt, she confronts Justin for an explanation, which he cannot offer satisfactorily, so she reports the suspicious behaviour. In the final episode, Erin is called into her superior's office, where she is reprimanded because there was no evidence of her claim:

> CARROWAY: What angle are you trying to work, Erin? Is there a plan? I hope you've got a plan. This isn't just random game playing.
> ERIN: Ma'am, I'm confused.
> CARROWAY: If you're so keen to smear a superior officer, you're going to have to be smarter than that. A lot smarter. Now get out of my sight. Go for a walk. Do some serious thinking about your future in this department. In this service.

Realising that someone must have erased the evidence, Erin unleashes on John, Justin and Benny Silver (portrayed by Michael Smiley). As she leaves, she quotes George Orwell's *Animal Farm*: 'And the creatures outside looked from pig to man and from man to pig. And still it was impossible to tell which was which.' Her sense of betrayal is palpable. Near the episode's conclusion, Justin confesses that he erased the computer history to protect John:

> JUSTIN: She was only trying to do the right thing. She doesn't deserve to be punished for it. It's wrong.
> JOHN: Yea, it is wrong.
> JUSTIN: I need to make it right.

This is one moment in the show where John and his team are shown to be clearly in the wrong. John's ability to walk that fine line between right and wrong is an important feature of his characterisation. Not only does Justin step over that line, John barely registers the infraction. And, contrary to his assertion that he would make it right, Erin returns in series three a changed person.

When she re-emerges – now a DCI (and John's equal) – Erin is harder, somewhat less naive and embittered. She returns as a member of the 'Judas Division', as Justin refers to the Internal Affairs Bureau, heading an investigation of John with DSU George Stark (David O'Hara). She contends that she is satisfied 'rooting out dirty coppers' although it is ever present in her mind that she is there because Justin sabotaged her career. Erin's story arc in this series is significant in the ways in which the show highlights her marginality. If a feature of John's characterisation is that he *is* a police officer, fully assimilated, Erin is consistently denied that same acceptance. And, in many ways, John is passively complicit in her isolation.

In some ways Erin's series three storyline mirrors that of series two. In each episode she becomes less sure of what she is doing and more disaffected with her superiors. John's moral ambiguity is partially mirrored in Stark, even though the latter becomes increasingly unhinged by his alcoholism. Erin's career, which at the beginning of series two was on the rise, seems to end in series three. She is again tricked and betrayed by police officers who bend the law toward their own ends. These different paths Erin and John travel demonstrate the fickle quality of the multicultural myth. Regardless of their similarities, the benefits of assimilation are dispersed arbitrarily. With limited space, Black people become competitors for these fragile benefits and everything becomes a liability. In this case, Erin's moral correctness does not assure her security. The only thing that will save her is to be cleverer, thus more valuable, than John. When she is not, she becomes expendable.

Ultimately, Erin and John become competitors for the meagre rewards of assimilation that only one of them can claim. What is lost is the chance to present John in the context of another Black character. The questions Lenny Henry posed to BAFTA become most prescient in this moment. Where is John's Black community? Where is Erin's? And why can they not provide that for one another?

The viewer's final glimpse of Erin shows her on a stretcher having suffered a gunshot wound. She and John gaze at one another and it is clear that this is the end of their road. Even this final parting is layered with significance. Throughout the third series John's tentative relationship with Mary, a white woman, has always contained an element of fear at putting her in harm's way; so much so that protecting her becomes a minor storyline. In fact, many of John's conflicts throughout the show centre on protecting various women (Zoe, Alice and Mary as his love interests and Jenny in series two). But Erin, even after Justin's statement that he would make things right, is left to flounder. The women John cannot protect are the women of colour, whose innocence and morality are often liabilities and derided, even though these same traits can be celebrated in white female characters. While John does try to save Zoe, there is a significant lack of such care for Erin. That 'she's a good woman', is not enough. Thus *Luther* presents a world in which Black police officers are isolated from their communities as well as from one another.

The Macpherson and Scarman reports recommended that BAME police officers be recruited as a means to improve community relations, however this goal has been generally unfulfilled. In 2013, the London branch of the NBPA noted that the Met ranks did not reflect the city's population:

> The 2011 census indicated that over 40% of Londoners were from BAME backgrounds, whilst only 10% of MPS police officers were from BAME communities. These officers disproportionately hug the lower ranks, face significantly slower rates of career progression and are over-represented in disciplinary actions, in comparison to their white counterparts.[29]

The difficulty of recruiting Black officers is a narrative with a long history. Black people's reluctance to join the police ranks cannot be divorced from that long history of animosity between the police services and Black communities. *The Future of Multi-ethnic Britain* suggests that hostility between BAME community and the police can highlight the severe chasm between the two groups:

> For black, Irish and Asian communities, contacts with the police are a microcosm of their contact with the state ... They can engender a sense of security and justice, but also much distrust and anger ... the anger is about both heavy policing and police neglect – criminalization and harassment on the one hand and inadequate attention to racist crime and behaviour on the other.[30]

This sentiment was echoed in the Scarman and Macpherson reports, which cited evidence of a general distrust of police by West Indian communities:

> Independent research undertaken for the Home Office in 1979 underlined the fact that the reluctance of young West Indians to join the police is deeply rooted in the attitude of many members of that community to the police. The reasons most commonly given for lack of interest in a police

career were a basic lack of interest in the job, a fear of being alienated from family and friends, and a fear of being ostracised because of colour prejudice within the service.[31]

And in her evidence to the Macpherson committee, Doreen Lawrence asserted: 'No black person can ever trust the police. This idea is not pre-conceived. It is based on experience and people that I know who have had bad experiences with the police. They don't seem to understand, we are not accustomed to visiting police stations, we are not accustomed to dealing with police and we have no reason to trust them.'[32] Thus, the decision to join the police might run counter to community knowledge and might, eventually, necessitate substantial sacrifices of family, community and culture as a prerequisite for belonging and advancement.

Inadvertently, *Luther* suggests that the (more than) thirty-year scheme to hire more Black officers as a panacea for troublesome race relations would only have served as a sticking plaster, even if it had been success-ful. The tense and confrontational relationship between BAME com-munities and the police do not change through the presence of Black officers. This is especially true when those Black officers face their own struggles within the service. Rather, the institutional racism that the Macpherson report diagnosed, can include Black officers without chang-ing the nature of its treatment of BAME communities. Black officers, like John Luther, become tokens who can be used as evidence that the police are not racist, but who are themselves subject to harsh policing when they do not conform to – or dare challenge – the status quo. To be fully accepted is to become part of the pre-existing racist structure.

The concept of a multicultural Britain has long been a popular public relations narrative, very often transmitted globally. This image presents the country as representative of civic cooperation and tolerance and at ease with its multi-ethnic character. However, Gabriel argues that in media, 'Multi-ethnic/racial themes are possible so long as the principle of liberal white superiority remains intact'.[33] The hidden catch is that whiteness is really the centre of the narrative. Contemporary British multiculturalism tolerates 'the other' to the extent that it conforms, as much as possible, to Englishness. Thus, *Luther* presents an image of a Black police officer whose blackness is never mentioned, because it does not have to be. The preferred narrative that can, and has, emerged sug-gests that John is not Black he is just a copper. The reality, however, is that John *is* Black. Idris Elba is Black. The insistence on, and praise of, colourblind casting did not result in a diverse cast. Rather, it hinged on John Luther being the token even as he is the lead. With him, the show needs no other people of colour, because one is enough. One 'other', even when that other is extraordinary (or maybe especially when this is the case) is the multicultural ideal.

A multicultural Britain would not want a concentration of the other because that would signify that England is no longer a white nation – if it ever was. In a multicultural framework not predicated on total assimilation, Luther would not have to be stripped of a community to be understood as a detective. John Luther achieves his acceptance, such that it is, but at the expense of his 'other' identities. This multicultural ideal does not respect ethnic and cultural diversity, rather it privileges and insists 'on the absolute superiority of' Englishness and whiteness.

To present the Met as overwhelmingly white is not new or even groundbreaking, but its overwhelming whiteness on *Luther* is heightened when a Black man becomes the entry point through which the audience views this world. In *Luther*, Whiteness is not critiqued because of John's presence; in many ways it is normalised. John can be 'a character, purely and simply' because were he to be a 'black character' he would be weighed down with the stereotypes that have defined other Black television characters.

In the first episode of *Luther*, the emotional underpinnings of the narrative help to set a level of drama and intrigue for the series. John meets Alice Morgan who, he realises during his initial interrogation, has killed her parents but has left no evidence of her guilt. When faced with a dearth of evidence to tie her to the crime he asserts, 'There's not enough anything. Absence is the point ... She doesn't leave evidence – just an evidence-shaped absence.' This is a useful way of understanding how race operates in *Luther* as a microcosm of the multicultural myth. It is not that Black people do not exist in contemporary London; rather their cultural heritages are the price they pay for full assimilation. And it is not that there are no Black characters in *Luther*, but that none of them can exhibit any of the cultural markers that might distinguish them as connected to countries or ethnic heritages outside the British Isles. In the context of *Luther*, the absence of John's blackness, in any cultural, community or familial forms, has marked that heritage as a liability. To be fully accepted, or have any hope of such, he has had to conform in such a way that he is also diminished.

Idris Elba began his speech to Parliament in January 2016, 'I could almost feel at home', and the remarks that follow belie a severe ambivalence about his place in British media and, potentially, the country itself. Speaking specifically to, and about, public service broadcasting, Elba makes clear that the British television industry has far to go in the quest to more accurately represent Britain's diversity. It seems significant that Elba does not exempt the BBC, the bastion of British public television and home to *Luther*, from his critiques. Instead he notes, 'Too many of our creative decision-makers share the same background. They decide which stories get told, and those stories decide how Britain is viewed. Even to ourselves. Especially to ourselves.'[34]

What the television industry considers 'diverse' does not represent the world as it exists and characters of colour are often tokenised: the Asian man, the woman. This phenomenon is not specific to British television; however, this particular iteration is a product of problems in the larger society. As Elba notes, 'however far we have to travel onscreen, we have many more rivers to cross off screen. A consistent theme in Elba's public remarks concerning his career has been a refusal to be understood only by his race. He says, 'on the whole, I don't think of myself as just a "black actor". I'm an actor, not a number.'[35] It would be easy to read this statement as support for the kind of colourblind multicultural-ism that this chapter has critiqued. However, one can argue that what Elba is seeking, and what *Luther* for all of its brilliance misses, is that 'colourblind' is as tone deaf as the myth of a multicultural Britain. In this situation, BAME actors would remain under-utilised in domestic media and BAME citizens continue to be marginalised in representations of the larger society. As Ross asserts for Black viewership, and what *Luther* could have achieved when it premiered 'is not something huge and extravagant but something small and relatively easy to provide: the opportunity to see themselves, in all their diversity, portrayed credibly on that most powerful of media – television'.[36]

Figure 7.1 Still image from the opening credits of *Luther* shows John Luther's (Idris Elba) silhouette against a darkened backdrop (BBC, tx. 17/10/10)

Figure 7.2 Luther and Zoe Luther (Indira Varma) – one of only two significant women of colour from the series *Luther* (BBC, tx. 17/10/10)

Figure 7.3 Erin Gray (Nikki Amuka-Bird) is the second of only two women of colour on *Luther*, noting the limits of British multicultural inclusion (BBC, tx. 17/10/10)

Figure 7.4 Luther and Gray discuss their concerns during a contentious relationship in series three of *Luther* (BBC, tx. 17/10/10)

Figure 7.5 John Luther kneeling over the body of his murdered wife, Zoe: *Luther*, end of series one (BBC, tx. 1/6/10)

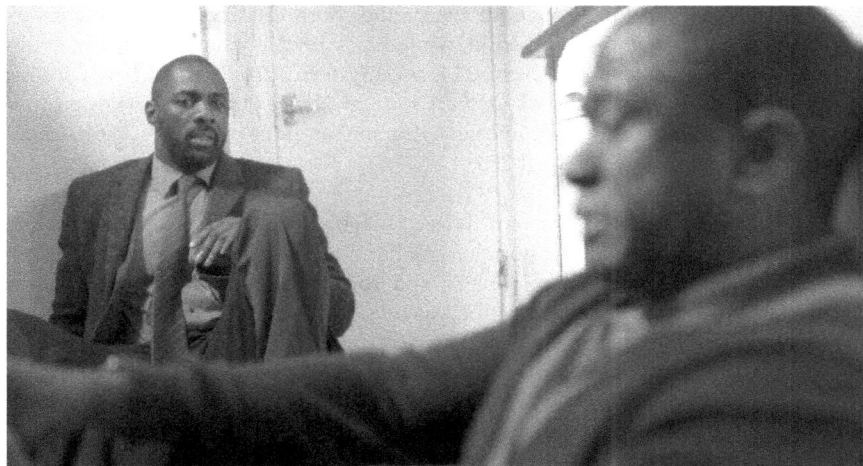

Figure 7.6 Luther attempts to console a father (Lucian Msamti) who must recount his daughter's suicide in series three of *Luther* (BBC, tx. 3/9/13)

Notes

1　Jaafar, Ali, 'Idris Elba Posts Full Text of Powerful Diversity Speech Online', Deadline, 20 January 2016, http://deadline.com/2016/01/idris-elba-posts-full-text-of-powerful-diversity-speech-online-1201686614/ (accessed 15 April 2016).

2　See the television series *Wallander* (2008–16), *Cracker* (1993–96) and *Prime Suspect* (1991–2006).

3　Bettinger, Brendan, 'Idris Elba's *LUTHER* to Air in America; Joins THE BIG C', *Collider*, 8 June 2010.

4　There were black detectives in secondary roles on a number of these shows including *DCI Banks*, *Dirk Gently* and *Law & Order: UK*.

5　Busby, Margaret and Doreen Lawrence, *And Still I Rise: Seeking Justice for Stephen* (London: Faber & Faber, 2006), p. 87.

6　*Ibid.*, p. xi.

7　MacPherson, William, *The Stephen Lawrence Inquiry* (London: Stationery Office Ltd, 1999), p. 4.

8　Rosenberg, Alyssa, '*Luther* Producer Phillippa Giles on Race and The Show's Approach to Casting', Thinkprogress.org, 19 October 2011.

9　Macpherson, *The Stephen Lawrence Inquiry*, p. 328.

10　Scarman, Lord Leslie, *The Brixton Disorders 10–12 April 1981: Report of an Inquiry by the Rt. Hon. The Lord Scarman, OBE* (Her Majesty's Stationery Office, 1981), p. 76.

11　*Ibid.*, p. 79.

12　This data separates those who identified themselves as 'mixed'. In 2010, this group was 1.3 per cent of police officers, and Asians were 1.8 per cent, the

highest BAME group throughout the period. Both classifications saw consistent increase throughout the period, while Black officers remained steady. From
*Statistics on Race and the Criminal Justice System 2010: A Ministry of Justice
publication under Section 95 of the Criminal Justice Act 1991*, www.gov.uk/
government/uploads/system/uploads/attachment_data/file/219967/stats-race-
cjs-2010.pdf (accessed 8 April 2016)

13 *Ibid.*
14 In the third series, Erin Gray returns as a DCI, but in the context of the storyline
the audience gets the impression that she has not fully earned the rank.
15 From a report on the development and role of a Black Police Association
in the wider police modernisation agenda, by Superintendent Paul Wilson,
Metropolitan Police, London, England, September 2006 (For the Conference on
Rank-And-File participation in Police Reform – CA, 12–13 October 2006).
16 Rosenberg, '*Luther* Producer Phillippa Giles on Race and The Show's Approach
to Casting', p. 4.
17 Scarman, *The Brixton Disorders 10–12 April 1981*, p. 8.
18 *Ibid.*, p. 9.
19 Ross, Karen, *Black and White Media: Black Images in Popular Film and
Television* (Cambridge, UK: Polity, 1996), p. 140.
20 Ross, Karen, 'In Whose Image? TV Criticism and Black Minority Viewers',
in Simon Cottle (ed.), *Ethnic Minorities and the Media: Changing Cultural
Boundaries* (Buckingham and Philadelphia: Open University Press, 2000), p. 140.
21 Henry, Lenny, 'BAFTA Television Lecture', 17 March 2014. Online (accessed
April 15, 2016)
22 Ross, 'In Whose Image?', p. 140.
23 Gilroy, Paul, *'There Ain't No Black in the Union Jack': The Cultural Politics of
Race and Nation* (Chicago: University of Chicago Press, 1991), p. 59.
24 *Ibid.*, p. 46.
25 Gutzmore, Cecil, 'Carnival, the State and the Black Masses in the United
Kingdom', in Winston James and Clive Harris (eds), *Inside Babylon: The
Caribbean Diaspora in Britain* (Verso, 1993), p. 208.
26 Bradley, Ian, '"Sus law" is Not Aimed at Blacks, MPs told', *The Times*,
22 February 1980, p. 2.
27 Timmins, Nicholas, 'Trial by Judge and Jury Urged in place of "Sus" Law', *The
London*, 28 March 1980, p. 4.
28 Ross, Karen, 'In Whose Image?', p. 143.
29 From a report on the development and role of a Black Police Association in the
wider police modernisation agenda by Superintendent Paul Wilson Metropolitan
Police, London, England.
30 Parekh, Bhikhu C., *The Future of Multi-ethnic Britain: Report of the Commission
on the Future of Multi-Ethnic Britain* (London: Profile, 2000), pp. 110–12.
31 Scarman, *The Brixton Disorders 10–12 April 1981*, p. 76.
32 MacPherson, *The Stephen Lawrence Inquiry*, p. 8089.
33 Gabriel, Deborah, 'Challenging the Whiteness of Britishness: Co-creating
British Social History in the Blogosphere', Academia.edu. www.academia.

edu/16545071/Challenging_the_Whiteness_of_Britishness_Co-creating_ British_Social_History_in_the_Blogosphere (accessed 2 May 2016), p. 80.

34 Jaafar, 'Idris Elba Posts Full Text of Powerful Diversity Speech Online'.

35 *Ibid.*

36 Ross, Karen, 'In Whose Image?' p. 146.

8

Framing *The Fosters*: jokes, racism and Black and Asian voices in British comedy television

Gavin Schaffer

This chapter interrogates the relationship among television comedy, power and racial politics in post-war Britain. In a period where Black and Asian Britons were forced to negotiate racism as a day-to-day reality, I want to question the role played by television comedy in reflecting and shaping British multicultural society.[1] This chapter probes Black and Asian agency in comedy production, questioning who the joke makers were, and what impact this had on the development of comedy and its reception. The work by scholars of Black and Asian comedy television such as Sarita Malik, and of Black stand-up comedy such as Stephen Small, has helped us to understand that Black and Asian-led British comedy emerged belatedly in the 1980s and 1990s, hindered by the historical under-representation of these communities in British cultural production and the disinclination of British cultural leaders to address this problem.[2] This chapter uses these scholarly frames of reference, alongside research that addresses the social and political functions of comedy, to reopen the social history of Black British communities in post-war Britain through the story of sitcom.

This chapter explores some of the history that led to the belated breakthrough of Black and Asian British comedy, looking at the production of jokes about race and colour prior to the 1980s and 1990s, and questioning what these jokes tell us about British multiculturalism in this period. It questions the ways in which jokes about Black and Asian minorities functioned in a period of overwhelming white control, and, specifically, looks at one early attempt to give voice to Black British comedy, the production of *London Weekend Television*'s (LWT) family comedy, *The Fosters*, in 1976–77.[3] The chapter ultimately questions how contemporary representations of Black and Asian people in comedy came to be, and the role of television as a medium in shaping jokes about race.

Historically, many scholars, writers and performers have ascribed to comedy the power, or at least the potential, to affect change. George Orwell, in this context, famously suggested that jokes were 'tiny revolution[s]', an idea that empowers humour to puncture the contradictions and frustrations of serious society, to express radical and liberating ideas which otherwise cannot find a space.[4] Mikhail Bakhtin, in this context, argued that laughter could give voice, albeit fleetingly, to the political subaltern. 'This laughing truth', he asserted, 'expressed in curses and abusive words, degraded power'.[5] In this frame of mind, humour is a serious matter. As Eddie Waters, Trevor Griffiths' teacher of comedy in the influential play, *Comedians*, explained to his students, 'Comedy is medicine. Not coloured sweeties to rot their teeth with.'[6] Not only can a joke express frustration, Griffiths' character asserted, but a 'true joke … has to do more than release tension, it has to liberate the will and the desire, it has to change the situation'.[7]

However, many scholars have questioned whether comedy really has such radical potential. Henri Bergson famously argued that jokes were more likely to police social borders than promote revolution, an argument which has been nurtured by a series of contemporary analysts.[8] Aside from the comic tendency to reinforce the status quo, jokes, even when radically intended, struggle to assert meaning beyond their immediate context.[9] Even at the time of telling, people laugh at jokes for different reasons, so that it is difficult to argue that humour can serve a role in bolstering a political platform. Crucially, as James English quipped, 'laughing together is not the same as reaching agreement'.[10] Indeed, the unstable nature of jokes and laughter has led some scholars of race to argue that humour is no medium to make any kind of political point.[11] As comedian Jenny Lecoat explained in the 1980s, those seeking change should pursue other avenues of action: 'If you really want to change the world, you don't go into comedy – you learn to fire a gun and you go to fight in El Salvador'.[12]

If comedy cannot be expected to serve political ends in any substantial sense, it may instead support struggling communities by boosting morale and allowing for tension release, performing a valuable function, as Gareth Stedman Jones has suggested, as a 'culture of consolation'.[13] In this vein, it is arguable that Black and Asian comedy came of age not by promoting a Black and Asian British presence in Britain to white audiences, or by moving forward British race relations, but when Black and Asian voices began to articulate the feelings and frustrations of these communities for their own enjoyment.[14] Here programmes such as *Desmond's*, *The Lenny Henry Show* and, later, *Goodness Gracious Me*, have been historicised as particularly significant.[15] But long before the arrival of any Black and Asian written and performed comedy, a glut of eclectic comedy material about Black and Asian communities, immigration and racism, had appeared on British television – programmes that were about Black and Asian people, but mostly written, produced and performed by whites.

Race in early British sitcoms

The first sitcom on British television to deal substantially with issues of race and immigration was Johnny Speight's *Till Death Us Do Part* (figure 8.1), a programme that included no regular Black characters.[16] Speight did not consider this Black absence within the programme to be a significant obstacle to discussing racial issues, a tendency which reflected broader trends in British sitcom in the 1960s and 1970s. While actors such as Rudolph Walker, Thomas Baptiste and Kenny Lynch played pioneering roles in establishing Black voices in British television comedy, just as often 'black' characters were played by blacked-up white men, most significantly in Speight's 1969 sitcom *Curry and Chips* (LWT, 1969) (figure 8.2), and Jimmy Perry and David Croft's *It Ain't Half Hot Mum* (BBC, 1974–81).[17] When criticised for casting Spike Milligan instead of an Asian lead in *Curry and Chips*, Speight's response revealed his indifference when speaking to the *Daily Mirror*:

> One do-gooder protested that [Milligan] shouldn't have been given the role in the first place. It should have been played, he said, by any out-of-work Pakistani actor who was as funny and brilliant as Spike Milligan. If you know one, let us know.[18]

While organisations such as the Campaign against Racial Discrimination (CARD) and The Runnymede Trust increasingly vocalised disquiet about the practice, television executives did not seemingly see Black absence, or blacking up, as an obstacle to comedy about race and immigration.[19] In *Till Death*, while the story focused on racial issues time and again, real Black voices were almost entirely absent. Instead, this programme's stance was voiced through the leading character, Alf Garnett, played by Warren Mitchell.

Alf Garnett was a conservative bigot, extremely hostile to Black and Asian immigration to Britain and convinced of the superiority of white people. Over the course of six series, between 1965 and 1975, Garnett time and again attacked multicultural society, and railed against the Black and Asian presence in Britain. A fervent imperialist, Alf mourned the end of empire and what he perceived as the consequences for immigration:

In the old days mate when them coons come over here, they come for instructions mate, they was told what to go back and do. Chop chop. Not now though. They come over now an' tell us what to do. An old Wilson sits there and takes it. Blimey, if that had been old Winnie Churchill he'd have told 'em where they got off, mate. Get back to the jungle, he'd have told 'em. Get your bloody drums out.[20]

To Alf, Black and Asian immigrants were inferior interlopers in every respect. Back in Africa and Asia, Alf explained, these were people 'sitting on the pavements with flies crawling all over 'em', and had never 'even seen a proper toilet'.[21] Alf was sceptical that these migrant workers in Britain could play significant roles in the public services. 'It's not safe to go into hospital because of 'em', he argued. 'You go in with a broken thumb and they take your arm off … there's people around here that's frightened to go into hospital because of 'em … frightened they'd end up in a bloody stew pot.'[22]

While Alf made remarks of this nature in numerous episodes, they rarely went unchallenged. The idea of the programme, according to Speight and the BBC, was that Alf would vent his ignorance, which would then be confronted and refuted by other characters, most frequently his left-wing son-in-law, Mike (portrayed by Tony Booth). As one journalist in the *Financial Times* explained, Garnett was designed in this way to serve an educational, cleansing function. The audience would see his ignorance and be alienated and chastened by it: 'see these backward attitudes given the full treatment of Alf Garnett's profane invective, and we recover our sanity and learn to laugh at ourselves as we laugh at him'. Speight, in his own words, made this case repeatedly, 'You can't encourage racists to be any worse than they are. And the fact that you raise these points of view and make fun of them makes people more inclined to think about them. If you never mention them, they just go on.'

In observing the unpredictable and diverse nature of audience reception, and the questionable principles behind the programme, several scholars have highlighted the problematic nature of this anti-racist strategy,[23] which was undermined even at the time by BBC research, which suggested that audiences were more likely than not to agree with Alf and his bigoted racism. Yet Speight's approach defined and shaped the handling of race in British sitcom for a generation. Specifically, through *Till Death* and *Curry and Chips* Speight presented as legitimate the idea that racism could be expressed in comedy so long as the racist was presented as foolish. Alf always lost his arguments, and the anti-racist challenge expressed in *Till Death* by his family and occasionally by Black characters, was presented as sensible and superior. For example, in one

1974 episode, Alf was forced to call in a repair man to fix his television, only to find a Black worker sent to do the job (portrayed by Olu Jacobs). While Alf expressed incredulity that the repair man would be up to the task, the television was fixed in minutes and Jacobs's character mocked Alf's racism. He told Alf, 'Magic. Black magic … I bet you never thought when you bought this you'd have to get a native out of the jungle to repair it for you … it's knowing where to rub the rabbit's foot annit?'[24] Leaving Alf's home, the teasing continued, the repair man departing with the words, 'if you want me again … just beat the drums'.

Following Speight's example, the idea that racism could be given centre stage in sitcom, so long as the racist was always seen to lose, became a recurring feature of the genre in the 1970s. Most notably, it was harnessed week in week out as a comic device by writers Vince Powell and Harry Driver, in their race-focused sitcom *Love Thy Neighbour* (figure 8.3) and then later in Powell's *Mind Your Language*. Powell and Driver began writing together in the early 1960s and soon became successful sitcom scriptwriters for the independent networks.[25] The pair first explored racial themes in a long-running sitcom about the work relationship between a Jewish and Catholic tailor, *Never Mind the Quality, Feel the Width*, which ran for six series on ABC television between 1967 and 1971.[26] In, the wake of its success, they penned *Love Thy Neighbour* (Thames, 1972–76), a story about two married couples (one black and one white) who lived next door to each other.[27]

While the two wives (Joan Booth portrayed by Kate Williams and Barbie Reynolds by Nina Baden Semper) strove to be good neighbours, *Love Thy Neighbour* was constructed around the fractious relations between the two husbands (Eddie Booth portrayed by Jack Smethurst and Bill Reynolds portrayed by Rudolph Walker). As work colleagues as well as neighbours, Booth and Reynolds fought each other in every episode, arguments that were always underpinned by Eddie Booth's ignorant racism. Like Alf Garnett, Booth was constructed as a fool, who always lost his battles. In contrast, Bill was presented as more intelligent, suave and reasonable, always ready to show up Eddie's racism and ignorance. In the pilot episode, Bill dressed up as an African warrior, semi-naked with face paint and a knife, to show up the ludicrousness of Eddie's construction of him. He explained to the other three characters, 'This is how you expect us to behave and we don't want to disappoint you.' In another episode, Bill and Eddie donated blood together, during which Eddie dismissed Bill's contribution with his usual bigotry. There was, he argued, a difference between white and Black blood, 'Mine's civilised – yours is primitive … It wouldn't do for you to have our blood.' Predictably, this episode concluded with Eddie needing a blood transfusion and using Bill's blood after all, while Bill gloated, 'Hello, blood brother.'[28]

The extent to which Eddie was constructed as the programme's fool was not lost on the press. As Mary Malone wrote in her column in the *Daily Mirror*, 'The only characters who leave the screen with their dignity intact are the blacks. Now that's what I call prejudice.' This tendency to make a fool of the racist remained a recurring feature of Vince Powell's comedy writing. In his later sitcom, *Mind Your Language* (LWT 1977–79, 1986), a story based around a group of immigrants learning English (figure 8.4), Powell again focused on the humour value of racial difference, while simultaneously pressing the cautionary message that racism doesn't pay. For example, when the class teacher Mr Brown (portrayed by Barry Evans) awaited an external inspector, he made a fool of himself by not anticipating that his visitor might be Black. Dismissing the inspector as a new student, Brown patronised him when asking if he flew in on a 'big iron bird', only to be shamed into realising his mistake.[29]

In the emerging genre of racial sitcom, developed by Speight, and Powell and Driver, this principle of racists being the butt of jokes remained key. Indeed, this joke-play legitimised the genre, justifying repeated tirades of racist invective by supposedly showing audiences the right way to behave. In Yorkshire Television's *Rising Damp* (1974–78), bigoted landlord Rigsby (portrayed by Leonard Rossiter) time and again made a fool of himself in the face of suave, sophisticated African medical student, Philip (Don Warrington) (figure 8.5). In *It Ain't Half Hot Mum*, the Indian bearers repeatedly got the better of their English masters. In both cases, fools were made of those racist characters who underestimated Black and Asian people by buying into discourses of primitivism. In *It Ain't Half Hot Mum*, the Indian bearers capitalised on British naiveté, selling glass from Birmingham as precious mystical rubies.[30] Famously, in *Rising Damp*, Philip convinced Rigsby that a piece of his wardrobe was actually magical African love wood.[31] In this way, the failure of racists to see the common humanity of Black and Asian characters led to disaster, a clear message about race, but far from the only one that emerged from this body of work.

While racist characters in these programmes generally lost their battles, the broader messages about racial difference that emerged reflected a society still deeply unsure about the merits of multiculturalism, where television, both in front and behind the screen, still largely excluded Black Britons. Racism, constructed as unneighbourly intolerance and bigotry, may have been held to ridicule, but so to was the exoticism of Black and Asian people. Both Philip in *Rising Damp*, and Bill and Barbie Reynolds in *Love thy Neighbour*, were constructed as super-sexual in a way that separated them clearly from all the white characters. As a result of a long history of colonialism, Black people were not, it seemed, susceptible to the physical inadequacies or insecurities of everyone else. In *Mind Your Language*, the foreign students were frequently held up as primitive and culturally inferior to their British teacher. Jamila Ranja (portrayed by Jamila Massey) was so excited by her ability to mispronounce 'good evening' that she walked around the class manically greeting everyone. In another episode, she accidentally stole from supermarkets because she did not understand the concept of free offers.[32] Ranjeet Singh (Albert Moses) had to be taught that, now in Britain, he needn't fear an arranged marriage. Mr Brown told him: 'This isn't the Punjab, it's England, a civilised country.'[33]

Legitimised by the idea that they were on the side of anti-racism, sitcoms of this kind reinforced racial difference and held up multiculturalism as a field of conflict, where it was normal to highlight race at every turn.[34] As one journalist commented of *Love thy Neighbour*, 'The adage about destroying prejudice by laughter seems to be translated here as attempting to say "Nig nog" as many times as possible.'[35] Where Black and Asian actors were not altogether excluded from these programmes, they were faced with two choices, either to go along with the jokes as they stood, or refuse to take badly needed parts. While it would be inaccurate to entirely dismiss Black agency in these productions, it is unarguable that such agency was limited. Rudolph Walker, for example, recalled that he only agreed to take part in *Love thy Neighbour* on the basis that he was allowed to give as good as he got.[36] This, no doubt, he did, but the programme still left the impression that he and Nina Baden Semper were left to absorb much of the underlying racism that underpinned the show's premise. As one journalist in the *Sunday Times* argued, 'the humour of this series invariably panders to white prejudice with the black man (Rudolph Walker) laughing desperately at thick-skulled sallies like "Nig nogs are affected by the moon"'.[37]

Without doubt, the Black actors who took part in such programmes were vulnerable to anxiety that they were contributing to the problem of racism, and failing to stand up for the rights of Black people. Finishing his time on *Love thy Neighbour*, Rudolph Walker was quick to state that he would not again take part in a similar programme. He told the *West Indian World* in 1977, 'The series was stretching me to my limits mentally. I have now moved away from that sort of thing and, have no intention of being involved in a series of that nature any more.'[38]

While Walker's frustrations were understandable, we should be wary of dismissing the significance of Black and Asian presence in British sitcoms in the 1960s and 1970s. For one thing, the recruitment of Black actors was itself a breakthrough, set in context of the earlier practice of blacking up. Seeing Black and Asian people on screen in lead roles sent a message to the next generation that it was possible, as a Black or Asian actor, to make a career in television comedy. As Walker told Jim Pines, he hoped aspiring Black actors saw him in *Love thy Neighbour* and thought, 'If Rudolph can do it, why the hell can't I?'[39] For many Black and Asian people in Britain and beyond, seeing people of colour on British television was inherently desirable and pleasurable, even in sitcoms of this nature.[40] *Mind Your Language*, for example, was hugely popular in Sri Lanka, much to the irritation of one analyst, who could not fathom the nation's affection for a programme that he saw as a 'disturbing and saddening phenomenon'.[41] Why, the author noted, were 'thousands of households in Colombo and elsewhere in the country laughing themselves sick every Wednesday over the language-jokes in the programme, and why are people writing to the papers saying that Mr Moses (the Sri Lankan who plays Ranjeet Singh) has done Sri Lanka proud and put us on the map?'[42] The answer to this rhetorically posed question perhaps relates to the instability of comedy discussed at the start of this chapter.

People laughed at *Mind Your Language* in Sri Lanka, as everywhere, because of highly personal cultural cues, that could never be reduced to the intentions of writers and performers. It is, moreover, entirely inappropriate to assume that Black and Asian audiences were necessarily any less susceptible to the lure of racist jokes than white audiences. What was beyond doubt, however, was that laughter in this period, at least on television, was firmly controlled by white writers, producers and actors, and that this led to a particular representation of Black and Asian worlds to the exasperation of many Black and Asian people. Significant change began to occur only when Black and Asian people gained space to write and perform their own television comedy, but this, in the mid-1970s, mostly remained some years away. There was, however, one bold attempt to do Black comedy differently in this period, a programme that saw the beginnings of significant change in a range of ways. Though it was originally written by African American writers as US comedy *Good Times*, and adapted by a white British screenwriter, Jon Watkins, *The Fosters* (LWT 1976–7), with an all-Black cast, began to take British sitcom in new directions.

The Fosters: the rise of Black-led comedy?

The Fosters starred Norman Beaton and Isabelle Lucas, as husband and wife Sam and Pearl Foster, living in social housing in London with their three children (Sonny, portrayed by Lenny Henry, Sharon Rosita as Shirley, and Benjamin played by Lawrie Mark). A gentle, family-friendly comedy, *The Fosters* (figure 8.6) did not have any of the sharp taboo-breaking dialogue of *Till Death*, nor the adversarial day-to-day racism of *Love thy Neighbour*. Instead, *The Fosters* tried to emphasise the ordinary nature of Black British families, stressing the extent to which London was now a functioning multicultural space. *The Fosters'* opening credits, for example, showed two members of the police force (one Black, one white) walking the beat together, Black and white children playing, and a harmonious exchange between Black and white bus conductors. Thus *The Fosters* set a different tone, even before a word of dialogue had been spoken. This was not to be another race sitcom, at least not in the mould of its predecessors. Instead, the story strove to present the Fosters as typical Londoners.

As Beaton himself recalled, *The Fosters* was about a Black family, 'without referring to the fact that they were black'.[43] This decision was heralded as highly original in some parts of the press. For example, the *Guardian* claimed, amid some exaggeration, that it was 'the first time a series has gone out on British television based on black people as human beings, not as black people'. While, as the *Guardian* pointed out, producing a story about the ordinariness of Black British life was in-and-of-itself 'very political', for the actors involved, *The Fosters* seems to have provided a much desired break from didactic and dramatic treatments of racial themes on British television. As Beaton explained in the *Guardian* interview, 'We don't have to holler revolution all the time. After all, even revolutionaries have fun. They don't make bombs all the time.'[44]

Where politics functioned in *The Fosters*, the *Guardian* suggested, was at a more subtle level. In depicting an working-class family, the programme sent a strong message about the moral fibre of Black Britons and their legitimate place within society. Newton has observed that, 'The programme, like *Good Times*, had an ongoing theme that no matter the circumstances, these families could endure.'[45] When, in one episode, Sam Foster found £13,000 of money stolen from a supermarket in a rubbish bin, his honesty ensured that he returned it all despite his family's need.[46] In most episodes, the story followed Sam's search for employment. Throughout, the character was portrayed as desperate to pay his way and support his family, and as a positive role model.[47] By focusing on employment rather than racial conflict, *The Fosters* attempted to speak to the primary challenges of the Black community as seen from within.

The series also focused on cross-generational conflict and, in particular, disagreements between first and second generation Black Britons, a theme which went on to dominate much Black and Asian-written television and theatre in Britain.[48] For example, at two points in the first series, the increasing militancy of the second generation was addressed through the character of the youngest son Benjamin, in both cases resulting in Sam and Pearl supporting his political challenges. In one episode, Benjamin replaced the white effigy of Jesus in the family home with a Black one, which his brother had painted.[49] At a later occasion, Benjamin was sent home from school for calling the Queen a 'racialist' because of British immigration policy. Although initially minded to beat him, Sam ended up deeply proud of his son's knowledge of Black history, which, he explained to his father, 'was illegitimately not taught in his school'.[50] Through these themes, and by downplaying politics in most instances, *The Fosters* refocused the representation of Black people in British comedy. Instead of merely being portrayed as victims and provokers of racial conflict, characters began to come through who spoke more to the real challenges of Black British life, creating a space for Black comedy that was not only about race.

Despite *The Fosters*' original approach to Black British comedy, its limitations attracted considerable criticism. Most significantly, the programme was attacked repeatedly for failing to represent Black British life authentically. Some obvious issues underpinned these challenges, in particular the ethnic composition of the production team, and the harvesting of the script from *Good Times* in the USA. Carol Dix in the *Guardian* pointed out, for example, that while the show's actors were Black, 'the director, writer, stage crew and TV PA's are all white'.[51] The issue here was not only about colour but also concerned the track record of some of the people involved, who came directly from the stable of racial sitcoms. Most obviously, producer Stuart Allen came to *The Fosters* having worked previously on *Love thy Neighbour* and *Never Mind the Quality, Feel the Width;* and he went on, after the series, to produce *Mind Your Language*.

Its American origins led to criticism that *The Fosters* could not speak to Black Britons. It was not, as journalist Sylvia Clayton in the *Daily Telegraph* complained, 'a series about immigrants, it is an immigrant series', which ignored the talents of Black British writers. This review continued:

> We have in this country some highly-gifted West Indian writers and a fine tradition of comedy rooted in social observation … However, London Weekend Television preferred to have their humour canned and bland, with the odd reference to North Sea oil to show that they were on this side of the Atlantic.[52]

At the time, Carmen Munroe (who played Vilma, a friend of the family), conceded that it would have been preferable for the show to have had a Black British writer: 'Of course, it would have been more desirable to have a script written by a West Indian using idioms in and situations that are indigenous to the British scene ... but there you are.' This seeming failure to articulate a specifically Black British viewpoint was also criticised by British civil rights activists. For example, Cliff Lynch from the West Indian Standing Conference told the *Daily Mail* that *The Fosters* 'was a superficial stereotyped comedy which didn't really illustrate West Indian life in Britain'. For some, the light-hearted and optimistic responses of *The Fosters* to the drudgery of their lives continued an undesirable trope of colonial representation, and undermined the serious realities of British racial politics. Dismissing the character of Sonny, Lenny Henry's happy-go-lucky teenager, race and media scholar Charles Husband described 'the most recent media portrayal of Sambo – the all-smiling, all-gibbering, eyeball-rolling clown'.[53] Similarly, a Black community leader interviewed in the *Daily Mail* complained that the show was wrong to present Black families laughing and joking all day and talking about sex. Norman Beaton, out at a party in London, recalled being verbally attacked by Black youth who were critical of representation in *The Fosters*. The show, one young man told him, 'don't show the black community like it is. It's foolishness.' Another went even further, 'You're a fucking Uncle Tom ... You don't represent none of we'.[54]

For many within Britain's diverse Black communities, *The Fosters* was a missed opportunity, as banality and unthreatening humour was prioritised over highlighting some of the gritty challenges of Black life in a racist society. At the start of the series, the *West Indian World* promised a competition to publish the ten best audience reviews of the show's second episode. But the only letter to actually appear, seemingly reflecting the show's failure to capture the imagination of Black young people, came from a 13-year-old London boy who dismissed the series as 'a meaningless joke and an embarrassment to the black community'. Arguably, as the programme's makers would go on to suggest, ITV sitcom was not the vehicle through which to seek authentic representation. But the perception that *The Fosters* had failed even to try to reflect British Black lives meant that for some Black Britons the programme was a missed opportunity.

It would be easy in the context of these audience responses and some of *The Fosters*' more obvious limitations to write off the programme as a false dawn, an insignificant missed opportunity to give a voice to British Black and Asian comedy, by programmes in subsequent decades. But to dismiss the series in this way undermines what was in fact a striking contribution to change, foundations on which later comedy could build. At the heart of *The Fosters*' importance was the message it sent to aspiring Black artists, who could see in the series the possibility of being in a television programme that wasn't, at least ostensibly, only about race and which had numerous Black characters. Interviewed in the *West Indian World*, Isabelle Lucas defended the series in these terms, explaining that it had 'triggered off a wave of plays centred around black people'. And while some Black people did not recognise themselves in the programme, for others it provided valuable morale-boosting representation. One Jamaican family from South London told journalists that *The Fosters* were 'just like' them. Moreover, the mother hoped, 'it will help whites understand our way of life'.[55]

Objections to the programme were ultimately rooted in unrealistic expectations. The absence of significant numbers of Black and Asian actors on British television put an unbearable strain on those who were forced, in a way unheard of for their white peers, to attempt to represent entire communities. For many, this burden was stifling. Norman Beaton recalled feeling, before filming *The Fosters*, 'we're picking up the tab here for a whole community, a whole generation, please God don't let us fail'.[56] What failure meant to Beaton in this context was the seemingly inadequate explanation of the everyday realities and challenges of British Black lives. The vehicle of an ITV family sitcom, as saccharine and banal a genre as one could imagine, could hardly recreate the streets of Black London in any serious way. As television critic Chris Dunkley observed, the series needed to be understood as a Black entry into the canon of British sitcom. Responding to one viewer's complaint that the series prevented the proper illustration of Black lives, Dunkley was dismissive: 'Why should it "illustrate" rather than parody, satirise, or totally misrepresent just as other comedies and other people do?' *The Fosters* was, after all, consciously set up in terms of universal human relations. As Isabelle Lucas told the *Guardian*, 'We're now at the point that Lorraine Hansberry's *Raisin in the Sun* was at many years ago. Critics attacked that at the time saying it could have been about any family. So could this, thankfully.' In a period where Black comedy was largely silenced, *The Fosters* enabled Black comic actors to take their place in the sitcom stable. And unlike shows such as *Love thy Neighbour*, it did so without defaulting to race as a continual site of conflict. In this way, *The Fosters* gave British sitcom 'a new accent to play on the ears', as noted by *The Times*: one that would grow significantly stronger in the later work of its stars, Munroe and Beaton in *Desmond's*, and Lenny Henry in his own show.

Some of the frustrations about the limited impacts of *The Fosters* reflect broader realities about television comedy, and television more generally, which can seldom be said to be a reliable vehicle for political challenge or able to affect political change. Nonetheless, comedy merits historical attention for other reasons. Unlike news and current affairs, and even drama, the study of comedy allows us to peer at least some way into the subconscious rationales of past societies, because in comedy, writers and performers can give voice to views that would otherwise be impossible to present, justifying themselves as only joking. Undeniably, Alf Garnett and Eddie Booth, with their extreme racism, spoke something of the dark underbelly of British prejudice, venting views that were prominent, but to which only 'fools' could publicly give voice. These views, and the raft of British racial comedy of the 1960s and 1970s, tell us next to nothing about the realities of Black and Asian lives in Britain. They do, however, speak volumes about what white writers and performers thought these communities were, and how they saw fit to represent multicultural Britain.

The ascription of such authority to sitcoms may seem perverse, given the ephemeral and light-hearted nature of these productions. But, as Brett Mills cautioned in 2005, it is elitist and misguided to ignore programmes that were watched by so many, just because scholars may dismiss the content as low brow.[57] Indeed, the racial sitcoms of the 1960s and 1970s attest powerfully to some of the core realities of British racism in this period. While overt displays of racism, such as those of Garnett and Booth, were presented as wrongheaded and unpleasant, Black and Asian people were continually constructed as inherently worth laughing at, as exotic, and, ultimately, as outsiders.

Change, in the form of more diverse images of Black and Asian people, which broke with colonial representative tropes, came only when Black and Asian actors, writers and producers were able to make their own mark on British television comedy. While never entirely banishing from the screen problematic colonial constructions of Black and Asian life, these artists managed, to a far greater extent than previously, to present Black and Asian Britishness as every day, domestic and normal. In this way, Black and Asian comedy stopped being about racial conflict, and started to be about Black and Asian lives. Slowly, unevenly, different cultures and jokes won space in British television comedy, changing the historical pattern of laughter (where white people laughed at Black people) and driving Black and Asian cultures into the centre of British comedy. While it cannot be said that *The Fosters* did much to bring black cultures on to British screens, it gave space to Black performers who would go on to do so in the future. Moreover, by banishing jokes about race to the margins and focusing on a Black family as everyday Britons, the programme broke new ground, challenging the trope of racial sitcom, thereby offering hope and opportunities to the next generation of Black writers and performers. For this reason, this rarely remembered programme merits greater historical attention and recognition than it has hitherto been afforded.

Figure 8.1 The *Till Death Us Do Part* cast (Anthony Booth, Una Stubbs, Dandy Nichols and Warren Mitchell), in a 'discussion' of racial issues (BBC, tx. 26/12/72)

Figure 8.2 A 'blacked-up' Spike Milligan in Johnny Speight's 1969 sitcom *Curry and Chips* (LWT, 1969)

Figure 8.3 The race-focused sitcom *Love Thy Neighbour*, featuring Jack Smethurst and Rudolph Walker (Thames, 1972–76)

Figure 8.4 *Mind Your Language*, featuring Barry Evans and Francoise Pascal, revolved around a class of immigrants learning English (LWT 1977–79, 1986)

Figure 8.5 *Rising Damp*'s bigoted landlord Rigsby (Leonard Rossiter), sophisticated African medical student, Philip (Don Warrington), and actor Richard Beckinsale (Yorkshire Television, 1974–78)

Figure 8.6 *The Fosters* emphasised the ordinary nature of Black British families, stressing London as a functioning multicultural space. Among other talented actors, the cast included Lenny Henry (left), and singer Linda Lewis (right) who joined in 1977 (BBC, tx. 18/6/77).

Notes

1 For the persistence of racism amid post-war multiculturalism see Paul, Kathleen, *Whitewashing Britain: Race and Citizenship in the Postwar Era* (Ithaca: Cornell University Press, 1997); Panayi, Panikos, *An Immigration History of Britain: Multicultural Racism since 1800* (London: Pearson, 2010); Solomos, John, *Race and Racism in Britain* (Macmillan, 1993); Gilroy, Paul, *'There Ain't No Black in the Union Jack': the Cultural Politics of Race and Nation* (London: Hutchinson, 1997); and Goulbourne, Harry, *Race Relations in Britain since 1945* (London: Macmillan, 1998).

2 See Malik, Sarita, *Representing Black Britain: Black and Asian Images on Television* (London: Sage, 2002), pp. 101–3; Small, Stephen, '"Serious T'ing": The Black Comedy Circuit in England' in Stephen Wagg (ed.), *Because I Tell a Joke or Two: Comedy, Politics and Social Difference* (London: Routledge, 2004), pp. 221–43, Newton, Darrell, *Paving the Empire Road: BBC Television and Black Britons* (Manchester: Manchester University Press, 2011), pp. 208–9.

3 For a short history of *The Fosters* see Newton, *Paving the Empire Road*, pp. 166–8.

4 See Zupančič, Alenka, *The Odd One In: On Comedy* (Cambridge, MA: MIT Press, 2008), pp. 182–218; and Orwell, George, *As I Please: The Collected Essays, Journalism and Letters of George Orwell, Volume 3* (Penguin, 1970), p. 325.

5 Bakhtin, Mikhail, *Rabelais and his World* (Bloomington, IN: Indiana University Press, 1984), p. 93.

6 Griffiths, Trevor, *Comedians* (London: Faber, 1976), p. 20.

7 *Ibid.*, p. 23.

8 See Bergson, Henri, *Laughter: An Essay on the Meaning of the Comic* (Basingstoke: Macmillan, 1911).

9 Bailey, Peter, *Popular Culture and Performance in the Victorian City* (Cambridge University Press, 1998), p. 149 and Bakhtin, *Rabelais and his World*, p. 94.

10 English, James, *Comic Transactions: Literature, Humor, and the Politics of Community in Twentieth-Century Britain* (Ithaca: Cornell University Press, 1994), p. 14.

11 Davies, Christie, *Ethnic Humor around the World: A Comparative Analysis* (Bloomington, IN: Indiana University Press, 1990), p. 8.

12 Wilmut, Roger, and Rosengard, Peter, *Didn't You Kill My Mother-in-Law? The Story of Alternative Comedy in Britain from the Comedy Store to Saturday Live* (London: Methuen, 1989), p. 273.

13 Jones, G. Stedman, 'Working class culture and working class politics in London: Sport, Politics and the Working Class: 1870–1900; notes on the remaking of a working class', *Journal of Social History*, 7 (1974), p. 237.

14 Bailey, Peter, *Popular Culture and Performance in the Victorian City* (Cambridge University Press, 1998), p. 149.

15 Malik, *Representing Black Britain*, pp. 100–3.

16 For analysis see Schaffer, Gavin, 'Till Death Us Do Part and the BBC: Racial Politics and the British Working Classes 1965–75', *Journal of Contemporary History*, 45:4 (2010), pp. 454–77. Also see Malik *Representing Black Britain*, p. 94; Newton, *Paving the Empire Road*, pp. 165–6; and Schaffer, Gavin, *The Vision of a Nation: Making Multiculturalism on British Television 1960–80* (New York: Palgrave Macmillan, 2014), pp. 187–201. There was a recurring black character in the BBC's spin-off of *Till Death*, *In Sickness and in Health* (BBC, 1985–92), Alf's carer Winston (played by Eamonn Walker). Typically, Alf dismissed Winston as a 'gay, sambo pufta', Episode 5. *In Sickness and In Health*, 6 October 1985. Television.

17 In *Curry and Chips*, the lead character, Pakistani-Irishman Kevin O'Grady, was played by Spike Milligan. In *It Ain't Half Hot Mum*, the role of Rangi Ram the Bearer was played by Michael Bates.

18 See Malone, Mary, 'That Old Black Magic', *Daily Mirror*, 13 December 1973.

19 For example, in evidence submitted to the Annan Committee on the future of broadcasting, the Runnymede Trust complained: 'The use of white actors to play "coloured" characters is particularly deplorable. This has happened frequently – most notably in the ITV comedy series *Curry and Chips*. It is an irresponsible practice because it ensures that the coloured person portrayed will correspond to white society's humorous stereotype of a coloured person rather than to reality: it is insulting to the groups caricatured and perpetuates hostile attitudes on both sides.' BBC Written Archive Centre (WAC), Caversham, Reading, File R78/1625/1, 'Race Relations and Broadcasting': Submission of the Runnymede Trust to the Committee on the Future of Broadcasting', 31 January 1975. CARD expressed their concern about blacking up in the *Black and White Minstrel Show* in 1967, sending the BBC a petition against the practice from black Londoners. See ITA Archive, File 3995803, David Pitt to the Director General of the BBC, 16 May 1967.

20 'Peace and Goodwill', *Till Death Us Do Part*, BBC, 26 December 1966. Television.

21 'Alf's Dilemma', *Till Death Us Do Part*, BBC, 27 February 1967. Television.

22 'TV Licence', *Till Death Us Do Part*, BBC, 2 January 1974. Television.

23 See Malik, *Representing Black Britain*, p. 97; Husband, Charles, 'Racist Humour and Racist Ideology in British Television: Or I Laughed till You Cried', in George Paton and Chris Powell (eds), *Humour in Society: Resistance and Control* (Basingstoke: Palgrave Macmillan, 1988), p. 167; and Schaffer, *The Vision of a Nation*, pp. 178–230.

24 'Strikes and Blackouts', *Till Death Us Do Part*, BBC, 23 January 1974. Television.

25 The two wrote scripts for *Harry Worth* and for *Coronation Street* before writing sitcoms such *George and the Dragon* for ATV between 1966 and 1968.

26 Schaffer, *The Vision of a Nation*, pp. 193–6.

27 See Shaw, Sally, '"Light Entertainment" as Contested Socio-Political Space: Audience and Institutional Responses to Love thy Neighbour (1972–76)', *Critical Studies in Television*, 7:1 (2012), pp. 64–78; Schaffer, *The Vision of a Nation*, pp. 196–201; and Malik, *Representing Black Britain*, pp. 97–8.

28 Itself a parody of Tony Hancock's famous sketch, this theme was also famously visited in *Till Death Us Do Part*. See Schaffer, 'Till Death', p. 464.

29 'An Inspector Calls', *Mind Your Language*, LWT, 5 January 1978. Television.

30 'The Night of the Thugs', *It Ain't Half Hot Mum*, BBC, 20 February 1975. Television.

31 'Charisma', *Rising Damp*, Yorkshire Television, 27 December 1974. Television.

32 'An Inspector Calls', *Mind Your Language*, LWT, 5 January 1978. Television. 'The Best Things in Life', *Mind Your Language*, LWT, 27 January 1978. Television.

33 'A Fate Worse than Death', *Mind Your Language*, LWT, 13 January 1978. Television.

34 Malik, *Representing Black Britain*, p. 97.

35 Philpot, Terry, 'Does Our Television Reinforce Racialism?' *Tribune*, 6 April 1974.

36 Pines, Jim (ed.), *Black and White in Colour: Black People in British Television since 1936* (BFI, 1992), p. 78.

37 Dunn, Peter, *The Sunday Times*, 17 March, 1974.

38 Pierre, Russell, 'Roots: A Success for Whom?' *West Indian World*, 15–21 April 1977. Print.

39 *Ibid*.

40 See Newton, Darrell, *Paving the Empire Road*, p. 191.

41 In Vince Powell's autobiography he recalled that the programme topped the charts in India and was shown 'every night' in Singapore. See Powell, Vince, *From Rags to Gags: The Memoirs of a Comedy Writer* (Westborough, MA: Apex, 2008), p. 239. Also, Siriwardena, Reggie, *Race, the English Language and TV* (Colombo Sri Lanka: Council for Communal Harmony through the Media, 1982), p. 15.

42 Siriwardena, *Race, the English Language and TV*, p. 4.

43 Pines, *Black and White in Colour*, p. 116.

44 Dix, Carol, 'Black Comedy', *Guardian*, 9 April 1976.

45 See Newton, *Paving the Empire Road*, p. 160.

46 'The Windfall', *The Fosters*, LWT, 11 June 1976. Television.

47 For example see 'The Man I Most Admire', *The Fosters*, LWT, 14 May 1976; 'Situations Vacant', *The Fosters*, 21 May 1976; and 'Over the Hill', *The Fosters*, LWT, 18 June 1976. Television.

48 Generational conflict was a repeated theme in Michael Abbensetts' *Empire Road* (1978–79) which also starred Norman Beaton. For analysis see Newton, *Paving the Empire Road*, pp. 157–62. These issues have been extremely prominent in Black and Asian British drama such as Hanif Kureishi's early plays and novels (*Sammy and Rosie Get Laid*, 1987; *My Beautiful Laundrette*, 1985; and the *Buddha of Suburbia*, 1990), Gurinder Chadha's and Meera Syal's *Bhaji on the Beach*, 1993 and Ayub Khan Din's *East is East*, 1999, as well as in comedies like *Goodness Gracious Me* (See Malik, *Representing Black Britain*, 103). For more recent coverage of this issue in Black theatre see Kwame Kwei-Armah's play *Elmina's Kitchen* (2003).

49 'Black Jesus', *The Fosters*, LWT, 7 May 1976. Television.
50 'Benjamin's Rebellion', *The Fosters*, LWT, 2 July 1976. Television.
51 Dix, 'Black Comedy'.
52 Clayton, Sylvia, 'Facetious Format of "The Fosters"', *Daily Telegraph*, 10 April 1976. Print.
53 Husband, Charles, 'Racist Humour and Racist Ideology in British Television', p. 167.
54 Beaton, Norman, *Beaton but Unbowed: An Autobiography* (London: Methuen, 1986), p. 206.
55 Diaz, Herma, Interview with Isabelle Lucas, *West Indian World*, 20–26 January 1978. Print.
56 *Ibid.*, p. 190.
57 Mills, Brett, *Television Sitcom* (London: BFI, 2005), p. 154.

Selected bibliography

Ali, Amir, 'UK: Chicken Tikka Multiculturalism', *Economic and Political Weekly*, 36:30 (2001), pp. 21–8.

Anderson, Benedict, *Imagined Communities: Reflections on the Origin and Spread of Nationalism* (New York: Verso, 1991).

Anderson, Elijah, *The Cosmopolitan Canopy: Race and Civility in Everyday Life* (New York: W. W. Norton & Company, 2012).

Anderson, Elijah, 'The Iconic Ghetto', *The ANNALS of the American Academy of Political and Social Science*, 642:1 (2012), pp. 8–24.

Andrews, K., 'Black is a Country: Building Solidarity Across Borders', *World Policy Journal*, 33:1 (2016), pp. 15–19.

Andrews, K., 'From the "Bad Nigger" to the "Good Nigga": An Unintended Legacy of Black radicalism', *Race & Class*, 55:3 (2014), pp. 22–37.

Ang, Ien, *Desperately Seeking the Audience* (London: Routledge, 2006).

Anonymous, '*Luther* Creator Preparing Big-screen Version of the Idris Elba Drama', *Radio Times*, 22 March 2012.

Arata, Stephen D., 'The Occidental Tourist: Dracula and the Anxiety of Reverse Colonization', *Victorian Studies*, 33:4 (1990), pp. 621–45.

Awooner-Renner, Marilyn, 'Carmen Munroe belongs to the Human Race', *West Indian World*, 3–9 September 1976.

Baggaley, Jon, *Psychology of the Television Image* (Ann Arbor, MI: Saxon House, 1980).

Bailey, O., Georgiou, M., and Harindranath, R. (eds), *Transnational Lives and the Media: Re-Imagining Diasporas* (Basingstoke: Palgrave Macmillan, 2007).

Bailey, Peter, *Popular Culture and Performance in the Victorian City* (Cambridge: Cambridge University Press, 1998).

Bakhtin, Mikhail, *Rabelais and his World* (Bloomington, IN: Indiana University Press, 1984).

Balfe, Myles, 'Incredible Geographies? Orientalism and Genre Fantasy', *Social & Cultural Geography*, 5:1 (2004), p. 75.

Banks, Lynne Reid, 'TV News in the 50s was More Thrilling than The Hour', *Guardian*, 14 August 2011.

Barker, Chris, *Television, Globalization, and Cultural Identities* (Maidenhead and New York: Open University Press, 2005).

Beaton, Norman, *Beaton but Unbowed: An Autobiography* (London: Methuen, 1986).

Becker, Christine, 'From High Culture to Hip Culture: Transforming the BBC into BBC America', in Joel H. Wiener and Mark Hampton (eds), *Anglo-American Media Interactions, 1850–2000* (Basingstoke: Palgrave Macmillan, 2007).

Bellin, Joshua David, *Framing Monsters: Fantasy Film and Social Alienation* (Carbondale: Southern Illinois University Press, 2005).

Bergson, Henri, *Laughter: An Essay on the Meaning of the Comic* (Basingstoke: Macmillan, 1911).

Bernardi, Daniel, 'Introduction: Race and Contemporary Hollywood Cinema', in Daniel Bernardi (ed.), *The Persistence of Whiteness: Race and Contemporary Hollywood Cinema* (London: Routledge, 2008).

Bettinger, Brendan, 'Idris Elba's *LUTHER* to Air in America; Joins THE BIG C', *Collider*, 8 June 2010.

Bignell, Jonathan, *An Introduction to Television Studies* (London: Routledge, 2012).

Bignell, Jonathan, and Orlebar, Jeremy, *The Television Handbook* (Philadelphia: Taylor & Francis, 2005).

Billig, Michael, *Laughter and Ridicule: Towards a Social Critique of Humour* (London: Sage, 2005).

Bogle, Donald, *Toms, Coons, Mulattoes, Mammies and Bucks: An Interpretive History of Blacks in American Films* (New York: Continuum, 1989).

Bonilla-Silva, Eduardo, and Ashe, Austin, 'The End of Racism? Colorblind Racism and Popular Media', in Sarah Nilsen and Sarah E. Turner (eds), *The Colorblind Screen: Television in Post-Racial America* (New York University Press, 2014).

Born, Georgina, *Uncertain Vision: Birt, Dyke and the Reinvention of the BBC* (New York: Random House, 2005).

Bourne, Stephen, *Black in the British Frame: Black people in British Film and Television 1896–1996* (London: Cassell, 1998).

Boylorn, Robin M., 'As Seen On TV: An Autoethnographic Reflection on Race and Reality Television', *Critical Studies in Media Communication*, 25:4 (2008), pp. 413–33.

Brandt, George W. (ed.), *British Television Drama in the 1980s* (Cambridge: Cambridge University Press, 1993).

Brantlinger, Patrick, 'Victorians and Africans: The Genealogy of the Myth of the Dark Continent', *Critical Inquiry*, 12:1 (1985), pp. 166–203.

Brighton, Shane, 'British Muslims, Multiculturalism and UK Foreign Policy: "Integration" and "Cohesion" in and beyond the State', *International Affairs*, 83:1 (2007), p. 6.

Brixton Disorders: 10–12 April 1981: Report of an Inquiry (Her Majesty's Stationery Office, 1986).

Brooks, Dianne L., 'Television and Legal Identity in Prime Suspect', *Studies in Law, Politics and Society*, 14 (1994), p. 90.

Brunsdon, Charlotte, 'What is the "Television" of Television Studies?' in Christine Geraghty and David Lusted (eds), *The Television Studies Book* (London: Arnold, 1998), pp. 95–113.

Burton, Antoinette, 'When Was Britain?' Nostalgia for the Nation at the End of the 'American Century', *Journal of Modern History*, 75:2 (2003), p. 360.

Busby, Margaret, and Lawrence, Doreen, *And Still I Rise: Seeking Justice for Stephen* (London: Faber & Faber, 2006).

Butler, Jeremy, *Television: Critical Methods and Applications* (New York: Routledge, 2001).

Calvert, Ben, Casey, Neil, Casey, Bernadette, French, Liam, and Lewis, Justin, *Television Studies: The Key Concepts* (New York: Routledge, 2007).

Campion, M. J., *Look Who's Talking: Cultural Diversity, Public Service Broadcasting and the National Conversation* (Nuffield College, 2005).

Cantor, Muriel G., 'The American Family on Television: from Molly Goldberg to Bill Cosby', *Journal of Comparative Family Studies*, 22:2 (1991), pp. 205.

Carpenter, Humphrey, *The Envy of the World: Fifty Years of the BBC Third Programme and Radio Three* (London: Weidenfeld & Nicolson, 1996).

Centre for Contemporary Cultural Studies, *Policing the Crisis: Mugging, the State and Law and Order* (London: Macmillan, 1978).

Césaire, Aimé, *Discourse on Colonialism* (Monthly Review Press, 1972).

Charles, Alec, 'The Ideology of Anachronism: Television, History, and the Nature of Time', in David Butler (ed.), *Time and Relative Dissertations in Space: Critical Perspectives on 'Doctor Who'* (Manchester University Press, 2007).

Clark, Phenderson Djèlí, '*Doctor Who* (?) – Racey-Wacey-Timey-Wimey', blog-post, *The Musings of a Disgruntled Haradrim*, 3 June 2013.

Clarke, Alan, 'Holding the Blue Lamp: Television and the Police in Britain', *Crime and Social Justice*, 19, 'Crisis in Theory and Social Policy' (1983), pp. 44–51.

Clarke, Simon and Garner, Steven, *White Identities: A Critical Sociological Approach* (New York: Pluto Press, 2009).

Collins, Marcus, 'Pride and Prejudice: West Indian Men in Mid-Twentieth-Century Britain', *Journal of British Studies*, 40 (2001), pp. 391–418.

Communications Act (The Stationery Office, 2003).

Cooke, Lez, *British Television Drama: A History* (London: BFI, 2003).

Corner, John, *Critical Ideas in Television Studies* (Oxford: Oxford University Press, 1999).

Corner, John, 'Once Upon a Time … Visual Design and Documentary Openings', in Ann Gray and Erin Bell (eds), *Televising History: Mediating the Past in Postwar Europe* (Basingstoke: Palgrave, 2010), pp. 13–27.

Cottle, Simon (ed.), *Ethnic Minorities and the Media: Changing Cultural Boundaries* (Buckingham and Philadelphia: Open University Press, 2000).

Cross, Neil, *Luther: The Calling* (New York: Simon & Schuster, 2011).

Daniels, Therese and Jane Gerson (eds), *The Colour Black* (London: BFI, 1989).

Davies, Christie, *Ethnic Humor around the World: A Comparative Analysis* (Bloomington, IN: Indiana University Press, 1990).

Davies, Serena, '*Luther*, BBC One, Review', *Telegraph*, 5 May 2010.

Davis, David Brion, *Inhuman Bondage: The Rise and fall of Slavery in the New World* (Oxford: Oxford University Press, 2006).

Davis, J. Madison, 'He Do the Police in Different Voices: The Rise of the Police Procedural', *World Literature Today*, 86:1 (January/February 2012), p. 9.

Deacon, Michael, '*The Hour*, BBC Two, episode 1, review', *The Telegraph*, 19 July 2011.

Diaz, Herma, Interview with Isabelle Lucas, *West Indian World*, 20–26 January 1978.

Dines, Gail and Humez, Jean M. (eds) *Gender, Race, and Class in Media: A Text Reader* (London: Sage, 2013).

Dix, Carol, 'Black Comedy', *Guardian*, 9 April 1976.

Doane, Ashley, 'Shades of Colorblindness: Rethinking Racial Ideology in the United States', in Sarah Nilsen and Sarah E. Turner (eds), *The Colorblind Screen: Television in Post-Racial America* (New York: New York University Press, 2014).

Downing, Neil, and Husband, John, *Representing Race: Racisms, Ethnicity and the Media* (London: Sage 2005).

DuBois, W. E. B., *The Souls of Black Folk* (Minneola, NY: Dover Publications, 1994).

Elliott, Jane, 'Suffering Agency: Imagining Neoliberal Personhood in North America and Britain', *Social Text*, 31:2 (2013), pp. 83–101.

Ellis, John, 'Scheduling: The Last Creative Act in Television?' *Media, Culture & Society*, 22:1 (2000), pp. 25–38.

English, James, *Comic Transactions: Literature, Humor, and the Politics of Community in Twentieth-Century Britain* (Ithaca, NY: Cornell University Press, 1994).

Fanon, Franz, *Black Skin, White Masks* (New York: Grove Publishers, 1994).

Fanthome, Christine, 'Commissioning Television Programmes', in Douglas Gomery and Luke Hockley (eds), *Television Industries* (London: BFI, 2006).

Fitzgerald, Louise, 'Taking a Pregnant Pause: Interrogating the Feminist Potential of Call the Midwife', in James Leggott and Julie Anne Taddeo (eds), *Upstairs and Downstairs: British Costume Drama Television from the Forsyth Saga to Downton Abbey* (Lanham, MD: Rowman & Littlefield, 2015).

Fly, Fire, 'The White Doctor', in Lindy Orthia (ed.), *Doctor Who & Race* (Bristol: Intellect Ltd, 2013).

Foss, Eric, 'The Ood as a Slave Race: Colonial Continuity in the Second Great and Bountiful Human Empire', in Lindy Orthia (ed.), *Doctor Who & Race* (Bristol: Intellect Ltd, 2013).

Franklin, Bob (ed.), *British Television Policy: A Reader* (London: Routledge, 2001).

Freud, Sigmund, *Jokes and their Relation to the Unconscious* (London: Routledge & Kegan Paul, 1960).

Gabriel, Deborah, 'Challenging the Whiteness of Britishness: Co-creating British Social History in the Blogosphere', Academia.edu., 2 May 2016.

Garnham, Nicholas, 'Concepts of Culture: Public Policy and the Cultural Industries', *Cultural Studies*, 1:1 (1987), pp. 23–37.

Geraghty, Christine and Lusted, David (eds), *The Television Studies Book* (London: Arnold, 1998).

Gillespie, Marie, *Television, Ethnicity and Cultural Change* (London: Routledge, 1995).

Gilroy, Paul, *The Black Atlantic: Modernity and Double-Consciousness* (Cambridge. MA: Harvard University Press, 1993).

Gilroy, Paul, *'There Ain't No Black in the Union Jack': The Cultural Politics of Race and Nation* (London: Hutchinson, 1997).

Goodwin, Peter, *Television under the Tories: Broadcasting Policy 1979–1997* (London: BFI, 1998).

Goulbourne, Harry, *Race Relations in Britain since 1945* (London: Macmillan, 1998).

Graham, M. and Robinson, G., '"The Silent Catastrophe": Institutional Racism in the British Educational System and the Underachievement of Black Boys', *Journal of Black Studies*, 34:5 (2004), pp. 653–71.

Gray, Herman, *Watching Race: Television and the Struggle for Blackness* (Minneapolis: University of Minnesota Press, 1995).

Gray, Jonathan, Cornel Sandvoss and C. Lee Harrington (eds), *Fandom: Identities and Communities in a Mediated World* (London, Routledge: 2007).

Greene, Eric, *Planet of the Apes as American Myth: Race, Politics, and Popular Culture* (Middletown, CT: Wesleyan Publishing, 1998).

Griffiths, Trevor, *Comedians* (London: Faber, 1976).

Gripsrud, J. (ed.), *Television and Common Knowledge* (London: Routledge, 1999).

Guerrero, Ed, *Framing Blackness: The African American Image in Film* (Philadelphia: Temple University Press, 1993).

Gutzmore, Cecil, 'Carnival, the State and the Black Masses in the United Kingdom', in Winston James and Clive Harris (eds), *Inside Babylon: The Caribbean Diaspora in Britain* (London: Verso, 1993).

Hall, Catherine, *White Male and Middle Class* (Polity Press, 1992).

Hall, Stuart, 'The Whites of their Eyes: Racist Ideologies and the Media', in Hugh Mackay (ed.), *The Media Reader* (London: BFI, 1990).

Hallam, Julia, 'Power Plays: Gender, Genre and Lynda La Plante', in Jonathan Bignell, Stephen Lacey and Madeleine Macmurraugh-Kavanagh (eds), *British Television Drama: Past, Present and Future* (London: Palgrave, 2000).

Harrison, A. (ed.), *Black Exodus: The Great Migration from the American South* (Jackson, MS: University Press of Mississippi, 1992).

Hartmann, Paul, and Husband, Charles, *Racism and the Mass Media: A Study of the Role of the Mass Media in the Formation of White Beliefs and Attitudes in Britain* (Davis-Poynter, 1974).

Havens, Timothy, *Black Television Travels: African American Media around the Globe* (New York: New York University Press, 2013).

Havens, Timothy, 'Media Industry Sociology: Mainstream, Critical, and Cultural Perspectives', in Silvio Waisbord (ed.), *Media Sociology: A Reappraisal* (Cambridge and Malden, MA: Polity Press, 2014).

Henry, Lenny, 'BAFTA Television Lecture', British Academy of Film and Television Awards, 17 March 2014.

Hesmondhalgh, David, 'Cultural and Creative Industries', in Tony Bennett and J. Frow (eds), *The SAGE Handbook of Cultural Analysis* (Los Angeles: London: Sage, 2008).

Hesmondhalgh, David and Saha, Anamik, 'Race, Ethnicity, and Cultural Production.' *Popular Communication*, 11:3 (2013), pp. 179–95.

Higgins, David M., 'Toward a Cosmopolitan Science Fiction', *American Literature*, 88:2 (2011), pp. 331–54.

Higgins, John (ed.), *The Raymond Williams Reader* (Hoboken, NJ: Wiley Blackwell, 2001).

Hill Collins, P., *Black Feminist Thought: Knowledge, Consciousness, and the Politics of Empowerment* (London: Routledge, 2000).

Hilmes, Michele, 'Transnational TV: What Do We Mean by "Co-production" Anymore?' *Media Industries*, 1:2 (2014), pp. 12–13.

Hilmes, Michele, 'Who we are, who we are not: Battle of the Global Paradigms', in Lisa Parks and Shanti Kumar (eds), *Planet TV: A Global Television Reader* (New York: New York University Press, 2003).

Holdsworth, A., *Television, Memory and Nostalgia* (Basingstoke: Palgrave, 2011).

Holmes, Su, *Entertaining Television: The BBC and Popular Television Culture in the 1950s* (Manchester: Manchester University Press, 2008).

Holzman, Linda, *Media Messages: What Film, Television and Popular Music Teach us About Race, Class, Gender, and Sexual Orientation* (Armonk, NY: M. F. Sharpe, 2000).

Hood, Stuart (ed.), *Behind the Scenes: The Structure of British Television in the Nineties* (London: Lawrence & Wishart, 1994).

Horsti, Karina, Hultén, Gunilla, and Titley, Gavan (eds), *National Conversations: Public Service Media and Cultural Diversity in Europe* (London: Intellect, 2014).

Horton, D., and Wohl, R. R., 'Mass Communication and Para-social Interaction: Observations on Intimacy at a Distance', *Psychiatry*, 19 (1956), pp. 215–29.

Howitt, Dennis, and Owusu-Bempah, Kwame, 'Race and Ethnicity in Popular Humour', in Sharon Lockyer and Michael Pickering (eds), *Beyond a Joke: The Limits of Humour* (London: Macmillan, 2005).

Hughey, Matthew, *The White Savior Film: Content, Critics, and Consumption* (Philadelphia: Temple University Press, 2014).

Husband, Charles, 'Racist Humour and Racist Ideology in British Television: Or I Laughed till You Cried', in George Paton and Chris Powell (eds), *Humour in Society: Resistance and Control* (New York: Palgrave Macmillan, 1988).

James, Robin, 'Notes on a Theory of Multi-Racial White Supremacist Patriarchy', *It's Her Factory*, 19 November 2013.

Jancovich, Mark and Lyons, James (eds), *Quality Popular Television: Cult TV, the Industry and Fans* (London: BFI, 2008).

Jenkins, Henry, *Textual Poachers: Television Fans & Participatory Culture: Studies in culture and communication* (New York: Routledge, 1992).

Jones, G. Stedman, 'Working Class Culture and Working Class Politics in London: Sport, Politics and the Working Class: 1870–1900; Notes on the Remaking of a Working class', *Journal of Social History*, 7:4 (1974), pp. 460–508.

Jurik, Nancy C. and Cavender, Gray, 'Policing Race and Gender: An Analysis of *Prime Suspect 2*', *Women's Studies Quarterly*, 32:3/4 (Fall–Winter, 2004), p. 226.

Kalra, V. S. and N. Kapoor, 'Interrogating Segregation, Integration and the Community Cohesion Agenda', *Journal of Ethnic and Migration Studies*, 35:9 (2009), pp. 1397–415.

Kruse, K., *White Flight: Atlanta and the Making of Modern Conservatism* (Princeton, NJ: Princeton University Press, 2002).

Kubrin, C., 'Gangstas, Thugs, and Hustlas: Identity and the Code of the Street in Rap Music', *Social Problems*, 52 (2005), pp. 360–78.

LaGrone, K. L., 'From Minstrelsy to Gangsta Rap: the "Nigger" as a Commodity for Popular American Entertainment', *Journal of African American Studies*, 5:2 (2000), pp. 117–31.

Lavender III, Isiah, *Race in American Science Fiction* (Bloomington, IN: Indiana University Press, 2011).

Lawrence, Doreen and Margaret Busby, *And Still I Rise* (London: Faber & Faber, 2006).

Lewis, Melinda, 'Renegotiating British Identity through Comedy Television', thesis, Bowling Green State University, 2009.

Lionett, Francoise and Shih, Shu-mei, *Minor Transnationalism* (Durham, NC: Duke University Press, 2005).

Loader, Ian, 'Policing and the Social: Questions of Symbolic Power', *The British Journal of Sociology*, 8:1 (March 1997), pp. 1–18.

Lotz, Amanda D., *The Television Will Be Revolutionized* (New York: New York University Press, 2007).

Machado, Sam, '*Call the Midwife* Season 4 Premiere: Pregnant Woman Will Experience Racism, How Is She Going To Handle It?' *Enstars*, Claire Entertainment Inc., 24 January 2015.

MacPherson, William, *The Stephen Lawrence Inquiry* (London: Stationery Office Ltd, 1999).

Melamed, Jodi, *Represent and Destroy: Rationalizing Violence in the New Racial Capitalism* (Minneapolis: University of Minnesota Press, 2011).

Malik, Sarita, *Representing Black Britain: Black and Asian Images on Television* (London: Sage, 2002).

Malik, Sarita, '"Creative Diversity": UK Public Service Broadcasting After Multiculturalism', *Popular Communication*, 11:3 (2013), pp. 227–41.

Malik, Sarita, '"Keeping It Real": The Politics of Channel 4's Multiculturalism, Mainstreaming and Mandates', *Screen*, 49:3 (2008), pp. 343–53.

Malone, Mary, 'That Old Black Magic', *The Daily Mirror*, 13 December 1973.

Marcus, Daniel, *Happy Days and Wonder Years: The Fifties and the Sixties in Contemporary Cultural Politics* (New Brunswick, NJ: Rutgers University Press, 2004).

Martinson, Jane, '*Call the Midwife* to Film Episode in South Africa', *Guardian*, 21 March 2016.

Massey, S. and N. A. Denton, *American Apartheid: Segregation and the Making of the Underclass* (Cambridge, MA: Harvard University Press, 1993).

Mavhunga, Clapperton Chakanetsa, 'Vermin Beings, On Pestiferous Animals and Human Game', *Social Text*, 29:1 (2011), pp. 151–76.

McVeigh, Tim, 'Top Boy Gets a Mixed Reception from Hackney's Youth', *Observer*, 29 October 2011.

Mercer, K., *Welcome to the Jungle: New Positions in Black Cultural Studies* (London: Routledge, 1994).

Miller, Jeffrey S., *Something Completely Different: British Television and American Culture* (Minneapolis: University Of Minnesota Press, 2000).

Mills, Brett, *Television Sitcom* (London: BFI, 2005).

Mills, Charles Wade, *The Racial Contract* (Ithaca, NY: Cornell University Press, 1997).

Monk, Claire, 'The British Heritage-Film Debate Revisited', in Claire Monk and Amy Sargeant (eds), *British Historical Cinema: The History, Heritage and Costume Film* (London: Routledge, 2002).

Morley, David, *Home Territories: Media, Mobility and Identity* (London: Routledge, 2000).

Muir, Hugh, 'Metropolitan Police Still Institutionally Racist, say Black and Asian Officers', *Guardian*, 21 April 2013.

Murdock, Graham, 'Radical drama, Radical Theatre', *Media, Culture and Society*, 2 (1980), pp. 151–68.

Nama, Adilifu, *Black Space: Imagining Race in Science Fiction Film* (Austin: University of Texas Press, 2008).

National Statistics, 'Police Workforce, England and Wales: 31 March 2015'.

Neal, Larry, *Visions of a Liberated Future: Black Arts Movement Writings* (New York: Thunder's Mouth Press, 1989).

Newton, Darrell, *Paving the Empire Road: BBC Television and Black Britons* (Manchester: Manchester University Press, 2011).

Newton, Darrell, 'Calling the West Indies: The BBC World Service and Caribbean Voices', *The Historical Journal of Film, Radio, and Television*, 28:4 (2010), pp. 489–97.

Newton, Darrell, '"How Can we Help You"? Director General Greene and the BBC Coloured Conference of 1965', *Ethnicity and Race in a Changing World*, 3:2 (2012), pp. 113–26.

Newton, Darrell, 'Shifting Sentiments: West Indians Immigrants, the BBC, and Cultural Production', in Helen Wheatley (ed.), *Re-viewing Television History: Critical Issues in Television Historiography* (London: I. B. Tauris, 2007).

Nijhar, Preeti, *Law and Imperialism: Criminality and Constitution in Colonial India and Victorian England* (London: Routledge, 2015).

Nilsen, Sarah and Sarah E. Turner, 'Introduction', in Sarah Nilsen and Sarah E. Turner (eds), *The Colorblind Screen: Television in Post-Racial America* (New York: New York University Press, 2014).

Nishime, Leilani, 'Aliens: Narrating U.S. Global Identity through Transnational Adoption and Interracial Marriage in Battlestar Galactica', *Critical Studies in Media Communication*, 28:5 (2011).

Orfield, G., *Reviving the goal of an Integrated Society: A 21st Century Challenge* (Los Angeles, CA: The Civil Rights Project/Proyecto Derechos Civiles at UCLA, 2009).

Orthia, Lindy A., '"Sociopathetic Abscess" or "Yawning Chasm"? The Absent Postcolonial Transition in Doctor Who', *The Journal of Commonwealth Literature*, 45:2 (2010), pp. 207–25.

Orwell, George, *As I Please: The Collected Essays, Journalism and Letters of George Orwell, Volume 3* (London: Penguin, 1970).

Panayi, Panikos, *An Immigration History of Britain: Multicultural Racism since 1800* (London: Pearson, 2010).

Parekh, Bhikhu C., *The Future of Multi-ethnic Britain: Report of the Commission on the Future of Multi-Ethnic Britain* (London: Profile, 2000).

Paul, Kathleen, *Whitewashing Britain: Race and Citizenship in the Postwar Era* (Ithaca, NY: Cornell University Press, 1997).

Phillips, D., 'Ethnic and Racial Segregation: A Critical Perspective', *Geography Compass*, 1:5 (2007), pp. 1138–59.

Phillips, D., and Harrison, M., 'Constructing an Integrated Society: Historical Lessons for Tackling Black and Minority Ethnic Housing Segregation in Britain', *Housing Studies*, 25:2 (2010), pp. 221–35.

Phillips, Mike, and Phillips, Trevor, *Windrush: The Irresistible Rise of Multi-Racial Britain* (New York: Harper Collins, 1999).

Pines, Jim (ed.), *Black and White in Colour: Black People in British Television since 1936* (London: BFI, 1992).

Pollard, E. et al., *Researching the Independent Production Sector: A Focus on Minority Ethnic Led Companies. Report Produced for Pact and the UK Film Council* (Institute for Employment Studies, 2004).

Powell, Vince, *From Rags to Gags: The Memoirs of a Comedy Writer* (Westborough, MA: Apex, 2008).

Prashad, Vijay, *The Karma of Brown Folk* (Minneapolis: University of Minnesota Press, 2000).

Rex. J., and Moore, R., *Race, Community and Conflict: A Study of Sparkbrook* (Oxford: Oxford University Press, 1971).

Rieder, John, *Colonialism and the Emergence of Science Fiction* (Middleton, CT: Wesleyan University Press, 2008).

Riggan, William, *Picaros, Madmen, Naifs, and Clowns: The Unreliable First-Person Narrator* (Norman, OK: University of Oklahoma Press, 1982).

Rigoni, I., and Saitta, E. (eds), *Mediating Cultural Diversity in a Globalised Public Space* (Basingstoke: Palgrave Macmillan, 2012).

Roediger, David, *Towards the Abolition of Whiteness: Essays on Race, Politics, and Working Class History* (New York: Verso, 1994).

Ross, Karen, 'In Whose Image? TV Criticism and Black Minority Viewers', in Simon Cottle (ed.), *Ethnic Minorities and the Media: Changing Cultural Boundaries* (Buckingham and Philadelphia: Open University Press, 2000), 133–48.

Ryan, Bill, *Making Capital from Culture: The Corporate Form of Capitalist Production* (Berlin and New York: Walter de Gruyter, 1991).

Saha, Anamik, 'Beards, Scarves, Halal Meat, Terrorists, Forced Marriage: Television Industries and the Production of "Race,"' *Media Culture & Society*, 34:4 (May 2012), pp. 424–38.

Sarikakis, Katherine, *British Media in a Global Era* (London: Arnold, 2004).

Scannell, Paddy, 'Radio, Television, and Modern Life: A Phenomenological Approach' (Google Scholar, 1996).

Scarman, Lord Leslie, *The Brixton Disorders 10–12 April 1981: Report of an Inquiry by the Rt. Hon. The Lord Scarman, OBE* (London: Her Majesty's Stationery Office, November 1981).

Schaffer, Gavin, *The Vision of a Nation: Making Multiculturalism on British Television 1960–80* (New York: Palgrave Macmillan, 2014).

Schaffer, Gavin, 'Till Death Us Do Part and the BBC: Racial Politics and the British Working Classes 1965–75', *Journal of Contemporary History*, 45:4 (2010), pp. 454–77.

Seale, B., *Seize the Time: The Story of the Black Panther Party* (New York: Random House, 1970).

Selznick, Barbara J., *Global Television: Co-Producing Culture* (Philadelphia: Temple University Press, 2008).

Shaw, Sally, '"Light Entertainment" as Contested Socio-Political Space: Audience and Institutional Responses to Love thy Neighbour (1972–76)', *Critical Studies in Television*, 7:1 (2012), pp. 64–78.

Siapera, Eugenia, *Cultural Diversity and Global Media: The Mediation of Difference* (Hoboken, NJ: Wiley Blackwell, 2010).

Siriwardena, Reggie, *Race, the English Language and TV* (Colombo, Sri Lanka: Council for Communal Harmony through the Media, 1982).

Small, Stephen, '"Serious T'ing": The Black Comedy Circuit in England', in Stephen Wagg (ed.), *Because I Tell a Joke or Two: Comedy, Politics and Social Difference* (London: Routledge, 2004).

Solomos, John, *Race and Racism in Britain* (London: Macmillan, 1993).

Spaulding, Timothy A., *Re-Forming the Past: History, the Fantastic, and the Postmodern Slave Narrative* (Columbus, OH: Ohio State University Press, 2005).

Spigel, Lynn, *Welcome to the Dreamhouse: Popular Media and Postwar Suburbs* (Durham, NC: Duke, 2001).

Squires, Catherine, *The Post-Racial Mystique Media and Race in the Twenty-First Century* (New York: New York University Press, 2014).

Stedman-Jones, Gareth, *Languages of Class: Studies in English Working-Class History 1832–1982* (Cambridge: Cambridge University Press, 1983).

Steve Garner, 'The Uses of Whiteness: What Sociologists Working on Europe Can Draw from US Research on Whiteness', *Sociology*, 40:2 (2006), pp. 257–75.

Sturken, Marita, *Tangled Memories: The Vietnam War: the AIDS Epidemic, and the Politics of Remembering* (Berkeley: University of California Press, 1997).

Sunak, R., and Rajeswaran, S., *A Portrait of Modern Britain* (London: The Policy Exchange, 2014).

The Communications Market Report (Ofcom, 2015).

Thompson, Ethan, and Mittell, Jason, *How to Watch Television* (New York: New York University Press, 2013).

Tracey, Michael, *Decline and Fall of Public Service Broadcasting* (Oxford: Clarendon Press, 1998).

Twitchin, John (ed.), *The Black and White Media Show Book* (Stoke-on-Trent: Trentham, 1988).

Waters, Chris, 'Dark Strangers in Our Midst: Discourses of Race and Nation in Britain, 1947–1963', *Journal of British Studies*, 36 (1997), pp. 207–38.

Webster, Wendy, 'There'll Always be an England: Representations of Colonial Wars and Immigration, 1948–1968', *Journal of British Studies*, 40:4 (2001), pp. 557–84.

Williams, Raymond, and Williams, Ederyn, *Television: Technology and Cultural Form* (Oxford: Psychology Press, 2003).

Wilmut, Roger and Rosengard, Peter, *Didn't You Kill my Mother-in-Law? The Story of Alternative Comedy in Britain from the Comedy Store to Saturday Live* (London: Methuen, 1989).

Woolaston, Sam, 'Call the Midwife Review – Could be Much Improved by Morphine', *Guardian*, 19 January 2015.

Worth, Jennifer, *Call the Midwife: A Memoir of Birth, Joy, and Hard Times* (London: Penguin, 2002).

X, M., 'Message to the Grassroots', speech at the Northern Negro Grassroots Leadership Conference, Detroit, 1963.

Yuen, Nancy Wang, 'Playing "Ghetto": Black Actors, Stereotypes, and Authenticity', in Darnell Hunt and Ana-Christina Ramon (eds), *Black Los Angeles: American Dreams and Racial Realities* (New York: New York University Press, 2010), pp. 232–42.

Zupančič, Alenka, *The Odd One In: On Comedy* (Cambridge, MA: MIT Press, 2008).

Index

EU authorised representative for GPSR:
Easy Access System Europe, Mustamäe tee 50,
10621 Tallinn, Estonia
gpsr.requests@easproject.com